Women's Consciousness,
Women's Conscience

Women's Consciousness, Women's Conscience

A READER IN FEMINIST ETHICS

edited by

Barbara Hilkert Andolsen
Christine E. Gudorf
Mary D. Pellauer

A SEABURY BOOK
Winston Press
MINNEAPOLIS • CHICAGO • NEW YORK

Library of Congress Catalog Card Number: 85–50124

ISBN: 0–86683–958–5 (Cloth)
          0–86683–970–4 (Paper)

Printed in the United States of America

5 4 3 2 1

Winston Press, 430 Oak Grove,
Minneapolis, MN 55403

For Beverly Wildung Harrison

teacher, colleague, sister, friend,
who has taught us what a passion for justice means.

Table of Contents

Acknowledgments   ix

Introduction   xi

Part 1: *Exploring New Territory:*
Bringing Women's Experience into Ethics

A Woman's Work Is Never Done: Unpaid Household Labor
    as a Social Justice Issue
    Barbara Hilkert Andolsen   3

Women in the Cutback Economy: Ethics, Ideology, and
    Class
    Nancy Bancroft   19

Moral Callousness and Moral Sensitivity: Violence against
    Women
    Mary D. Pellauer   33

Toward an Understanding of *Feminismo Hispano* in the
    U.S.A.
    Ada Maria Isasi-Diaz   51

Feminism and Peace
    Rosemary Radford Ruether   63

Anti-Semitism: The Unacknowledged Racism
    Judith Plaskow   75

On Healing the Nature/History Split in Feminist Thought
    Joan L. Griscom   85

Table of Contents

Part 2: *Mapping Paths and Dreaming Dreams:*
Retrieving Norms from Experience

Our Right to Choose: The Morality of Procreative Choice
Beverly Wildung Harrison   101

While Love Is Unfashionable: An Exploration of Black
Spirituality and Sexuality
Toinette M. Eugene   121

Discipleship and Patriarchy: Early Christian Ethos and
Christian Ethics in a Feminist Theological Perspective
Elisabeth Schüssler Fiorenza   143

Female Friendship and Feminist Ethics
Janice Raymond   161

Parenting, Mutual Love, and Sacrifice
Christine E. Gudorf   175

Ethics and Justice in Goddess Religion
Starhawk   193

Where Is the Love?
June Jordan   201

Part 3: *Staking Our Claims:*
Situating Feminist Ethical Claims in the Ethics Enterprise

A Framework for Feminist Ethics
Carol S. Robb   211

Feminism and the Moral Subject
Ruth L. Smith   235

Feminism and the Ethic of Inseparability
Catherine Keller   251

On Doing Religious Ethics
June O'Connor   265

Feminist Theology and Bioethics
Margaret A. Farley   285

Acknowledgments

Nancy Bancroft's "Women in the Cutback Economy," originally published as "But Can She Type? The Changing Context of Ethics for Sexual Equality," reprinted by permission of *Cross Currents*. Copyright © 1980 by *Cross Currents*.

Margaret A. Farley's "Feminist Theology and Bioethics" from *Theology and Bioethics: Exploring the Foundations and Frontiers*, ed. Earl E. Shelp (forthcoming, 1985) by permission of the publisher. Copyright © D. Reidel Publishing Company, Dordrecht, Holland.

Elisabeth Schüssler Fiorenza's "Discipleship and Patriarchy: Early Christian Ethos and Ethics in a Feminist Theological Perspective" reprinted by permission of the author. First published in *The Annual of the Society of Christian Ethics*, 1982.

Joan Griscom's "On Healing the Nature/History Split in Feminist Thought" first published in *Heresies*, reprinted by permission of the author.

Beverly Wildung Harrison's "Our Right to Choose: The Morality of Procreative Choice" from *Our Right to Choose: Toward a New Ethic of Abortion* by Beverly Wildung Harrison. Copyright © 1983 by Beverly Wildung Harrison. Reprinted by permission of Beacon Press.

June Jordan's "Where Is the Love?" from *Civil Wars* by June Jordan. Copyright © 1981 by Beacon Press. Reprinted by permission of Beacon Press.

June O'Connor's "On Doing Religious Ethics" reprinted by permission of *The Journal of Religious Ethics*. Copyright © 1980 by *The Journal of Religious Ethics*.

Judith Plaskow's "Anti-Semitism: The Unacknowledged Racism," adapted by permission of the publisher from *Women's Spirit*

Acknowledgments

Bonding, ed. Janet Kalven and Mary I. Buckley. Copyright © 1984 The Pilgrim Press.

Carol S. Robb's "A Framework for Feminist Ethics" reprinted by permission of *The Journal of Religious Ethics*. Copyright © 1981 by *The Journal of Religious Ethics*.

Rosemary Radford Ruether's "Feminism and Peace," copyright © 1983 Christian Century Foundation. Reprinted by permission from the 31 August–7 September 1983 issue of *The Christian Century*.

Starhawk's "Justice and Ethics in Goddess Religion" reprinted from *The Politics of Women's Spirituality*, ed. Charlene Spretnak, by permission of the author. Copyright © 1979 Starhawk (Miriam Simos).

Introduction

The last fifteen years have witnessed enormous changes in women's consciousness, but the accompanying changes in our ethical styles—changes in our consciences—have received little sustained attention. The women's movement is deeply ethical in nature, both because it often relies upon concepts from the moral traditions of the West (such as rights or justice) and because the women's movement has challenged, criticized, and worked to reconstruct that tradition. Our ethics, like our education, politics, laws, and religion, have been deeply patriarchal, embodying firmly entrenched double standards of behavior for men and women. Ethical systems have been articulated, refined, and extended by men. When women and morality are discussed together in the western world, the subject too often becomes sexual morality, rather than the full range of human actions, struggles to create a good society, or human yearnings for justice and fulfillment. Ethicists have often spoken of women's moral capacities contemptuously. "Woman" is carnal and hence too closely associated with the evil impulses of the body; she is without that self-control necessary for disciplined moral action; she is too emotional and lacks the dispassionate rationality necessary for good moral judgment.

Women's own voices and insights have rarely been recognized in ethics. One result of the legacy of sexism has been the small numbers of women trained in the field of ethics as a specialty, whether in departments of philosophy or religion.[1] With the rise of the women's

1 Phillipa Foote, Dorothy Emmet, and Simone de Beauvoir are among the handful of women identifiable as ethicists before the 1970s. Women make up less than ten per cent of the Society of Christian Ethics, a major American professional association for religious ethicists. Only one of the three editors of this volume had the opportunity to study ethics with a woman faculty member. This

movement, our numbers have increased slightly but our questions and discontents have mushroomed. Why do so few courses in ethics take the women's movement seriously? Why do we too often feel out of place as women during gatherings of our professional colleagues? Why do our moral passions appear marginal or invisible to traditional authorities on ethics? Gradually, we began to imagine other ways of doing ethics; we spoke of "feminist ethics" as we had learned to speak of "feminist theology."

We do not offer a definition of "feminist ethics." Definitions arise after initial explorations have succeeded, after investigation and classification have gone on awhile, after there is some collective understanding about the perimeters of the territory. Surveying feminist ethics, we feel less like laboratory scientists carefully categorizing phenomena, and more like explorers venturing into new terrain, unsure what there is to find, at times lost in a wilderness unmapped before us, at other times exhilarated by unknown vistas and valleys.

As Adrienne Rich puts it:

> the rules break like a thermometer,
> quicksilver spills across the charted systems,
> we're out in a country that has no language,
> no laws, we're chasing the raven and the wren
> through gorges unexplored since dawn
> whatever we do together is pure invention
> the maps they gave us were out of date
> by years. . . .[2]

The patriarchal legacy of the West has hidden women's experience from ethical view, covering the lives, voices and insights of women with darkness, hedging them about with fences, falsifying landmarks, forbidding exploration altogether or, more often, simply ignoring reports. Sometimes we have had the sense that our training has outfitted us poorly for this work, as though we were sent into deserts with goose down parkas or into snowcapped mountains with

volume was initiated in the only "professional association" of women in ethics we know, the Feminist Ethicists of the Northeast, a study group whose members are drawn primarily from Boston and New York.

2 Adrienne Rich, *The Dream of a Common Language: Poems 1974–1977* (New York: W. W. Norton, 1978), 31.

sandals and camels. We are learning the hard way what equipment is best suited for the exploration we do.

We know that the adventurous spirits of our students, colleagues, and sisters will take them into regions where we have never gone. We find this prospect exciting, and even more, filled with *joy*. Despite grim caricatures of humorless feminists, despite the pain from which our struggles arise, our own experience of the women's movement is that it is joyful. Our laughter, smiles, hugs, and pleasure in each other's company are the truest evidence that this is the work we are called to do. The women's movement has taught us that justice is less the arithmetical calculations of an Aristotle than a joyous assent to the deepest possibilities of human existence.

We have learned that sensitivity to the concrete experience of women (what Mary Daly calls "experiencing our experience")[3] is the foundation for feminist ethics. First we outline a few points about this concentration on the daily textures of our lives. Second, we find that experiencing our experience leads us to social analysis, to the work of examining social data and creating social theories which illuminate our experience against a larger social backdrop. Last, our personal experience and social analysis lead us beyond the confines of what is called "secular" life—forcing us to ask religious questions and to affirm religious insights. After comments upon these three areas, we shall note some points of special interest in the essays which follow.

WOMEN'S EXPERIENCE AND FEMINIST ETHICS

Feminist ethics begins with female experience. But here feminists confront a first major problem. What is female experience? It is difficult for us to describe our own experience accurately or perceptively, for we have had few opportunities to examine our own lives in the common world where social definitions of reality are articulated. Too often, society creates a vision of "feminine" experience which keeps women subservient to men, alienated from our own human wholeness, and isolated from other women.

---

3 Mary Daly, *Beyond God the Father: Toward a Philosophy of Women's Liberation* (Boston: Beacon Press, 1973), 12.

Women's Consciousness, Women's Conscience

In the early days of the women's liberation movement, as we talked with one another, we found ourselves, in the words of sociologist C. Wright Mills, "turning private troubles into public issues."[4] Our individual experiences of discrimination, trivialization, damage, and distortion were not unique. They were shared. Social dynamics which caused us pain and suffering as individuals generally affected women as a group. Finding common ground where we did not expect it, we discovered a crucial, feminist, political/ethical insight of the women's movement: "the personal is the political."

Feminist ethics is rooted in this new effort by women to name our own experience in the public world. Pivotal to this process is the ongoing conversation of women's support groups, such as women's studies classes, friendship groups, or consciousness raising groups.[5] For the three of us, who became active in the women's liberation movement in the late 1960s, consciousness-raising groups were formative.

In women's support groups, we employ a technique basic to feminism and, hence, to feminist ethics. We tell our own stories in a community of women. When telling our own stories, we use a traditional skill. Women have long gathered to share tales of our lives. For example, the novelist Paule Marshall attributes her grasp of language to listening to her mother and her mother's friends, first generation immigrants from Barbados, gathered around the kitchen table to discuss their day. Demeaned as domestic workers in the larger world, these women restored their sense of their own human dignity through conversation with one another.[6]

4 C. Wright Mills, "On Politics," in *The Sociological Imagination* (New York: Oxford University Press, 1959), 187.

5 For a description of consciousness-raising groups and a sample list of topics and questions such groups might use, see "Building a Movement," in *Radical Feminism*, ed. Anne Koedt, Ellen Levine, and Anita Rapone (New York: Quadrangle Books, 1973), 271–384. For more recent and more detailed exercises, see Part I of *Beyond Sex Roles*, ed. Alice Sargent (New York: West Publishing, 1977), 7–140. For exercises focusing specifically on racism, see Tia Cross et al., "Face-to-Face, Day-to-Day—Racism CR," in *But Some of Us Are Brave: Black Women's Studies*, ed. Gloria T. Hull et al. (Old Westbury, NY: Feminist Press, 1982), 52–60.

6 Paule Marshall, "From the Poets in the Kitchens," *New York Times Book Review* (9 January 1983), 3, 34–35.

Introduction

What is new about feminist support groups is the attitude of members toward society's norms for women. Members of feminist support groups question all societal principles concerning how women's lives *ought* to be lived. When we gather to share our lives, we are engaged in moral, not just therapeutic, activity. Naming our own experience honestly, we assert our own worth and dignity as persons. For us to assert our dignity is, in itself, a morally courageous act in a world where women are too often defined as inferior. Feminists, listening to one another, also manifest a clear respect for the human worth of our partners in conversation.

In the process of listening to our stories we discover common themes. All of us have, at some time or other, been treated unfairly because we are women. Women's individual problems arise out of, or are exacerbated by, social structures which perpetuate female subordination.

However, listening to one another's stories, we also confront our differences sharply and often uncomfortably. There is no homogeneous woman's experience. Women's lives are very different. Among the differences which seem the most significant are the following: Some women are mothers; others are not. Some women come from upper class backgrounds; others, from the middle class; still others, from the working class or from poverty. Some are lesbian; some, heterosexual. Women are black, white, native American, Asian American, or Latina. Women are Jewish, Catholic, Protestant, adherents to other traditional world religions, followers of the Goddess, or nonreligious. Women have very different work experiences as homemakers, clerical workers, service workers, factory operatives, managers, or professionals. If feminist ethics is to be based upon the experience of *all* women, then such differences in experience must be acknowledged and incorporated into feminist theory.

One of the more serious challenges facing feminist ethics is to maintain genuinely open and fair dialogue about women's experiences. How can women with very different degrees of social power meet as equals in the feminist community? What process for framing our questions would allow all participants to speak about their own most pressing concerns? How can the women's movement confront those economic and racial/ethnic minority realities which make it so hard for us to converse? How can we *all* be active in the process of feminist ethics? These questions have no easy answers, but they are crucial to the future of feminism and to the well-being of women everywhere.

There are three strands of women's experience currently being used in feminist ethics. First, many published materials about feminist ethics have emerged out of the experience of rage against sexist injustice.

But, second, some of us claim there is another stratum of female experience which has barely been opened up for feminist ethics. In this discussion, some feminists say that there is something inherent in women's bodily, and perhaps even psychological, makeup which inclines women toward certain moral values. Some of us claim that the experience of menstruation links women to the rhythms of nature in a special way and that women are more likely to respect the Earth and its other creatures. Others suggest that women, as those uniquely capable of giving life, are more strongly opposed to the destruction of life than are men. Hence, women may oppose warfare and other life-threatening activities more consistently than do men. Other feminists repudiate these claims of innate female virtues, emphasizing instead the role of culture in shaping female values.

Third, lesbian feminists have raised other central questions. Feminists emphasize the virtue of female solidarity, calling upon all women to be loyal to other women. Many emphasize women's capacity for deep and sustaining relationships. Lesbians discover in a special way that women have the power to love other women with a passion that both recognizes profound sameness and cherishes surprising, enriching differences. Lesbian feminists have spotlighted intimate dimensions of sexist, social structures which make it nearly impossible for even well-intentioned men and women to maintain equal relationships. Both lesbian and heterosexual women are investigating the dynamics of homophobia and "compulsory heterosexuality"—social patterns, particularly economic patterns, which force women into a crippling dependency upon men.[7]

---

7 Adrienne Rich, "Compulsory Heterosexuality and Lesbian Existence," *Signs* 5 (Summer, 1980), 631–60 is an important discussion of these issues.

Introduction

The process of turning private troubles into public issues involves many moral judgments about our society. It is not fair that female workers are so poorly paid. It is not right that so many women carry the double burden of household maintenance and labor force participation. It is not just for society to burden so many women with the double yoke of sexism and racism or ethnic prejudice. It is not right that so many women face the crushing weight of poverty. A society in which so many women are brutally beaten and raped is not a good society. And when we make such judgments, they are not merely abstract statements. They are based upon sensitivity to the stories of women's lives.

Furthermore, telling our stories to each other and making judgments about injustice and justice leads women into *action*. Such actions may be as simple as helping another woman to see what options she has tomorrow. Or they may be as complex and long range as commitments and actions to change the balance of political power between the sexes or to revamp the economic system. From such small beginnings as women's consciousness-raising groups have come rape crisis centers and battered women's shelters; caucuses, networks, and coalitions of professional and political women; community organizations; newsletters, magazines, and presses for sharing information and insights; feminist-oriented small businesses—a whole host of new organizations and institutions which have transformed the social landscape.

Sharing our experience, naming the injustices in our lives, we imagined a new future, one in which society respects the human worth of women and promotes our well-being. We acted and created institutions to work toward making our visions real, reshaping society. Crucial to that process are our developing social analyses.

SOCIAL ANALYSES

Inherent in the women's movement are social analyses—sometimes implicit, sometimes self-consciously articulated—of the ways in which our social institutions work, of the social forces that shape our experiences as women, and of the possibilities for change in our social structures. Our social analyses center on diagnoses of the wrongs done to women, an estimation or assessment of the state of injustice. Such social analyses may be vague or inchoate, more assumed than consciously worked out; they may consist more of pictures and images of the social order than social science theories; or they may be more fully explicit. They vary in sophistication, insight, accuracy, and practical usefulness.

Moreover, feminist social analysis is a process, not a finished product. Facing new experiences daily, engaging in ongoing conversations with other women about our lives, and acting to change our experiences, all this generates new experiences and hence new analyses. Feminist social analysis is a spiraling process, rather than a linear one.

Included in such a social assessment are several interwoven, but distinct, threads:

—assertions about what is natural and what is the result of human choice, that is, a sense of what can be changed and what cannot be;

—some understanding of social causality, identification of the most fundamental dimensions of our common life;

—an assignment of priorities for action, a sense of what is urgent to change and what may be less urgent at present;

—visions of just alternatives to the present injustice;

—suggestions about strategies for social transformation.

While there is no *one* social analysis adopted by all feminists, most feminists agree we must develop an analysis broad enough to account for the experience of *all* women, not merely a few. We must investigate the social situation of women from racial, ethnic, and economic groups other than our own. But how these different oppressions are related is a matter of some disagreement. Some feminists believe that sexism is the primordial injustice, the model upon which race and class oppression are constructed. Some argue that patriarchy is built on mind/body dualisms which identify ruling class men with rational, objective mind and women and minority and poor men with the irrational, subjective body. In such systems, rational mind is always to rule the irrational body; ruling class men, to reign over women, minority and poor men. Feminists from nonwestern (particularly African or Asian) backgrounds may disagree with women from North America and Europe on this point, insisting that their cultures manifest patriarchy without possessing a mind/body split.

Feminists agree however, that to understand and to transform the doubly (or triply) unjust situations faced by racial/ethnic minority women, poor women, or lesbians, we must have an analysis of interlocking injustices in our social order. Furthermore, a merely "additive" understanding of injustices will not do; we cannot simply append racism and class oppression to sexism as though an analysis could be reduced to a list. As Toinette Eugene, June Jordan, Ada Maria Isasi-Diaz, and Judith Plaskow demonstrate in their essays here, analyses of the situations of black, Hispanic, or Jewish women must begin from the inside out.

This means that "sisterhood is complicated."[8] It is complicated not least by the fact that simple good will on the part of white women or Christian women or middle-class women or heterosexual women will not insure that we do not ourselves perpetuate the injustices against which we claim to fight. Struggles against racism, anti-Semitism, ethnic prejudice, class oppression, and heterosexual privilege must go on within the women's movement, too. Remedying wrongs done to some women by exacerbating or perpetuating wrongs done to other persons seems far from the visions of justice we hold dear. Only a complex understanding of social injustice can enable participants in the women's movement to acknowledge occasions on which we too are oppressors.

Other variations of a broad philosophical and political nature have developed among feminists over the last decade. These divergent positions are most often labeled liberal feminist, radical feminist, and socialist or Marxist feminist. Distinctions between these approaches are not hard and fast; it is difficult to describe them briefly without caricaturing someone. *Liberal feminists* are perhaps most familiar to North Americans. They describe oppression as resulting from the unequal treatment of women and men within our social institutions; such unequal treatment results in unfairness to individuals. Changes in the legal and political structures are important liberal mechanisms for redressing injustices. *Radical feminists*

8 Michele Russell, "Sisterhood is Complicated," in *Beyond Sex Roles*, 259-66.

highlight patriarchy described as an oppressive gender-related pattern pervading our entire culture. They stress change in the patriarchal family and elimination of violence against women. They emphasize cultural aspects of the social order, rather than legal, political, or economic ones. *Socialist or Marxist feminists* stand within those traditions. They criticize the women's movement for lack of a critique of capitalism and the socialist movement or Marxism for failure to take patriarchy seriously. They are particularly sensitive to economic issues, especially those of concern to poor and working-class women.[9]

Such variations in social analyses within the women's movement are directly relevant to feminist ethics. They flesh out our felt sense of injustice to women, help identify those social trends which undermine or enhance women's well-being, suggest alternatives to existing social patterns, influence our priorities for action, and provide models of how social change occurs. Thus, they undergird our sense of moral obligation, right action, of the good society.

Feminist modes of social analysis require us to look beyond the ordinary limits of the field of ethics (narrowly construed) and beyond the disciplinary boundaries of the usual university curriculum. Sexism works as a whole; we cannot accept disciplinary lines which force us to see it only in narrow fragments. Justice for women is "wholistic." Working on our life experience, building our insights into social analysis that can do justice both to the complicated nature of sisterhood and to the complex nature of modern social institutions, we must insist on making interdisciplinary inquiries.

Furthermore, we cannot accept rifts between knowing and doing or among separated areas of life. What happens in the kitchen or the bedroom is significant for what happens in boardrooms and on city streets. In ethics, this means that we cannot accept artificial dichotomies between "personal ethics" and "social ethics" or "public ethics."

---

9 For a more complete treatment of these views, see Alison M. Jaggar and Paula Rothenberg Struhl, *Feminist Frameworks: Alternative Theoretical Accounts of the Relations Between Women and Men* (New York: McGraw-Hill, 1978).

Introduction

The impetus implicit within the women's movement for larger and deeper pathways of connection does not stop with the boundaries of the social order. Increasing numbers of feminists go on to explore the religious implications of our experiences and analyses. Just as we emphasized the diversity of women's experiences and of feminist social analyses, so too there is no single, simple way to describe the religious ferment among feminists or its implications for feminist ethics.[10]

Relationships between ethics and religious faith are a matter of controversy in the modern world. Before the Enlightenment, many, if not most, people believed something was right because a deity or deities commanded it or because it was in harmony with the cosmos as the divine being(s) established it. For the last several centuries in the West, these connections between the religious and the ethical have ceased to be self-evident for many. Indeed, some ethicists argue that merely because a god commands a certain action does not, in itself, determine the morality of the action. Others have responded that no ethical perspective or endeavor can be adequately "grounded" apart from some understanding of the Ultimate.

For many feminist ethicists, (feminist) morality takes priority over religion. A religious duty, institution, or ceremony is morally acceptable because it is consistent with the well-being of women, not solely because a god requires it. Religious authority, including Scripture, is subject to feminist norms, not *vice versa*. When religious beliefs or practices demean women, they must be challenged. There is no religious reality outside ourselves to which we will sacrifice our dignity as persons.

Fundamental to feminist spiritual growth have been critiques of patriarchy within traditional western religions, especially Judaism and Christianity. To our horror, feminists have discovered a record of blatantly misogynist comments among these traditions, from Scriptural texts through classic theological works to the daily prac-

10 In addition to the references cited in many of the following essays, we commend *Womanspirit Rising: A Feminist Reader in Religion*, ed. Carol P. Christ and Judith Plaskow (New York: Harper & Row, 1979) as an introduction to the issues and options current in feminism and religion.

tices of grassroots religious communities. The image of God as Father, of Israel/Church as the Bride of Yahweh/Christ, and of woman as Eve have come under attack. Feminists challenge hierarchical patterns in which religious superiors dominate those "divinely ordained" to be subordinates—God, humanity; priest, people; man, woman; husband, wife; master, servant; master race, racial inferiors; parent, child. We repudiate assertions that sexuality, and hence women's bodies, pose a primary danger to the (male) spirit.

We have probed deeper into central theological categories of western religion, exploring concepts which did not, at first glance, contain gender references. For instance, many modern Christian theologians describe sin as selfish pride and prescribe self-giving love—agape—as the remedy. Such theologians purport to describe the universal human condition; but feminists, scanning the contours of female experience, respond that such concepts are more expressive of typical *male* experiences. For women, taught to pour themselves out in "sacrificial" service to others, sin more often takes the form of a loss of personal identity, a waste of "God-given" talents, and a covert manipulation of those one "serves." To call pride *the* basic sin could only distort and conceal the experience of women under patriarchy.

Such critiques led many feminists to conclude that the usual western religious options were fundamentally patriarchal. Many left churches and synagogues in order to remain faithful to feminist values. Other feminists disagreed. They responded that feminist commitments were consistent with the most basic values of Judaism and Christianity. The God of Moses and Miriam, of Jesus and Mary of Magdala, is a God who actively seeks human liberation and justice rather than oppression and the status quo.

Still other feminists remaining in the traditional religions warned we should not evaluate Judaism or Christianity entirely on the basis of the records which Jewish or Christian *men* have compiled, rather we should strive to uncover the religious experience of our foremothers in those religions. Women played a powerful role in the Galilean Jesus movement and in the house churches of early missionary Christianity. Christian women denied power in male-dominated ecclesiastical structures have been religiously empowered through mystical experiences or the direct inspiration of the

Spirit. There are strands of female imagery for the divine to be found in Scripture and in later religious traditions.

These feminist religious debates have been complicated and enriched by the rise of yet another feminist religious option, a restoration of ancient female symbols of the divine, most notably through the revival of *wicca* or the worship of the Goddess. Female-centered religions are immensely attractive to many feminists (including some who remain a part of Christian and Jewish communities). Goddess religion's female images for divine power, its rituals affirming women's being and celebrating sisterhood, and its fresh spiritual insights have drawn more and more attention. Many feminists resonate with Goddess religion's positive valuation of the female body, its ecological sensitivity, and its ability to inspire action on behalf of world peace.

Feminist spirituality, whether it is an extension of traditional western religions or a revival of Goddess religion, provides a "ground" in which feminists can root their visions of justice for women and a source of energy to struggle for that future. Feminists may name the wellspring of their hope differently. For example, Schüssler Fiorenza speaks of the Sophia-God of Jesus who holds out a future of human wholeness and fulfillment for *all*[11]; Daly evokes "the Witch within ourSelves, who spins and weaves the tapestries of Elemental creation."[12] We feminists do not yet have a common language to describe divine being, but we are beginning to mold new images. So, too, feminist ethicists are just beginning the task of describing those actions and habits of life (virtues) which are consistent with our new visions of the Ultimate.

We have structured this book based on our understanding of feminist ethics as we have represented it above. We, the editors, make no claims to be representative of feminists doing ethics. We are three white, middle-class, Christian women trained in religious

11 Elisabeth Schüssler Fiorenza, *In Memory of Her: A Feminist Theological Reconstruction of Christian Origins* (New York: Crossroad Press, 1983), 130–54.

12 Mary Daly, *Pure Lust: Elemental Feminist Philosophy* (Boston: Beacon Press, 1984), xii. For Daly, all Goddess language is a metaphor for Be-ing which is not static, but rather "the Active Verb in whose potency all biophilic reality participates" (26).

ethics. All three of us are heterosexual, married, with children. But we have tried to present varied approaches in this volume.

The three sections of this book represent three moments in the doing of feminist ethics. The first section, "Exploring New Territory: Bringing Women's Experience into Ethics," presents particular perspectives on women's experience. Since no account of experience is ever uninterpreted, varieties of feminist social analysis undergird these accounts. We begin with women's experience because we have learned that we must constantly return to our own experience as our guide.

Furthermore, we notice how rarely certain subjects important to many women come up in most ethics courses, books, or discussions. We have not heard our colleagues raise distribution of housework and childcare responsibilities as an ethical issue, as Andolsen does. Until very recently, the violence against women discussed by Pellauer has been concealed under a heavy cloak of silence. Nor have we noted much consideration of the special economic problems of women workers (Bancroft) or the painful experiences of those women who are doubly oppressed (Isasi-Diaz, Plaskow). The diversity in women's experiences can lead to ideological splits within feminist ranks. Both Ruether and Griscom discuss such splits. We do not claim to provide a comprehensive guide to women's experience in this section, rather we offer some examples of the kinds of experience feminists find it important to scrutinize as ethical issues.

The second section, "Mapping Paths and Dreaming Dreams: Retrieving Norms from Experience," turns to the values and commitments to which we have been led by shared reflection on our experiences. In this section, Eugene proposes that feminism points the way to rediscovery of valuable links between sexuality and spirituality in black culture. Out of two very different contexts, Jordan and Gudorf signal the need for self-love and mutuality, an affirmation which has become an important theme in feminist religious ethics. Raymond develops the notion of female friendships as novel in the history of ideas and as a powerful force for the well-being of women.[13] Connections between concern for persons and

13 An excellent earlier essay in feminist ethics also highlighted female friendship. See Eleanor Humes Haney, "What is Feminist Ethics? A Proposal for Continuing Discussion," *Journal of Religious Ethics* 8 (Spring, 1980), 115–24.

care for the Earth emerge clearly from Starhawk's account of ethics in Goddess religion. Schüssler Fiorenza proposes that feminism grounds decisions about religious authority, especially the Scriptures, in a commitment to women's well-being. In the same vein, Harrison maintains that it is necessary to focus on the well-being of women as a primary concern in reproductive ethics.

Section Three, "Staking our Claims: Situating Feminist Ethics in the Ethical Enterprise," is the most academic of these three sections. It moves from the specific norms of feminists to the field of ethics as a discipline. Thus it is dependent upon the work of the earlier two sections. Robb analyzes what is distinctive about feminist ethics as a type of social ethics. Smith demonstrates how generally accepted notions of self are inadequate in feminist ethics, and Keller explores a relational understanding of the self as more appropriate to feminist experience. O'Connor emphasizes the importance of emotion in ethics, in contrast to an overemphasis on rationality as the crucial moral capacity. In the last essay, Farley uses issues in medical ethics as an occasion to examine the link between feminist ethics and feminist theology.

Some of these articles are very specialized, dotted with footnotes. Others were written for more popular audiences and rely more directly upon the experience and authority of the author herself. Furthermore, these authors work in many other fields besides ethics—in theology, Scripture studies, philosophy, journalism, psychology, and ministry. The cross-fertilization that occurs within the work of people from such different specializations is exciting to us. We hope that readers will find this diversity of voice true to their experiences of the women's movement.

We understand this work as no more than a first step. We hope that future volumes in feminist ethics will be forthcoming, for there are many issues we have not addressed here. Among these are connections between feminism in the United States and the liberation movements of the Third World, the impact of world trade on women, feminism and indigenous religions, feminist notions of the body and their implications for ethics, and militarism.

Finally, we want to say a word about the *process* of putting this reader together. We found our collaboration a fascinating example of women's doing ethics, for our behavior together was unlike most of our other professional relationships. We made soup together, we wept, we shouted at each other, we discussed our children—all interspersed with serious discussion of issues, proposals, and editing details. We admitted when we were confused, frightened, guilty, angry with one another, or just plain stuck. (Not every time, but often enough to move us through our blockages.) Making soup together while deep in discussion about feminist ethics became for us a sign of the kind of wholeness we could have together now while striving for larger wholeness. In this revolution, as poet Marge Piercy says, "we have to remember/ to sing and make soup."[14]

Barbara Hilkert Andolsen
Christine E. Gudorf
Mary D. Pellauer

14 Marge Piercy, "The Spring Offensive of the Snail," in *To Be of Use* (Garden City, NY: Doubleday and Co., 1973), 64.

Exploring New Territory

BRINGING WOMEN'S EXPERIENCE INTO ETHICS

Part One

1

A Woman's Work Is Never Done

UNPAID HOUSEHOLD LABOR
AS A SOCIAL JUSTICE ISSUE

Barbara Hilkert Andolsen

The old saying, "A man must work from sun to sun, but a woman's work is never done," may be more true now than at any time in the last hundred years. More women with husbands and/or children are working for wages than ever before.

In this paper I will use social science data to describe the household burdens borne by wage-earning women. I will demonstrate that Catholic social thought on women and the family supports, albeit with growing ambivalence, the notion that household work, especially the care of children, is women's responsiblity. I will assert that any distribution of family responsibilities which leaves the wage-earning woman with the major share of household tasks violates the norm of justice. Finally, I will insist that fair treatment of salaried women within the family requires significant social change, as well as personal commitment from household partners.

In this essay I will describe the situation of wage-earning women in the United States today. I will work within the limits of our present economic system—advanced industrial capitalism evolving toward post-industrial capitalism. Other feminist ethicists have raised important questions about capitalism's capacity to respond to the human needs of wage-earning women and their families.[1] However, such a discussion is beyond the scope of this paper.

1 For discussions of the underlying economic issues, see Bancroft, infra;

3

Barbara Hilkert Andolsen

BURDENS BORNE BY WAGE-EARNING WOMEN

Married women are moving into the American labor force in unprecedented numbers. This trend toward increased labor force participation began after the second World War and has continued unabated. There is a steady increase in the percentage of women with children who work outside the home.

By 1983 fifty-two percent of all wives were working for wages. Almost two-thirds of all women with children ages six to seventeen were working for wages. Fifty percent of mothers with children under six were working outside the home (an increase of seventeen percent in one decade.)[2] More than three-quarters of all divorced mothers are in the labor force.[3] American households in which a wage-earning husband supports a nonwage-earning wife—a wife presumably devoting her energies to household maintenance—are now a dwindling minority among families.

We should not anticipate that better economic times will reverse this trend. According to a 1981 Harris poll, women are working because they want to, not just because they have to. "Given a choice, most working women would continue to work, although many would prefer part-time to full-time jobs. . . ."[4] The heavy household responsibilities of many women are probably a factor in this expressed desire for part-time employment. On the basis of this long-established, continuous trend toward paid employment for married women, including mothers, it seems reasonable to conclude that meeting job requirements, family obligations, and personal needs will present a serious problem in many families for the foreseeable future.

Beverly Harrison, "Effet de L'Industrialisation Sur Le Role Des Femmes Dans La Société," *Concilium, Revue Internationale De Théologie* 111, 91–103; and Rosemary Radford Ruether, *New Women, New Earth* (New York: Seabury Press, 1975) and *Sexism and God-Talk: Toward a Feminist Theology* (Boston: Beacon Press, 1983).

2 Elizabeth Waldman, "Labor Force Statistics From a Family Perspective," *Monthly Labor Review* 106 (December 1983), 17–18.

3 Beverly Johnson and Elizabeth Waldman, "Most Women Who Maintain Families Receive Poor Labor Market Returns," *Monthly Labor Review* 106 (December 1983), 31.

4 Sue Shellenbarger, "As More Women Take Jobs, They Affect Ads, Politics, Family Life," *Wall Street Journal* (29 June 1982).

4

Presently salaried women are making huge sacrifices to sustain family life. Sociological studies show that wage-earning women put in very long days. They do their jobs, then come home to put in more long hours doing the bulk of the household maintenance tasks. Although wage-earning women spend fewer hours on housework than do full-time homemakers, the total number of hours worked by wage-earning women with families exceeds the total number of hours worked by homemakers. Indeed, one researcher who surveyed fifty years of data on housework concluded: "... for married women in full time jobs the work day is probably longer than it was for their grandmothers."[5]

Other studies confirm the pattern; when a woman goes to work full time, her total work week is enormous by contemporary American standards. In a study done in Syracuse, women employed full time "had total work weeks of seventy-six hours on average. . . ."[6] An anthropologist, reviewing time allocation literature, concluded: "The most consistent patterns across all studies are those of the labor time of employed women. . . . they work longer hours than employed men and housewives. . . . for a seven-day work week employed women average from 10.5 to 12.6 hours per day. . . ."[7]

In a Cornell University study, husbands of wage-earning wives reported that they spent an average of 1.8 hours more doing household tasks and 2.7 hours more in childcare per week than did husbands of nonemployed wives.[8] In another set of studies, men's household labor ranged for .3 to 1.3 hours per day.[9] Husbands also tended to perform what I would describe as the more pleasant household tasks. According to one survey, husbands took on twenty-five percent of the social or educational care of children, twenty-five percent of the marketing, ten percent of the food preparation, and seven percent of the food clean-up chores.[10] There is some evidence

5 JoAnn Vanek, "Time Spent in Housework," *Scientific American* (November, 1974), 120.

6 Heidi I. Hartmann, "The Family as the Locus of Gender, Class and Political Study: The Example of Housework," *Signs* 6 (Spring 1981), 379.

7 Wanda Minge-Klevana, "Does Labor Time Decrease with Industrialization? A Survey of Time Allocation Studies," *Current Anthropology* 21 (June 1980), 285.

8 Hartmann, "Family as Locus of Gender: Housework," 379.

9 Minge-Klevana, "Time Allocation Studies," 283.

10 Hartmann, "Family as Locus of Gender: Housework," 380.

that younger, well-educated husbands are taking on a larger share of household responsibilities. Nevertheless, most wage-earning women spend far more time doing housework than do their husbands.[11]

Interviews with a small number of affluent dual-career couples revealed another problem area. What happens when the usual child-care arrangements fail? Who takes care of the child home on school vacation or ill? "Inevitably, there were times, such as emergencies when integration [of home and work] was vital; even so, it was not achieved without friction and, almost without exception, it was the woman who made the accommodation."[12]

Black families face these pressures in special ways. Since Reconstruction, proportionately more married black women have worked for wages than have married white women. These differences between the races are dwindling as more white women go to work. However, as of 1983, ten percent more married black women worked than did their white counterparts.[13] More black women are single heads of household. In 1983, thirty-one percent of black families were maintained by women, compared to nine percent of white households.[14] Hispanic women are also more likely than other white women to maintain a family alone.[15] However, Hispanic women are less likely to be in the labor force than are other white women or black women.

Strains in meeting family responsibilities are especially severe for single parents. The number of single parents has more than doubled between 1970 and 1983. "One parent families are maintained by the mother in the vast majority of cases (89%)."[16]

11 Maureen Dowd, "Poll Reports Many Men Are Shifting Views on Housework," *New York Times* (11 December 1983).

12 Donald St. John-Parsons, "Continuous Dual-Career Families: A Case Study," in *Dual Career Couples*, ed. Jeff Bryson and Rebecca Bryson (New York: Human Sciences Press, 1978), 33.

13 Howard Hayghe, "Married Couples Work and Income Patterns," *Monthly Labor Review* 106 (December 1983), 26.

14 U. S. Bureau of the Census. *Current Population Reports: Household and Family Characteristics, March, 1983* (Washington, 1984), 2.

15 Hispanic is a term which denotes ethnic background, not racial characteristics. Most Hispanic women are classified as white; some are black.

16 Bureau of the Census. *Household and Family Characteristics*, 6.

A *Woman's Work is Never Done*

DOMESTIC JUSTICE

I contend that justice requires that men who are in dual-salary families share equally with women in the burdens that arise out of paid work and household maintenance. Moreover, social justice requires that society recognize that workers are human beings who have domestic needs. Work and other social institutions should be organized in such a fashion that human beings can work, meet their personal and family needs, and enjoy leisure.

I have turned to justice because it is the virtue which challenges us to balance conflicting claims. Moreover, it is the virtue which we associate with public decision making, and the distribution of household burdens has an important public dimension. Turning to my own Catholic tradition, I returned to the thought of Thomas Aquinas. According to Thomas, justice is indeed the relevant category for justice is the virtue which regulates all one's treatment of other human beings.

However, in Thomas's thought there is a problematic tension between respect for the equal dignity of all persons and an assumption of enduring differences (including sexual differences) among human beings which legitimate unequal distribution of social benefits and burdens. Thomas assumed that society was based upon stable hierarchies of authority. He defined distributive justice as a mean which "consists in a certain proportion of equality."[17] Distributive justice means to give to each person his/her due in relation to his/her social location. "In distributive justice a person receives all the more of the common goods, according as he holds a more prominent position in the community."[18] And a person is relieved all the more of mundane social burdens, because he/she holds a more powerful position in the community.

According to Thomas, a specific sort of distributive justice—domestic justice—governs the relationship between a husband and wife. Within the household, a husband and wife are more nearly equal than father and son or master and servant. There is more

17 Thomas Aquinas, *Summa Theologica*, II, II, 58, 10.
18 Aquinas, *Summa Theologica*, II, II, 61, 2.

scope for justice between husband and wife, because the wife stands in a closer social relationship to the husband.

While Thomas acknowledged the dignity of wives within the marriage relationship, he took for granted a division of labor based upon sex. Indeed he believed that women were innately formed to be the bearers of children and the managers of household tasks. Within the household man and woman, exercising complementary male and female talents, were capable of satisfying domestic needs which neither could meet alone. For, "... among those works that are necessary for human life some are becoming to men, others to women."[19] Thomas was not specific about which duties were fitting for women, except that he observed that "the mother has more to do with the offspring than the father has."[20]

Thus Thomas's model of distributive justice, of which domestic justice is a subcategory, is a model based upon axiomatic human inequalities, including the inferiority of women. Yet within Thomas's discussion of justice there exists a countervailing recognition of a fundamental human equality which challenges a distribution of social goods and burdens based on social status. Thomas recognizes that sons and servants (and wives) when considered as human beings have a separate existence and are distinct individuals. As such their welfare is of concern to the whole community. Had Thomas pursued the implications of the fundamental dignity of each household member, it might have revolutionized his appropriation of Aristotle's domestic justice. However, Thomas could not rid himself of the notion that subordinate members of the household belong to its male head. Therefore, he overrode his own awareness of the human dignity of subordinates, each "considered as a person," and concluded "the perfect idea of right or just is wanting" to sons, servants (and wives).[21]

Pius XI This tendency to consider women, not as persons in their own right, but rather as functionaries within a naturally determined family system, continues to bedevil more recent Catholic discussions on the relationship between family and work. Over

19 Aquinas, *Summa Theologica*, Supplement, 41, 1.
20 Aquinas, *Summa Theologica*, Supplement, 44, 2, obj. 1.
21 Aquinas, *Summa Theologica*, II, II, 57, 4, obj. 2.

the past century the popes have gradually come to accept women as full persons within the public world, but they continue to view women as anomalous creatures within the family. This failure to recognize women as full persons within the family has resulted in social teachings on work and family which are inadequate to the situation of wage-earning wives and mothers.

In the early 1930s Pius XI took up questions of family and work in two of his most famous encyclicals—*Casti Connubii* and *Quadragesimo Anno*. Pius XI viewed the subordination of a submissive wife to a strong husband as "the structure of the family and its fundamental law, established and confirmed by God," which "must always and everywhere be maintained intact."[22] Both natural law and divine revelation confirm the traditional roles of husband and wife. The natural law is apparent in the self-evidently different characteristics of men and women. As for the Christian Scriptures, Pius relied on Eph 5:22–23: "Let women be subject to their husbands as to the Lord, because the husband is the head of the wife, as Christ is the head of the Church."

Like Thomas Aquinas, Pius XI recognized the innate human dignity of the wife as a human being in her own right. He insisted, "This subjection, however, does not deny or take away the liberty which fully belongs to the woman . . . in view of her dignity as a human person. . . ."[23] He concurred with Thomas that the wife was more nearly the equal of the husband than other family members. Nonetheless, Pius XI declared that in some human relationships strict equality is not possible. Marriage is one of those relationships in which "there must be a certain inequality and due accommodation, which is demanded by the good of the family and the right ordering and unity and stability of home life."[24]

Pius XI's response to the international feminist movement of the late nineteenth and early twentieth century was fear and rejection. He cautioned against secular talk about "women's emancipation." He condemned those who "do not scruple to do away with the honorable and trusting obedience which the woman owes to the

22 Pius XI, *Casti Connubii,* paragraph 28.
23 Pius XI, *Casti Connubii,* paragraph 27.
24 Pius XI, *Casti Connubii,* paragraph 76.

man. . . . [Who assert] that such a subjection of one party to the other is unworthy of human dignity, that the rights of husband and wife are equal. . . ."[25]

Pius XI linked questioning of woman's submission within the family with dangerous ideas about woman's place in the economic realm. He rejected proposals that married women should be allowed to engage in economic dealings without the permission of their husbands, for a woman engaged in independent economic enterprises would give her attention "chiefly to these rather than to children, husband, and family."[26]

Pius XI believed that God had created women for the express purpose of bearing children, nurturing those children, and serving as the center of life within the home. Therefore, he condemned economic arrangements that made it necessary for women to work outside the home. In a just order,

> mothers will above all perform their work at home or near the home, giving their time to domestic cares. Intolerable, and to be opposed with all our strength, is the abuse whereby mothers of families, because of the insufficiency of the father's salary, are forced to engage in gainful occupations outside the domestic walls, to the neglect of their own proper cares and duties, particularly the education of their children.[27]

It was precisely this concern to preserve the traditional family structure which led Pius XI to define a just wage as one "sufficient for the support of . . . the worker and his family."[28]

In Pius XI's writings, we find the same tension between a respect for universal human dignity as a principle and a notion of female nature which entails different duties for women than for men. Moreover, Pius XI is caught in an irreconcilable conflict when he appeals to a stable, unchanging nature of women in the face of massive social change in the roles of women. The pope expresses fear that women will leave home and babies to pursue political and business interests. However, he has already declared that women are by nature shaped to bear and nurture children, so that it should be

25 Pius XI, *Casti Connubii*, paragraph 74.
26 Pius XI, *Casti Connubii*, paragraph 74.
27 Pius XI, *Quadragesimo Anno*, paragraph 71.
28 Pius XI, *Quadragesimo Anno*, paragraph 71.

psychologically impossible for women to leave home voluntarily. The similarities between men and women must be as significant as their differences, if new social opportunities can so easily corrupt the character of women.

The Contemporary Catholic Position   There is a profound difference between Pius XI's statements concerning true emancipation for women and the resounding affirmation of the social and political rights of women found in "The Church in the Modern World" from Vatican II. Nonetheless, the bishops' special concern for women as nurturers remains in tension with their more general proclamations concerning human rights for all, including women.

In a context of approval, the bishops note, "Where they have not yet won it, women claim for themselves an equality with men before the law and in fact."[29] (The irony in this statement, of course, is that the bishops appear to believe that in 1965 women had indeed achieved equality in fact in many countries.) In a section entitled "The Essential Equality of Men; and Social Justice," the bishops declared unequivocally: "True, all persons are not alike from the point of view of varying physical power and the diversity of intellectual and moral resources. Nevertheless, with respect to the fundamental rights of the person, every type of discrimination, . . . whether based on sex, race, color, social condition, language or religion, is to be overcome and eradicated as contrary to God's intent."[30]

The language of the bishops with respect to marriage and family is one of partnership and mutual support largely devoid of sexually stereotyped prescriptions regarding the duties of husbands and wives. The Scriptural references describe marriage as the bonding of two in one flesh and as a covenant. There are no references from the *Haustafeln* in "The Church and the Modern World."[31]

29 "The Constitution on the Church in the Modern World," in *The Documents of Vatican II*, ed. Walter M. Abbott (New York: America Press, 1966), paragraph 9.

30 "The Constitution on the Church in the Modern World," paragraph 29.

31 The *Haustafeln* are the so-called household lists. These are the passages in the Christian New Testament which contain brief ethical codes describing moral obligations of household members. They advise "inferior" members of a Christian household (wives, children, slaves) to obey their superiors (husbands, parents,

Nonetheless, the bishops find themselves in a quandary because they believe that the welfare of young children requires intensive interaction between mother and child. Thus the bishops are led to declare: "The children, especially the younger among them, need the care of their mothers at home. This domestic role of hers must be safely preserved, though the legitimate social progress of women should not be underrated on that account."[32] It is not surprising that in 1965 this convocation of church leaders were unable to foresee the magnitude of social change which would be necessary, if the social progress of women was to be reconciled with the needs of young children. However, the bishops offer one avenue to pursue when they encourage the "active presence of the father" as "highly beneficial" to the development of children.[33]

The tension created by an affirmation of women as human persons entitled to full social rights and a view that women are uniquely essential to raising of children is also reflected in John Paul II's *Laborem Exercens*. John Paul II continues to assert that women are by nature different from men. This sexual difference is most clearly apparent in women's role as mothers. Therefore, the pope demands that industrial society be restructured to accommodate the needs of women. Recognizing that women now work in almost every type of job, John Paul insists that women "should be able to fulfill their task in accordance with their own nature ... [with] respect for their family aspirations and for their specific role in contributing ... to the good of society."[34] In light of centuries of Catholic tradition which describe the family as the basic unit of society, I think it is likely that John Paul has in mind here the contribution which women make to society through the maintenance of strong, loving families. John Paul is insistent that work for women should be organized in such a fashion that women's wage labor does not require "abandoning what is specific to them and at the expense of the family, in which women as mothers have an irreplaceable role."[35]

masters). See Eph 5:22–6:9 and Col 3:18–4:1.
32 "The Constitution on the Church in the Modern World," paragraph 52.
33 "The Constitution on the Church in the Modern World," paragraph 52.
34 John Paul II, *Laborem Exercens*, paragraph 92.
35 John Paul II, *Laborem Exercens*, paragraph 92.

In spite of his belief that women have a unique maternal nature, John Paul does not declare that society should facilitate a permanent return to the home for women. The pope is apparently reconciled to the idea that women work for wages. He asserts that women must not be discriminated against or excluded from jobs they are capable of performing, on account of their family responsibilities. Unfortunately John Paul does not talk about the importance of fathers to children, nor about the social contribution which fathers make through being good parents. Sadly, he does not demand that fathers must not be required "to pay for their advancement [on the job] . . . at the expense of the family."[36] (A demand he does make on behalf of women.)

Thus the family structure which church leaders are striving to safeguard marginalizes the father—neglecting his capacity for nurture and minimizing his contribution to the development of the child. At best, the father is the stern disciplinarian of Pius XI who lays down laws which insure right family order or the vague figure of Vatican II whose nurturing of his children is highly beneficial, but seemingly not essential.

The Catholic response to the justice issues which arise out of the combination of work and family in modern industrial society is hamstrung by static notions of the nature of women and of the family. Church leaders have acknowledged the historical reality of social change in almost every type of human relationship. Yet, when it comes to the family, church leaders regress to a static natural law methodology which draws conclusions based on a model of the unchanging maternal nature of women. Male clerics create an idealized vision of mother and child, then attempt to safeguard that static image by demanding that society preserve the ideal family structure.

A natural law approach which makes the maternal nature of women one constant in a changing world is no longer adequate. The same recognition of the historical, relational nature of the human person which has been used so fruitfully in Catholic discussions of other social justice issues must now be employed in discussions concerning women and the family.

36 John Paul II, *Laborem Exercens*, paragraph 92.

Barbara Hilkert Andolsen

The Second Vatican Council made the impact of history on humanity a significant theme in its discussion of the modern world. The Council unequivocally recognized ". . . the human race has passed from a rather static concept of reality, to a more dynamic, evolutionary one."[37] The bishops assembled for Vatican II acknowledged that modern individuals are always in the process of developing their full human personalities. These church fathers assert: "Modern humanity is developing a unique character and the manifestation of that character is in the ever greater discovery and affirmation of human rights."[38]

If these statements are true for humanity as a whole, they must be equally true for women. Women are experiencing profound changes as they struggle within history to achieve full personhood. Women do not remain stable, unchanging while men alone transform their humanity through the discovery of their human rights.

There are, of course, basic reproductive structures in the female body. Most women have bodies which confront them with the possibility of pregnancy, childbirth, and breastfeeding. Yet the ways in which women respond to those fundamental physical possibilities are shaped by the woman's personal response to her body, by her particular set of relationships, and by her culture.[39]

Each society must create patterns which integrate human reproductive biology into the social fabric. The job of Catholic theologians is not to baptize an idealized version of one social adaptation, but rather to challenge each society to create family structures and to integrate families into society in a fashion which respects human dignity of all persons.

We have seen that the Catholic church has rightly recognized the moral authenticity of women's demands to participate as full persons in the cultural, political, and economic affairs of their

37 "The Constitution on the Church in the Modern World," paragraph 5.

38 "Gaudium et Spes," in *Constitutiones Decreta Declarationes* (Rome: Cura et Studio Secretariae Generalis Concilii Oecumenici Vaticani II, 1966), paragraph 41 (private translation).

39 Of course, men's bodies also have basic reproductive structures. However, since a fertile man's physiological role in reproduction is limited to insemination, a man's physical experience in reproduction is less dramatic. A man's response to his procreative power is also shaped by his personal response to his body, his particular set of relationships and his culture.

societies. However, as long as women are expected to do double duty as workers and as household laborers, within social systems which refuse to acknowledge the reality of childcare and housework, the vast majority of women cannot participate equally in society.

SOCIAL JUSTICE FOR WORKING WOMEN REQUIRES SOCIAL CHANGE

In order for women to be equal participants with men in social affairs, men must shoulder an equal share of domestic tasks. In countries such as Sweden where programs have been introduced to integrate home and work more smoothly, the programs have had limited success because the majority of men have refused to participate fully. Even after seven years, only ten percent of eligible Swedish men have elected to take advantage of generous parental leave programs, and many of those few men have taken only short leaves.[40] Equality for women means that men must assume equal family obligations. They must give up the notion that housework is "woman's work" with which they magnanimously offer to "help."

A just distribution of family responsibilities requires that women and children revise their roles too. Women must be willing to relinquish some of the control over the home which they gained when they were its solitary full-time occupants. Women must review their standards for family living, critiquing the socially mediated role of "super-mom." Parents need to reexamine an overprotective attitude toward a mythic childhood meant for play, free of responsibility. Children are members of the family unit, and they should perform household tasks appropriate to their age.

But good will and cooperation among family members alone will not be sufficient to solve the problems of home and work. Equally important, social patterns must be restructured in a fashion which makes explicit provisions for domestic needs. Enormous changes will be required in order to integrate family and work in a structure humane to all parties.

Even matters which seem to have little to do with equality for

---

40 Kathleen Teltsch, "Swedish Feminists See a New Sense of Apathy," *New York Times* (9 July 1982).

women must be reexamined. For example, present land-use patterns which segregate businesses from residential housing need to be challenged. Pius XI was right in a sense he never imagined when he proclaimed that women's work should be located near where the children are. Relocating home, childcare, and work in close physical proximity would make it possible for working *parents* to participate more actively in the care of their children. Working mothers could also breastfeed their infants more conveniently.

Many workers need more flexible working hours so that they can adjust their work schedules to meet the particular needs of their own families. Flextime programs which allow workers to determine the starting and quitting times most conducive to their family needs are an example of redesigning work to mesh with personal lives.

In addition, the career track for many professional careers will certainly have to be changed in order to accommodate the demands of shared family life. It is not uncommon for employers to require that apprentice lawyers, doctors, and business executives work hours that absolutely preclude active participation in domestic life. The years between twenty-five and thirty-five are often the years in which professionals are challenged to demonstrate their ability to take the "fast track" to the top by working very long hours. Yet those are precisely the years in which many couples have young children and the heaviest household responsibilities. In my own profession, the tenure system results in the heaviest pressure for professional performance in those same key young family years. It is equally inhumane to require factory or service workers to work long hours of mandatory overtime to meet the convenience of the employer, or to pay such low wages that workers must moonlight to meet essential needs.

If we assume that contemporary women join men in a desire to enjoy the rewards of wage labor, then the question of childcare is of paramount social importance. Children are not the sole property of the parents who conceived them. Nor should the woman who gives birth to a child be considered naturally responsible for that child's total care. Children are society's future; therefore, society is responsible for the well-being of children. America gives lip service to such principles, but recent public policies show a callous disregard for the needs of children.

In order for parents to be full social participants, society must give priority to social programs which provide quality care for children. A parental leave program used equally by men and women to care for young infants without jeopardizing work relationships is essential. There is an urgent need for more good childcare facilities. The Children's Defense Fund estimates that only six million formal slots now exist for the thirteen million children with working parents who could benefit from such care.[41] Most families cannot finance quality daycare entirely out of their own salaries.[42] A few employers and many churches and synagogues have recognized a responsibility for children and are subsidizing childcare facilities.

More publicly sponsored programs are needed, too. Yet, the present federal administration's policies are making publicly subsidized childcare less available. Income eligibility requirements for subsidized childcare have been stiffened; the CETA program which paid the wages of many childcare workers has been abolished. This social trend must be reversed.

In fairness to the Reagan administration, it should be noted that Reagan did support a congressional revision of the tax law which allowed certain moderate-income parents to claim a larger tax credit for childcare expenses. Congress also provided attractive tax incentives for businesses which provided childcare facilities or which make direct payments to employees for childcare expenses. (As of 1984, it appears that few businesses have taken advantage of these childcare provisions.) While such tax reforms are better than nothing, credits do not benefit low-income parents (who owe no taxes and, hence, cannot claim a credit) or higher-income parents (who are not eligible for the larger credit). Neither have these tax policies significantly increased the number of childcare facilities available.

A significant number of American families have responsibility for

41 Alvin Sanoff and Jeannye Thornton, "Our Neglected Kids," *U. S. News and World Report* (9 August 1982), 55.
42 The problem of funding for childcare centers is actually even more severe than it seems, since daycare workers are presently, in effect, subsidizing daycare costs by working for low wages. In justice, the wages of these workers must be raised, so that some families do not gain increased time for paid work and leisure by exploiting other workers (usually minority group women).

the needs of disabled and/or elderly members. Since the senior citizen population of the United States is growing rapidly, this problem is becoming ever more acute. Social programs need to be devised which assist families in coping with illness, disability or aging without placing unfair burdens on the female members of the household. Programs which provide daytime care plus transportation for disabled or elderly relatives of workers are a step in the right direction. So are respite care programs, i.e., programs which provide facilities and personnel to care for disabled persons for short periods while family members who are the normal caretakers must be away from home.

The economic cost of justice for wage-earning women is high. Parental leave programs and work week redesign efforts often raise overhead and, unless accompanied by productivity increases, lessen profits. Social services which assist families in caring for children, the disabled, and the elderly are expensive and usually cannot be provided on a profit-making basis. Families often cannot afford the total cost of such care, therefore, such programs must be subsidized by government appropriations and/or private charity. Lessening the unfair burdens on working women and their families would require a significant reallocation of social resources.

Today the burden on women who work for wage and still carry the major share of household duties is severe. The virtue of justice challenges us to strive to distribute domestic burdens equitably. Justice for wage-earning women requires, not solely a fair division of chores among family members, but also greater social support for domestic life.

2

Women in the Cutback Economy

ETHICS, IDEOLOGY, AND CLASS[1]

Nancy Bancroft

Ethicists and feminist theologians were among those who helped to make permanent changes in American culture during the 1960s, but a sexist or neo-sexist trend since the mid-1970s has undermined the gains of the previous decade. Economically, women are losing ground they had conquered. Ideologically, there is danger that the very concept of male/female equality as a good or feasible goal will erode from the public mind. Women's enhanced role in 1984 electoral politics may obscure, but will not reverse the trend.

The purpose of this article is to delineate economic and ideological attacks on American women, and discuss the source of those attacks. A rapidly changing world situation has put extraordinary pressure on the dominant class in the United States. In order to maintain profits and a viable position in the world balance of power, the American business and governmental elite has had to pass its crisis onto the backs of poor and working citizens. In this context, women along with nonwhite Americans, bear the worst of the economic burden. As blacks face renewed racism, women also suffer the effects of neo-sexist ideology, which justifies their special plight.

My underlying thesis is that we will not do justice to ethics for sexual equality, if we separate it from certain other social-ethical issues. Racism, international affairs, and the oppression of poor and

1 The present article is based on my "'But Can She Type?' The Changing Context of Ethics for Sexual Equality," *Cross Currents* 30 (Summer, 1980).

19

working people are both interrelated and related to sexism. As practical policy and rigorous theory, ethics is weakened by compartmentalizing its subject matter. With few exceptions, social ethicists view problems in isolation which cannot be properly understood except as linked to each other and to a common source.[2]

WOMEN AND THE CUTBACK ECONOMY

According to figures from the United States Bureau of Labor Statistics, at the start of 1984 over half of all women sixteen years and older were either employed or looking for work. At first glance, the figures present a rosy picture of women no longer enslaved to home and hearth, but expressing their potential in widely-available careers. However, it is all too clear that most women work because they have to work. Labor economists cite inflation and family financial needs as main reasons for the steady growth of women in the work force. Unless one person works two jobs, it takes two wage-earners for families to achieve even a modest standard of living. In 1982, sixty-six percent of women in the labor force were single, widowed, divorced or separated, or had husbands who earned less than $15,000. These women worked from compelling economic necessity.[3] Most either held or sought full-time employment. The notion of working women as wives who are earning pin money is simply out of date.

Moreover, the largest increase among women workers is in low-paying job categories. Women are still badly paid, both in absolute terms and relative to men. In the 1980s, most women as a group earn less than two-thirds of what men earn. The glossy magazines which feature women executives make us forget their counterparts in garment sweatshops, increasingly reminiscent of the nineteenth century.

2 Beverly Wildung Harrison and Rosemary Ruether were among feminist theologians and ethicists who early began to examine interrelationships between racism, sexism and class. To date, there is more promise than fulfillment in this area, however. One helpful article, by black Marxist Michelle Russell, is "Women, Work and Politics" in *Theology in the Americas,* ed. Sergio Torres and John Eagleson (Maryknoll, NY: Orbis Books, 1976).

3 "20 Facts on Women Workers," U. S. Department of Labor, Office of the Secretary, Women's Bureau, 1982.

Women in the Cutback Economy

Women have not so much gained access to, as they have been forcibly injected into the labor market. Intensifying this process is the cutback economy of America since the early 1970s. Marked by inflated prices, diminished real wages, and intractable unemployment, the cutback economy brings paycheck concessions and mass layoffs of industrial workers. Often these workers are the husbands, sons, or sweethearts of women who take ill-paid jobs to keep the family intact. In myriad other ways, the cutback economy affects women directly. Daycare centers have raised prices or gone out of business. Now more than ever, women need free, public daycare for their children. But the demand for it is muted, because in a cutback economy people are led to believe that there is just not the money for such services. In addition, women are too tired from trying to survive to have much energy for demanding a little more. There are cutbacks in every area which make up the fabric of woman's life. It is harder and more expensive for her to find decent health care, education, and recreation for her children, transportation to stores or to her job.

The troubled economy means actual and *de facto* losses in welfare grants and services. Most welfare recipients are female heads of households and their dependent children. Here, too, women are under economic attack.

To speak of the cutback economy does not precisely identify the source of recent women's oppression: to name only processes is to lose sight of faces behind them. Cutbacks do not, after all, represent a sudden decrease in the world's wealth. They signify a changing distribution of wealth, from one set of people to another. The megacorporations and banks are making more money than ever. Nevertheless, since about 1973, it has become significantly harder for American corporate owners to maintain the profit rate they need for survival within world capitalist relations. The cutbacks here at home are the product of an international shift in the global balance of wealth and power. Our domestic economy, with its neo-sexist effects, represents an attempt by the American dominant class to pass its new burden on to the middle sectors, the working class, and the poor.

The dominant class includes less than one percent of the population. It consists of some of the highest-ranking intellectuals and public officials, the owners of the largest corporations (including American-based multinationals), and the heads of a few, giant financial groups which control and interlock with the large corporations. The members of this class need not conspire to rule America. But neither are they careless about their vast financial holdings. They organize, work, and plan together to protect and extend their interests. Partly open to public scrutiny, their policy organizations include the Council on Foreign Relations, the Business Council, the Committee for Economic Development, and the Trilateral Commission. Careful research suggests that these dominant-class organizations set in motion most if not all major decisions in American foreign and domestic life, regardless of which political party holds nominal power.[4]

The international crisis of the dominant class since the mid-1970s is more than a budget deficit or decline of the dollar. It stems from the fact that American owners are losing to world competitors in all the essentials of global empire. For the first time since World War II, the United States has fallen behind in capital accumulation, productivity, access to cheap labor, raw materials and markets, and in military power and political influence. Hence the profit rate is falling. Economists in the White House and at Harvard debate the cause, not the fact, of the falling profit rate of American business.[5]

The redistribution of wealth and power which the domestic cuts reflect is, in the first instance, from our dominant class to its counterparts in Europe, Japan, the Third World and the Soviet Union. Trilateral strategy by the American dominant class did not stem the tide of economic nationalism in Europe and Japan.[6] Japanese and

---

4 The literature on American dominant circles is substantial and includes several theoretical approaches (e.g., elite theory; Marxist and non-Marxist class theory). Some standard authors are Ferdinand Lund, C. Wright Mills, Gabriel Kolko and G. William Domhoff. My own approach comes closest to that set forth in "Who Rules America?" published in *PL* 8 nos. 5 and 6 (no author or page given). Reprinted in pamphlet from PLP, Box 808, Brooklyn, NY 11201.

5 An interesting if somewhat dated example is William Nordhaus, "The Falling Share of Profits," in *The Brookings Papers* (Washington, DC: The Brookings Institution, 1974) and Martin Feldstein's reply in the 1977 *Brookings Papers*.

6 See Richard Ullman, "Trilateralism: 'Partnership' for What?" *Foreign Affairs* (October, 1976).

European capitalists modernized production to the disadvantage of American business, while billions of dollars of unproductive American capital poured into Vietnam. Despite United States adventures in Grenada, Lebanon, and elsewhere, the Third World is no longer widely open for penetration by American interests. Rising middle powers like the OPEC nations challenge our dominant class. Africa, Asia, Latin America and even Europe have growing ties to the Soviet Union, which is the most important nation in the decline of American world hegemony.

Far from being communist in Marx's sense of replacing the profit system with distribution according to need, the Soviet Union rivals America as an imperialist power. For example, in India, as early as 1972, the Soviets controlled eighty percent of heavy engineering and electric-generating industries, thirty percent of iron and steel, and much of the export trade.[7] Today, Russia dominates a growing list of Third World countries where American interests once ruled. Particularly threatening the American dominant class are Soviet gains in strategic areas like southern Africa, the Horn of Africa, the Mid-East and Latin America, which is not only nearby, but also a new source of oil. The Russians have been self-sufficient in crude oil production and have much greater oil reserves than America does. This is not to speak of Soviet access to Eastern European oil and potential for control of Arab oilfields. Soviet economic and military growth have led even America's European allies to step up trade and banking with the U.S.S.R., while their citizens protest U.S. weapons on European soil.

The American dominant class cannot see this country become a second-rate world power without an all-out fight. In the competitive structure of advanced capitalism, not to fight would be to commit unprecedented, class suicide. Our dominant class is engaged in an international economic and political war. Increasingly, it prepares for and engages in military war, which historically accompanies global shifts in wealth and power. To recoup actual losses and

7 The figures on Soviet involvement in India are from Kathleen Gough and Hari P. Sharma, eds., *Imperialism and Revolution in South Asia* (New York: Monthly Review Press, 1973). Comparative figures on the United States and Soviet economic growth are available in UN *Statistical Yearbook* tables on Growth of World Industry.

prepare to avert future ones, the dominant class has had to initiate domestic cuts. These will deepen until the crisis of American capitalism is resolved, probably by war, in a new balance of power (or, conceivably, revolution).

In the light of the foregoing analysis, the outlook for women in the American economy is poor. Gains made during the height of the women's liberation movement are insufficient to withstand the effect of the cuts. The position of women is not only insecure, but likely to deteriorate dramatically. In a cutback economy, equality loses. Achievement of equality between the sexes would be a very expensive social reform. During periods of crisis, those who dominate American politics and economics are unwilling—in their own terms, unable—to pay for reforms of any kind.

This is the context in which religious and secular ethicists must begin to address women's oppression. Agendas formulated in the era of women's-liberation publicity are long out of date. The life situations which ethics addresses are never static. The ethics of sexual equality will remain abstract, unless we take into account the implications of the dominant class crisis for justice at home.

WOMEN AND NEO-SEXIST IDEOLOGY

In the new international situation, the American dominant class must do more than streamline the domestic economy. It must also attempt to avert political backlash against itself. Cutbacks always raise the spectre of resistance from poor and working people, particularly women and minorities, who are hit the hardest. Economic crises can become political crises for a dominant class. So another domestic priority for the dominant class in the present period is to encourage ideology which contains or forestalls political rebellion. Nationalist and militarist ideologies promote the tightening of citizens' belts, in what is called the national interest. These are consensus ideologies, which tend to blur intra-national class lines. Racism and sexism are divisive ideologies, which also blur class lines. They justify cutbacks in the case of particular groups, splitting women and minorities from potential allies and making all cuts easier. Like minorities, women are under ideological attack while their living standards decline.

Sociobiology illustrates the ideological attack on women since the 1960s. This would-be academic field won marked media attention after Harvard professor E. O. Wilson coined the word in his 1975 *Sociobiology: The New Synthesis.*[8] At the 1977 annual meeting of the American Society of Christian Ethics, Norman Faramelli correctly criticized sociobiology as a form of social Darwinism: that is, as pseudoscience.[9] Reviewing the sociobiology debate, Faramelli identified its religious, social and ethical implications. But he did not specifically address the sexism of sociobiology or its relation to the changing political economy of American women.

In the last decade and a half, various seemingly scientific works have suggested physical bases for contemporary differences in male/female social roles and characteristics. *Sociobiology* and its successors were the high point of this genre. Among many speculations, the Wilson book tells us the male/female division of labor is, over the long run, genetic. According to Wilson, we inherit our sex-role differences by natural selection, from hunter-gatherer societies in which ancient man hunted while ancient woman stayed at home. Sociobiology treats the nuclear family as a universal given, crudely biologizes social behavior, and incorrectly assumes that science can distinguish environmental from genetic causal factors. The outcome in regard to sexual equality is Professor Wilson's now-famous guess. I quote it in context:

> In hunter-gatherer societies, men hunt and women stay at home. This strong bias persists in most agricultural and industrial societies, and appears to have a genetic origin. My own guess is that the genetic bias is intense enough to cause a substantial division of labor even in the most free and egalitarian of future societies. . . .[10]

Sociobiology was rapidly taught as truth in high school textbooks. There is even a sociobiology movie aimed at high school audiences, called *Doing What Comes Naturally.* It features women in mini-

8 E. O. Wilson, *Sociobiology: The New Synthesis* (Cambridge, MA: Harvard University Press, 1975).

9 "The Religious, Social and Ethical Implications of Contemporary Sociobiology," presented at the eighteenth annual meeting of the American Society of Christian Ethics, Toronto, Canada, 14 January 1977. Unpublished paper.

10 E. O. Wilson, in the *New York Times Magazine* (12 October 1975).

skirts cheering men off to war. In 1979, Professor Wilson won the Pulitzer prize for another book, also with a misleading title: *On Human Nature.*[11] Again he wrote of constancies in human character, including sex roles, with an hereditary basis. He called for sociobiology to investigate constraints which limit options for improving social organization and ways of life.

Social improvement will indeed be under constraint, if hereditarian scholars continue to popularize the idea that inequality is a *structurally permanent* feature of human life. The genetic constraints that Wilson believes he is *finding* are actually ideological constraints he is *helping to create.*

The ideological function of the entire geneticist genre is related to the present vacuity of remaining affirmative action programs. Why fund affirmative action for women, if they are genetically apt to play only an inferior part in the division of labor? In a cutback economy, there likewise arises much questionable scholarship on race, heredity and IQ. Why help minorities with affirmative action or other costly programs, if Arthur Jensen was right that "the number of intelligence genes seem lower, overall, in the black population than in the white"?[12] Finally, ideology of the "reverse racism" sort goes one step further. Not only are minorities and women victims in the cutback economy; they are held responsible for taking jobs and education from other victims, who are white males. Forced by the international power crisis to lower the domestic living standard, the dominant class encourages us to blame each other instead of itself.

I am not arguing here that the immediate purveyors of sociobiology, or any racist or sexist ideology, consciously serve the dominant class. Nor need the dominant class consciously conspire to defraud the public. But the largest bankers and businessmen do dominate the mass media, the research foundations and the boards of the most influential universities. It is hardly surprising that

11 *On Human Nature* (Harvard University Press, 1978). There was a useful review by Stuart Hampshire in *The New York Review of Books* 25 (12 October 1978).

12 Quoted in Lee Edson, "Jensenism," *New York Times Magazine* (31 August 1969). See also Arthur Jensen, "How Much Can We Boost IQ and Scholastic Achievement?" *Harvard Educational Review,* Reprint Series No. 2, 1969.

money, prestige, and media coverage go disproportionately to writers whose ideas are consistent with business needs.[13]

Historically, both racism and sexism have performed several functions for any capitalist class. First, they justify the cheap labor status of minorities and women relative to whites and men. In America, the wage differentials between blacks and whites alone save the owners of business billions of dollars yearly. Despite a pseudo-progressive view that whites benefit from racism, studies have shown that white wages fall when the black-white income gap is greatest.[14] It is clear that women's relatively low wages keep the male wage floor down. Women are told, "Why should we pay you more? Your husbands are the breadwinners; you only supplement the income." But men are never paid more because their wives earn less.

Second, racism and sexism divide the population, making it difficult for minority and white women and men to unite for better wages, conditions, or public services. Third, sexism has a special payoff for capitalists. It saves them untold amounts in unpaid labor to keep house and raise children, maintaining present and future generations of workers.

Upon such functions as these has the enormous productivity of American capital been built. The dominant class could not afford to give up racism and sexism at the best of times. When, as now, it is in a period of hard times, the dominant class must insure a docile, divided, poorly-paid work force. In this context, hereditarian ideas

13 See note 4, above. "Who Rules America?" carefully documents the interlocking directorates which dominate media, university, and foundation boards. See also "The Ideology Process," pp. 169–201 in an excellent source on the dominant class: G. William Domhoff, *The Powers That Be: Process of Ruling Class Domination in America* (New York: Vintage Books, 1979). Domhoff's "ruling class" is at least as accurate a term as the phrase "dominant class" which I have used in this article.

14 See especially Michael Reich, "The Economics of Racism," in Richard C. Edwards et al., eds., *The Capitalist System* (Englewood Cliffs, NJ: Prentice-Hall, 1972). I know of no recent parallel studies on how women's wages hold down men's wages but I refer the interested reader to Joan Jordan's "The Place of American Women: Economic Exploitation of Women," *Revolutionary Age* 1:3 (1968), published by Freedom Socialist Publications, 3117 E. Thomas, Seattle, WA 98102 and reprinted in the early 1970s by New England Free Press, Boston, Massachusetts. Somewhat related is "The Structure of Women's Oppression" by Mary Burke in *Theology in the Americas*, 192–201.

revive which were last in currency as the Nazis began to grow, during the pre-World War II crisis of the world capitalism. It is no accident that since the mid-1970s women have found their issues trivialized, even in the liberal churches.[15] Unless people fight very hard for it, sexual equality is a luxury which the dominant class cannot allow us to see as possible or worthwhile.

IMPLICATIONS FOR THE ETHICS OF SEXUAL EQUALITY

As we have seen, the economic and ideological oppression of women in America fits a crisis-agenda of the American dominant class. Unless the crisis of the dominant class is to become permanently our own crisis, other Americans will need a different agenda. For people concerned with the discipline of ethics, the new agenda must include a reformulation of the ethics of sexual equality. Toward such reformulation, I submit three implications of the foregoing analysis. They concern three different levels of ethical inquiry.

1. At the level of ethical theory, we *should develop norms and policies that take more carefully into account the changing social facts* on which normative ethics always partly rest. Some time ago, Ralph Potter, James Gustafson, and other Christian ethicists delineated the permanent features of ethical policy, if not of norms. Potter usefully demonstrated that ethical policies all share certain elements. Specific policies differ along one or more of four dimensions: modes of moral reasoning; loyalties or reference groups; theological or quasi-theological concerns; view of the facts.[16] No ethicist would deny that our view of the facts, or interpretation of the situation, affects the ethical policy we recommend. I would go so far as to say that our view of the social and political facts determines how we choose and apply ethical norms for virtually any issue. All too often, however, we take our "facts" uncritically from established social and political scientists. Or we assume as empirically true the conclusions of the media or of popular wisdom. Others' blind spots become our own.

15 Carter Heyward and Suzanne R. Hiatt, "The Trivialization of Women," *Christianity and Crisis* 38 (26 June 1978).

16 Ralph Potter, "The Logic of Moral Argument," in *Toward a Discipline of Social Ethics*, ed. Paul Deats (Boston University Press, 1972), 93–114.

The most cunningly constructed ethical edifice will be weak—even dangerous—if its factual building blocks are outdated or wrong. This is not to say that we should uncritically accept facts from leftist media and social science, rather than establishment ones. But to apply ethical norms adequately requires both openness and hard social analysis. We need to do more primary research, particularly in economics and sociology as they bear on ethics. In secondary research, we need both to broaden our sources beyond the usual scope and to become more self-conscious about whom we trust.

2. At the level of intersection between ethical theory and ethical practice, I am suggesting that we should *never again conceive of women's liberation apart from liberation generally.* Whatever our "facts," it will not do to analyze only what currently appears as social reality. We must concentrate in particular on points of change, clues to long-range trends in the society which our norms and policies address. Women's liberation is fairly recent as a mass concept, but it rested in part on a social analysis which is at best out of date. Increased attacks on women's rights more than parallel racist attacks and the oppression of poor and working whites and males. To the extent that the women's liberation model for sexual equality did not let us see the connections between oppressions, it lacked truth and power for change.

We have lacked sophistication, in both religious and secular ethics, for probing the relation between racism, sexism and class oppression. In the 1970s some, women ethicists in particular, intuited and began to study the interconnections among the oppressed. But we still need to spell out in depth how the continuing racist, sexist and class attacks are all rooted in a single, dominant class effort to upgrade itself in the world economy at our expense.

If the issue was ever how women are to be liberated, now it is: what is happening to nearly everybody? We need to rethink the concept of liberation, before repressive ideologies remove it from all but a few, most oppressed and/or progressive minds.

3. Finally, at the level of ethical practice, social ethicists have a role to play in helping *develop unified strategy and movement among all the victims of dominant class ideology and economics.* This calls for a significant shift in our thinking, if we have been rooted in separatist social movements. In *Christianity and Crisis,* 26

June 1978, two spokespeople for women's equality in the churches said:

> the political right is gaining strength in its attack on human rights precisely because the male left, within and without the church, has made it clear that women and sexuality are not issues worth fighting very hard about. . . . As women . . . are denied full equality . . . so, too, will disappear the civil and ecclesiastical rights of other powerless people. Perhaps, sooner or later, the list will include the rights of straight, white, liberal Christian men.[17]

The authors correctly implied that concerned people need to forge a new unity, if we are to achieve sexual equality. But the authors themselves stood in the way of unity insofar as they were not abreast of changing social facts and the need for new formulations. "Straight, white, liberal Christian men" were *already* under attack at the time the authors prophesied it.

Women and minorities are the first victims of cutback economics and ideology. But dominant-class ideology aims to separate women from men, whites from nonwhites, precisely because *all* those groups are being hurt. The only people unscathed are in the dominant class or close to it (some but not all, white males). It serves this group well if we blame the victims—each other.

Racism and sexism certainly make domination and further cuts easier. But it also helps the dominant class when minorities blame all whites, or when women consider men *per se* the enemy. Our common quality and standard of life will continue to erode, unless we oppose the dominant class agenda with a more far-reaching strategy than in the separatist movements of the 1960s.

Clearly, our work is cut out for us. Many are weary from the new economic oppression and many are already poisoned by neo-sexist and racist ideas. Others are diverted by nationalism, or the false promises of seemingly progressive politicians. Even to win cuts in profit for minimal social reform would require a massive and militant movement. But the alternative to building a strong, unified movement of women and men of all colors is worse than we can easily imagine.

Religious and secular observers have suggested that there will be a gray-flannel fascism in America in the foreseeable future. I have

17 Heyward and Hiatt, "Trivialization of Women," 162.

argued elsewhere that the crisis of the dominant class impels them toward fascism, toward an anti-Soviet war.[18] Finally, however, there is another alternative—building a movement toward genuine communism. In contemporary thought, cynicism prevails about such a possibility. But as the crisis of the dominant class deepens, we may become even more cynical about expecting permanent reforms within the present system.

18 Theologian Joseph Holland poses fascism versus socialism as *the* alternatives for the American near future. See his "Marxist Class Analysis in American Society Today," *Theology of the Americas,* 317–28. Among secular sources, see Bertram Gross, *Friendly Fascism: The New Face of Power in America* (New York: M. Evans, 1980). My own analyses are in "American Fascism: Analysis and Call for Research," *Phylon* 43 (June 1982) and "Fascism and Religious Legitimation," *Radical Religion* 5 (Winter 1981).

3

Moral Callousness and Moral Sensitivity

VIOLENCE AGAINST WOMEN

Mary D. Pellauer

Violence has been a staple of ethical and theological reflection over the past several decades. The nonviolent philosophy of Martin Luther King, Jr., war and nuclear armaments, revolutionary violence, the diet of television violence fed to our children, all have been grist for the mill of the professional ethicist and theologian, as well as for makers of public policy in legislatures and churches. Given this range of attention, it is astonishing to note the profound silence in ethics regarding violence against women—rape, battering, child sexual abuse and incest. The exceptions are few, recent, and feminist.[1] This silence must be broken.

Only a feminist perspective can be adequate to guide reflection on violence against women. Only with the women's movement did we notice these abuses, let alone make strides toward understanding them, provide genuine healing for the victims, or make institutional changes to grapple with them. While we have not yet stopped rape,

---

1 Mary Daly, *Gyn/Ecology* (Boston: Beacon Press, 1978); James Nelson, *Embodiment* (Minneapolis, MN: Augsburg, 1978); Beverly Harrison, *Our Right to Choose* (Boston: Beacon Press, 1983); Marie Fortune, *Sexual Violence, the Unmentionable Sin: An Ethical and Pastoral Perspective* (New York: Pilgrim Press, 1983). I am indebted to all of these works in various ways.

battering, or child sexual abuse, we are closer today than ever before in human history to grasping the rudiments of what will be necessary to do so.

Feminism is not, in my view, a set of *a priori* answers, nor a commitment to a particular ideology. It is rather a willingness to follow questions wherever they lead us. Feminism insists upon a commitment to listening with open ears to women's experience in order to reformulate our actions and thought. It is thus more a method for creative inquiry than a set of predetermined points. Feminism *is* a commitment to women's well-being, to pursuing justice instead of patriarchy, but the substance of women's well-being is not necessarily known in advance.

Since there is so little guidance in ethics for proceeding on these topics, I shall rely upon a metaphor. The image, moral callousness, arises from my experience, so I begin in a narrative mode. Second, research of the past decade has disclosed shocking amounts of violence against women, even when we limit ourselves to rape, child sexual abuse, and battering. Section two briefly summarizes this data. Third, those dry numbers take on meaning as we understand the impact of this violence on the women victimized. Last, we shall explore briefly what we need in order to struggle for a way of life without violence against women. Moral sensitivity needs to replace our moral callousness.

MORAL CALLOUSNESS IN MY EXPERIENCE

The metaphor, moral callousness, comes directly from my experience as a woman. To describe that female experience is one preliminary way to guide discussion about violence against women. The moral callus I first discovered was my own.

More than a decade ago I was a graduate student in social ethics, living in Chicago, newly married, in the early days of the women's movement. During this period, feminists in the area began to discuss something new and deeply disturbing: rape and battered women.

I heard stories about battered women for months before something odd and eerie happened. I saw flickering and confused images in the back of my mind, images of my father picking up a butcher knife and going after my mother . . . her picking up a frying pan to fend him off ... him with a baseball bat ... her running away. These memories were confused. I saw similar scenes from different angles of vision at the same time—as though I were sitting in a kitchen chair, standing in a doorway, or in the stairwell. It dawned on me painfully that I knew something about battering out of my own life, out of my own family.

Almost more difficult to handle than these memories themselves (which drove me into therapy) was the realization that I had been hearing about battered women for almost a year without having the faintest clue that I had seen battering myself. Why had I not realized this before? What had happened to make me so distant to my own lifestory? I had escaped. I had forgotten. In escaping as an individual, in forgetting, I swept my pain and my personal experiences of life under the rug of my psyche. By denying my pain, I numbed myself to my own history. I didn't think about it; I ignored it. I grew a callus, a moral and emotional callus, over a portion of my self where once there had been sensitivity. I did so with such effectiveness that later on, hearing the stories of the pain of other women, I heard them as though they were distant and unusual, something novel, a new discovery. I was both numb and blind to the reality of my own life even when it had been named and described for me by others.

That sense of numbness, of not-feeling, is the primary reason that I settle upon the images of moral callousness and moral sensitivity to underscore what is happening to us as a people when we tolerate violence against women. The sense that I had tolerated an injustice that I had personally witnessed made me ask: how much more numb am I when I am not among the oppressed but among the oppressors? How many other injustices have I witnessed and taken for granted? What about those that I would never have directly before my own two eyes? This was the birth of a thoroughgoing hermeneutic of suspicion in my life.

Moral callousness does not describe the reactions I had as a child, sitting in those chairs or standing in those doorways, witnessing these scenes. As a child I was terrified and horrified and often afraid for my mother's life. I was often angry, frequently with both my parents, for I believed that this violence must have been my mother's fault. I was ashamed; certainly, I believed, "good" people

35

did not have these sordid scenes in their families. I was confused and bewildered, since I believed both that my family was exceptionally bad because of this violence, and that this was just par for the course, ordinary, to be expected if you were female. So I was afraid for my own future, for it seemed highly possible that this would also be my fate as a woman. As a child I took battering for granted, took it as a matter of course, in part because everyone else did too: churches, schools, media, books in the public library, relatives and friends, police and courts, hospitals, city government and county social service agencies, economic structures. All the resources and institutions which impinged on the life of our family, all participated in the web of interlocking social mechanisms which swept these issues under the rug, rendered us blind to the moral import of this behavior. I do not blame myself as a child for taking this violence for granted, for it was the only life and reality I knew.

On the other hand, I do blame myself as an adult for the thickened emotional and moral skin, the callus, which I had cultivated. While the callus I developed grew initially out of the denial which many victims go through (for no one can live with such awareness continually in the forefront of one's mind), still it took on dimensions of the larger societal denial. It made me hold battered women at arm's length during those initial months of having this abuse named and described. It short-circuited the normal transactions of empathizing and sympathizing with battered women. It made me numb on a number of levels. Dissolving that numbness, learning to respond and to feel, has been a long hard process.

Moral callousness is not an image or metaphor of our moral condition to berate or bludgeon others about moral faults I do not share. On the contrary. The fact of my experience is that good people, nice people, people of good will, whom I do not hesitate to call "moral" in the ordinary use of that term, myself included, all participate in and perpetuate, even extend and legitimate, violence against women simply by going about our business in an ordinary way. We do so primarily by our quotidian participation in social patterns and institutions which make up the bulk of everyday life. This is perplexing, not to say mystifying.

Feminist ethics does not dispel this perplexity. Indeed, it may even deepen it. But by refracting it at different angles, new dimensions may be perceived, reflected upon, discussed, and rendered actionable in new ways.

MASSIVE SOCIAL PATTERNS OF THE VICTIMIZATION OF WOMEN

Today we know a great deal more about violence against women than we did, say, fifteen years ago when I left home. Our new knowledge is due to the women's movement, which has generated intellectual and institutional resources about such issues with astonishing ingenuity and speed. There are now more than 500 battered women's shelters and 1500 rape crisis centers around the country. There has been advocacy for much-needed changes in laws and law enforcement agencies, hospital emergency rooms and psychological counselors.

It remains true that in the 1980s we still do not know the *precise* extent of any of these abuses. This cloud of ignorance is partly due to the nature of these crimes. To be raped still brings the shame and dishonorment that results in the very serious under-reporting of sexual assault. The sexually abused child is not only confused and frightened; she may also be explicitly commanded to secrecy under threats, emotional manipulation or fear. To be beaten by one's husband is still understood by many wives as part of the lot of married women, as embarrassing, or as the inevitable suffering of the human condition.

Our contemporary ignorance is also due to the definition of terms. In forty-two states, for instance, by legal definition rape cannot occur between a husband and wife.[2] Other classes of women are virtually defined as unrapeable, especially prostitutes and racial/ethnic minority women. "Battering" is not a legal, but a political, category. (Calls from battered women to authorities are often logged under "domestic disturbances.")

If we proceed by the legal definitions alone, there are massive amounts of these abuses occurring annually in the U.S.A. If we look beyond the legal definitions, the extent of each abuse correspondingly rises.

2 While eight progressive states struck the marital exemption, thirteen others expanded exemptions for assailants who had been in voluntary sexual relationships with their victims prior to the violent assault. See Diana Russell, *Rape in*

Mary D. Pellauer

The F.B.I. Uniform Crime Report informs us that in 1976 there were 56,000 completed or attempted rapes, a number which had swollen to 81,500 in 1981. Using the F.B.I.'s own guidelines (nine unreported rapes for every one reported), the early 1980s thus witnessed three-quarters of a million completed or attempted rapes. No one can say with certainty whether that increase is due to a change in the ratio of reported to unreported rapes, or to a genuine increase in sexual assaults in our nation; many feminists believe the latter.

Using these official figures, "a *conservative* estimate is that, under current conditions, 20–30 percent of girls now twelve years old will suffer a violent sexual attack during the remainder of their lives."[3] Whether that figure may stand equally for white women and for racial/ethnic minority women is disputed. Many in the anti-rape movement believe that minority women are in greater jeopardy than are white women, for they are prey both to the men of their own communities and to the white majority. In one study in Philadelphia, the proportions of black and white women among those reporting rape led researchers to note that "a black female is nearly six times as likely (5.7 to 1) to be a victim in a reported rape in Philadelphia as is a white female."[4] Others argue that the reporting rate for white women may be markedly lower than that for black women (but higher than that for Hispanic women), because white women either have other resources to which to turn or believe that they have more status to lose by reporting.[5]

Marriage (New York: Macmillan, 1983), 21–22.

3 Allan Griswold Johnson, "On the Prevalence of Rape in the United States," *Signs* 6 (Autumn, 1980), 145.

4 Thomas W. McCahill, Linda C. Meyer, Arthur M. Fischman, *The Aftermath of Rape* (Lexington, MA: Lexington Books, 1979), 7.

5 Thus that Philadelphia study reports that the most frequent reason for reporting was a desire for help and comfort (*The Aftermath of Rape*, 9). Since seventy percent of these women had median incomes of less than $9,000 per year (in 1973–74), and the incomes of fully ninety-five percent of them were below $12,000, and forty-five percent were on public assistance (7–8), researchers "hypothesized that victims who have the resources or the support to seek help and comfort privately (without relying on the public institutions) would be more likely to do so and not report to the police. Conversely, many victims of lower socioeconomic background are virtually forced to report to the police due to a lack of alternatives for receiving care and assistance" (83). Also in this study black women were slightly more likely than white women to participate in the

How far out of line may be those official rates is indicated by a recent groundbreaking study by Diana Russell based on a random sample rather than on self-selected or volunteer populations. Fully forty-four percent of the nearly one thousand women interviewed had experienced at least one completed or attempted sexual assault (thirty-three percent a completed rape). Furthermore, of the women who had ever been married in this population, fourteen percent, or one in seven, had been sexually assaulted by their husbands or ex-husbands during or after the marriage.[6]

The statistics on child sexual abuse, including incestuous abuse, are the most problematic. A worker at the National Center for Child Abuse and Neglect in the federal Department of Health and Human Services suggested to me on the phone in 1983 that 44,700, or seven percent, of the cases of substantiated maltreatment of children was the best national figure available for sexual abuse. Areas with new comprehensive laws on child sexual abuse, such as Minnesota, find higher rates even in official terms. Officers in the county agencies in my area suggest that sixteen percent of all abuse and neglect cases, or one-third of the abuse cases alone, are sexual abuse.

Other sociological studies suggest that rates are considerably higher than we get over the official channels. Independent research suggests that between one in five and one in three girls (and one in eleven boys) may be at risk sexually as children. Father-daughter incest represents the vast majority of such cases within the family (ninety-four percent).[7] Others indicate that when explicit education on sexual abuse prevention is given to school-age children, numbers of reports average around one child in six (and the proportion of male victims rises).[8] In Russell's random sample, thirty-eight percent

interviews (12).

6 Russell, *Rape in Marriage*, 64, 57. In this study rape rates for white and racial/ethnic minority women were not significantly different from the ratios in the population except for the lower rates for Asian-American women (or so Diana Russell commented at a conference on marital rape, 25 May 1984, in Minneapolis, MN). Data from this study will be further analyzed in her *Sexual Exploitation*, forthcoming from the Russell Sage Foundation, 1984.

7 This evidence is reviewed and summarized by Judith Herman, *Father-Daughter Incest* (Cambridge, MA: Harvard University Press, 1981), 7–21.

8 "Child Sexual Abuse Prevention Project," written and piloted by Cordelia Kent, Hennepin County Attorney's Office, Minneapolis, MN, 1979, 16–17.

of the women interviewed reported at least one experience of sexual abuse before age eighteen; sixteen percent reported one or more experiences of intrafamilial sexual abuse before that age. Only two percent of these cases of intrafamilial sexual abuse, and six percent of the extrafamilial abuse, were ever reported.[9]

The accuracy of our information is also hard to judge with regard to battering. But we do have some indications of the extent and seriousness of this abuse. In the mid-1960s in Chicago, domestic disturbance calls to the police exceeded the total for murder, rape, and aggravated assault put together. The F.B.I. estimates that one-quarter of all murders are family cases, and that one-half of these are spouse murders. While that proportion suggests a perverse equality, it is more apparent than real. Wives are seven times more likely than husbands to kill in self-defense—that is, in the course of being battered. Indeed, in the 1970s in Kansas City, forty percent of all the homicides were spouse murders, in half of which the police had previously been summoned five or more times to the home for "domestic disturbances." One random sample by Suzanne Steinmetz found that in fully ten percent of the families in the study, extreme physical abuse was present.[10] If we extrapolate from this group to the whole population of coupled adults, it suggests 4.7 million family situations in which battering occurs. Diana Russell also found evidence of battering in her random sample. Of the women who had been married, twenty-one percent had been battered, a proportion which would extend that estimate to 9.9 million battering families in this nation.[11]

Even considering all those qualifiers on who, where, and why numbers are tabulated about these abuses, these figures are astonishing. They astonish as much by their invisibility as by their extent. The fact that violence against women can be as prevalent as this suggests that we are both callous *and* blindered—and that the two are interrelated in our society as a whole as surely as they were in

9 Diana E. H. Russell, "The Incidence and Prevalence of Intrafamilial and Extrafamilial Sexual Abuse of Female Children," *Child Abuse and Neglect* 7 (1983), 133–46.

10 This evidence is reviewed in Del Martin, *Battered Wives* (San Francisco: Glide Publications, 1976), 11.

11 Russell, *Rape in Marriage*, 89.

my personal experience. In turning to the impact of these violent experiences on their victims, we must keep firmly in mind how hidden these crimes are from our ordinary view.

THE CLIMATE OF FEAR, DISTRUST, AND DENIAL

To ask what these numbers mean, we must begin with the meaning of these abuses to their victims. Listening seriously to the experiences of the victims has been fundamental to understanding these abuses. While there are individual differences and variations, there are some broad, common, and important patterns of responses in the experiences of victims.

The serious and often lethal nature of these abuses should alert us to the fundamental traumatic crises they precipitate in the lives of victims. Many raped and battered women perceive the assaults upon them as *life-threatening*. Women sexually assaulted report that they were afraid of being killed by the rapists, who often threaten to do precisely that, and may back up the threats by the use of a weapon. The perceptions of these women are not exaggerations. Even if the life of the victim is not taken by the assailant, we should not minimize the impact upon her. When rape victims were asked to rate the degree of crisis the assault inflicted upon their lives, forty-two percent responded that the rape was the most upsetting event of their entire lives; another quarter rated it eight to nine on a ten-point scale, as "highly stressful." The primary emotional response to rape is fear and terror. The trauma is compounded by the confrontation with powerlessness and helplessness, an attack on the sense of self, guilt and shame provoked by the violent intrusion into the most private personal space, feelings of grief and loss. All provoke great upheaval and disruption in the life of the rape victim. Some women may take years to recover from the assault, particularly if they do not have access to supportive networks to ease and enable the process of healing. Marital rape too is extremely traumatic, and has serious long-term effects on the lives of victims, increased and exacerbated by the use of other physical violence, the use of a weapon, and the duration of the assaults.

Similarly, battered women often report that they did not know how they survived the physical assaults. Battering husbands often threaten to kill their wives—and, as we indicated in the previous section, battering often results in homicide. Battered women are in effect trapped with their assailants, who may explode into violence during disagreements over household tasks, possessive jealousy, the husband's perception of his own authority, or sometimes for no reason at all. As the violence in such an intimate relationship becomes chronic, the effects become cumulative upon the battered woman. "Fear becomes an integral part of [her] daily life. . . . She remains in a state of apprehension and depression. She wonders if she will ever be free from fear and pain."[12] Such women may become hopeless and desperate, particularly if they turn to outside agencies and meet blame, misunderstanding, and unwillingness to aid.

Child sexual abuse too is perceived as frightening and shocking to the children. While the results of any kind of child sexual abuse are far from benign, father-daughter incest is most damaging. Serious difficulty as adults, including histories of divorce, institutionalization, prostitution, higher rates of adolescent pregnancy, runaway attempts, suicide attempts, drug or alcohol abuse, promiscuity, a sense of permanent stigmatization, often mark such women sexually abused as children.[13]

Fear and distrust are intimately related. The climate of fear in which victims live, perhaps for years, erodes their capacities to trust. Their jumpy edginess and caution may extend to everyone who comes into contact with them. Often it is men, unknown men, known men, men in general, who become the focus of such wariness. Rape victims and battered women remark that the assaults made them upset around men, increasingly suspicious of men, or simply unable to trust men any longer. These generalized feelings of distrust of men do not necessarily last forever. But they may be exacerbated by multiple experiences of assault into virtually a "negative worldview."[14]

Similar though perhaps more deepseated difficulties in trusting others are among the most painful of the effects of incestuous abuse.

12 R. Emerson Dobash and Russell Dobash, *Violence against Wives* (New York: The Free Press, 1979), 137, 139.
13 Herman, *Father-Daughter Incest*, 93–100.
14 McCahill, Meyer, and Fischman, *The Aftermath of Rape*, 31, 54.

"The most devastating result" of incest "is the irretrievable loss of the child's inviolability and trust in the adults in his or her life."[15] For child victims as for adult victims, mistrust is exacerbated by the reactions of those to whom these people turn for help. Children's disclosures of sexual abuse are greeted by disbelieving rejections or worse, by accusations of blame and lying:

> Unless specifically trained and sensitized, average adults, including mothers, relatives, teachers, counselors, doctors, psychotherapists, investigators, prosecutors, defense attorneys, judges and jurors cannot believe that a normal, truthful child would tolerate incest without immediately reporting it, or that an apparently normal father could be capable of repeated, unchallenged sexual molestation of his own daughter. The child of any age faces an unbelieving audience when she complains of ongoing incest. The troubled, angry adolescent risks not only disbelief, but scapegoating, humiliation, and punishment as well.[16]

Battered women similarly face disbelief and denial from an array of professionals and other persons to whom they turn. Like rape victims, battered women face an ideology which blames them, which minimizes the crises which they endure, which justifies the inattention and mercilessness to which they are subjected.[17]

Why do we deny, minimize, accuse, and blame women and girls when they ask for help? Why do we look away or do nothing, as did the bystanders on the city street when Kitty Genovese was raped and killed, or the spectators at the gang rape in the New Bedford bar? Why do neighbors who hear violent altercations next door fail to reach out? There are no simple or definitive answers to such questions, but we can suggest a few of the reasons for this moral callousness.

Our patriarchal history constructs the first and deepest layer of our moral calluses for us. The perverse patriarchal matrix mythologizes both victims and offenders. Patriarchal notions wear away at

15 Sandra Butler, *Conspiracy of Silence: The Trauma of Incest* (New York: Bantam Books, 1979), 3.

16 Roland Summit, "Beyond Belief: The Reluctant Discovery of Incest," in *Women's Sexual Experience: Explorations of the Dark Continent*, ed. Martha Kirkpatrick (New York: Plenum Press, 1982), 137.

17 See especially the chapters on "Relatives, Friends and Neighbors," "The Helping Professions," and "The Police and Judicial Response," in Dobash and Dobash, *Violence against Wives*.

the dignity and importance of women, justify the violence men do to women by claiming it is our fault, deflect our attention from abuse by claiming it as inevitable and immutable. It is a waste of tears and energy to become disturbed about what cannot be changed.

Blaming victims keeps those who are not yet victims feeling safe. That only luck, fortune, chance, circumstances, stand between any woman and such violence is difficult to accept, for it means that we must confront the risks and dangers inherent in our patriarchal way of life. Blaming victims thus may stem from

> a basic need for all individuals to find a rational explanation of violent crimes, particularly brutal crimes. Exposure to senseless, irrational, brutal behavior makes everyone feel vulnerable and helpless. It then can happen at any time, any place, and to anyone. It is relieving to find that the victim has done something or neglected something that plausibly contributed to the crime. It makes the other individual feel less helpless and less vulnerable and so feel safer.[18]

Similarly, falsehoods and stereotypes about offenders protect our illusions of safety. By attributing these crimes to sick, deranged, abnormal personalities, sex perverts and monsters and strangers on the street, we can assure ourselves that the men around us would never do such things. Unfortunately, assailants cannot be picked out from other peaceloving men by their psychopathology, looks, occupations, racial/ethnic minority status, or economic level. I have been agonized more than once to discover assailants among my acquaintances and even friends in churches and theological schools.

Keeping sexual and domestic violence at arm's length also serves to maintain our personal and social comfort. Maintaining our ignorance about such topics insures that we will not have to scrutinize ourselves for the ways in which we contribute to such evils, or it insures that we will not have to face our own pain.[19] If we do not

18 Martin Symonds, "The Accidental Victim of Violent Crime," in Stefan A. Pasternack, ed., *Violence and Victims* (New York: Spectrum Publications, 1975), 92.

19 During a pilot project for child sexual abuse prevention, for instance, workers met a teacher disturbed that the material would upset the children. Further exploration disclosed that his fears "stemmed from his own childhood victimization," with which he had not come to terms. *Child Sexual Abuse Prevention Program*, 22–23.

have to change, we can avoid the arduous struggles needed on both the personal and the societal fronts. We will not have to work to reorient our personal attitudes and behaviors. And we can sidestep the tedious, complicated, and time-consuming business of pressuring for change in public authorities—police, court systems and legislatures, the medical establishment, the social work bureaucracies, the clergy and churches, the housing industry, psychological treatment authorities, schools, and businesses.

It is important to note that healing and recovery are possible for victims of all these abuses, provided that the assaults are taken seriously by those to whom they turn, and provided that the helping agencies are sensitive and well-informed on the dynamics of each particular abuse. Rape victims *do* reorganize their lives and their senses of self; often they channel their anger and outrage into rape centers to reach out to others like them. Battered women who turn to shelters find both material support and empowerment towards making choices for their own health and well-being. Victims of child sexual assault are more likely, in the 1980s, to find agencies capable of dealing with their situations and groups in which to meet others with similar abusive experiences.

Understanding the dynamics of victimization, and healing the wounds from these abuses, are both essential. But they are also minimal. To heal the climate of fear, distrust, and denial that violence breeds is perhaps even more important. We need social transformation as much as we need understanding and succor to victims. We must struggle to stop this senseless round of patriarchal violations of women's integrity and life processes. We must confront the need and the possibility of *preventing* rape, battering, and child sexual abuse. To do so we must develop moral sensitivities to supplant our moral callousness.

MORAL SENSITIVITY:
STRUGGLING TO TRANSFORM PATRIARCHY

To struggle actively towards transforming the society, our moral calluses must be replaced with the moral sensitivity that is alive in response to the impact and meaning of violence against women. We must feel the pains, agonies, and confusions assaulted persons experience. We must allow ourselves to feel the moral indignation appropriate to such abuse. We must harness our moral passions to the admittedly large but possible and urgent task of working on the longterm overhaul of the social institutions that give rise to these pains. How we understand male power and dominance in the harsh light of violence against women, how we express its meaning and importance, is a fundamental issue for feminist ethics. Here we can only suggest some dimensions of this project which are most appropriate to the enterprise of ethics.

The most salient and perplexing dimension of violence against women is how ordinary and how taken for granted it is in our society. This ordinariness, this silence, this blindness, raise serious issues about whether in fact we approve of rape, battering, and child sexual abuse, verbal protestations to the contrary notwithstanding. When we stand by in silence, we give *tacit consent* to assailants and to these abuses. When we do not lift a finger to intervene, in effect we *collude* with assailants.[20] The fact that we ordinary people, in the ordinary actions of our daily lives, participate in the conditions that create and legitimate violence against women raises the suspicion that our ordinary terms of morality themselves are patriarchal. Adrienne Rich has put this most sharply.

> From a thoughtful woman's point of view, no ethical ideal has deserved our unconditional respect and adherence because in every ethics crimes against women are mysteriously unnamed or glossed over. . . . The absence of respect for women's lives is written into the heart of male theological doctrine, into the structure of the patriarchal family, and into the very language of patriarchal ethics.[21]

It has become common among feminists to note that the very word "virtue," so central to the western tradition's understanding of ethics, stems from the root *vir*, which literally meant "man" in the sense of male (in its turn related to *vis* meaning "force" or "strength").

This linguistic suspicion is not allayed by the fierce double

---

20 While John Harris does not put his points in this sharp fashion, the arguments about negative actions in *Violence and Responsibility* (London: Routledge and Kegan Paul, 1980) have similar conclusions.
21 Adrienne Rich, *Of Woman Born: Motherhood as Experience and Institution* (New York: W. W. Norton, 1976), 269–70.

standard for women and men in moral matters that has pervaded most of the tradition. For most of the history of the West, women have been viewed in principle as male property. That property presumption has skewed the terms of ethical reflection and action. Rape laws in the ancient world defined the crime as one against the property holder, whether husband or father; such laws confused rape with adultery and prescribed capital punishment for both the victim and the offender; children were of course property of their father to be disposed of as the father pleased, including into child marriage. Beating a wife, like beating a child, was not only legal but often recommended. Moral behavior for women has often been virtually coextensive with chastity and domesticity. These terms could only falsify and systematically distort the actual moral struggles of women victimized by male violence. When battered women are exhorted to keep the family together, for instance, they are prey to this pernicious ethical legacy. Rape victims queried about whether they resisted enough are treated as though they consented to an act which they experience as a danger of injury, mutilation or death, something which would be unthinkable in other cases of assault.

To undo those double standards does not mean simply to apply to women the ethical principles by which men have been exhorted or believed to live. It means rather to participate as equals in the process of the creation of the moral standards themselves. To do so will require us not simply to go looking for neatly stated propositions which can summarize our moral wisdom in a sentence or two. It requires us to listen carefully to the experiences women have of life, just as the movement against violence has done to victims. How our experiences and our ethics are related to each other, however, is a large and mostly unasked question in the field of ethics. In eliciting and attending to women's experiences, none are perhaps so crucial nor so ignored as our experiences of our *bodies*. To participate in creating nonpatriarchal moral standards we will need "to think through the body, to connect what has been so cruelly disorganized."[22]

22 Rich, *Of Woman Born: Motherhood as Experience and Institution*, 284. She continues, "There is an inexorable connection between every aspect of a

Mary D. Pellauer

To connect what has been so cruelly sundered may also have profound practical implications for preventing violence against women. It seems that *dissociation,* disconnection, is prominent in offenders' behaviors. It is risky to generalize about offenders, or course, particularly across the range of three such different crimes as rape, battering, and child sexual abuse, and particularly when so few offenders are identified and studied.[23] But persons who work with rapists, batterers, and sexual abusers of children point to themes that are directly relevant to moral callousness and moral sensitivity. The crimes of offenders are often related to an inability to feel their own feelings and a refusal to take responsibility for their own actions. Offenders often project responsibility on to victims. "She was asking for it" may be the most common rationalization for violence against women. Related to such insidious interpretations of the situation may be offenders' inability to express their own emotions, to be in touch with themselves. Therapists in treatment programs stress the "need to teach the patient how to recognize affect and describe it verbally."[24] Emotions unrecognized, particularly pain, depression, and anger, results in assault for lack of more proximate expression.

A callus is precisely an area which is tough, horny, hardened, *unfeeling;* the synonyms slide readily from the physical sense of hardened into the larger human ones of unresponsiveness: thick-skinned, impervious, inured, insensible; blind to, deaf to, dead to;

woman's being and every other; the scholar reading denies at her peril the blood on her tampon; the welfare mother accepts at her peril the derogation of her intelligence. These are issues of survival, because both the woman scholar and the welfare mother are engaged in fighting for the mere right to exist" (284–85). Hence I have begun this scholarly essay with an account of my experience of these topics.

23 Some offenders commit rape in the course of another felony, such as burglary. Some assailants are violent instrumentally, believing that violence is a legitimate means to achieve some overriding purpose. Other offenders were themselves victims as children. For the latter, our general ignoring of sexual and domestic violence takes its concrete toll in extending the dreary rollcall of bruises and blood into the next generation. See Richard T. Rada, *Clinical Aspects of the Rapist* (New York: Grune and Stratton, 1978); and A. Nicholas Groth with H. Jean Birnbaum, *Men Who Rape: The Psychology of the Offender* (New York: Plenum Press, 1979). At present there do not seem to be comparable studies of batterers and incest offenders.

24 John R. Lion, "Developing a Violence Clinic," in Pasternack, ed., *Violence and Victims,* 82.

48

neglectful, inattentive, unsusceptible. This range of meanings has to do with our feelings, our capacity to be touched by, to be sensitive to the human reality in question. In a callus the healthy transmission of messages along nerve fibers does not function; calluses neither receive nor send messages to and from the central nervous system.

Something analogous happens in the realm of morality when our emotional nerve system is impaired. More than two hundred years ago, Mary Wollstonecraft said, "Those who are able to see pain, unmoved, will soon learn to inflict it."[25] This insight suggests that perhaps it is because women in our society are encouraged and allowed a greater range of emotional expressiveness that we are as nonviolent as we are. Male socialization does not encourage them to express their feelings, especially those of pain, sadness, vulnerability, fear. To weep as a boy is to be a crybaby or a momma's boy. To weep as an adult is to be unmanly. It may be that our repression of the full range of emotional responsiveness in men is connected directly to violence against women. By dichtomizing human capacities across gender lines as we have so falsely and foolishly done under patriarchy, we have set the terms under which violence against women flourishes. We have focused the conditions for violence in the heart of the male role and male identity; correspondingly, we have established the conditions for victimization in the heart of the female role and female identity. That men are cool and rational—except when they run amok; that women are not to be trusted—except when we are firmly impressed into subordination at whatever cost; these strange premises are not merely evident in individual psychology but are built into a whole array of institutions that surround us.

Wollstonecraft's insight speaks to our capacities to weep, to mourn, to lament, to cry, over pain. It suggests that our ability to feel the pain of others is an ethical resource which may aid us in the larger task of learning to be actively gentle, to be healers of the vicious patterns of violence against women. I do not *know* if this is true. (Certainly the treatment programs for offenders are highly suggestive.) But it is true to my own experience of growth away

25 *A Vindication of the Rights of Woman* (1792; New York: W. W. Norton, 1967), 256.

from moral callousness. When I short-circuit my own pain, when I stuff it under the polite surface rug of my bland exterior, I also become less capable of responding to the pain of others. When I know my own pain for my own, explore it, feel it, talk it or act it out, it clears the air for me to respond to the suffering of others. The springs of action are cleared so that I can both feel with the other and respond to her. In the course of face-to-face relationships, pain cries out for relief. The spontaneous response is to be moved, to go forward in aid. Indeed, that response is virtually a physical one, an urge to move toward the suffering person, to touch them, to hold, to comfort, to assuage and allay. In the encounter between two persons, it requires a deliberate act of will to shunt aside this spontaneous desire to move toward the one who suffers. In doing so, one feels "callous," precisely as though one were refusing to be "moved" in the very most physical sense of that term. That sensitivity is only actual as we *act* to change the situations in which women are victimized.

To feel what we have been through, what others are going through: to be sensitive rather than hardened to pain in the lives of women. These may be frail resources for the moral tasks ahead of the women's movement as it confronts violence against women; they are not everything. Feeling pushes one forward to do analysis, to create institutions and networks and coalitions—to make intellectual and historical and spiritual and political connections.

To contribute to that future day of justice and peace is certainly the task of ethics, feminist or not. Our silence as a discipline only perpetuates the numbness and the taking-for-granted, the moral calluses of our present order.

4

Toward an Understanding of Feminismo Hispano *in the U.S.A.*

Ada Maria Isasi-Diaz

How more invisible than invisible can you be? And yet there is a quality of invisible invisibility which many of us women, feminists, of other than the dominant culture have. A *Feminista Hispana* is at home nowhere. Invisible invisibility has to do with people not even knowing that they do not know you. As *Feministas Hispanas* we are so irrelevant that the mind constructs needed to think about us do not exist. Society at large thinks of us as Hispanics and the majority of Hispanics think of us as women. Only among our very few is our name understood: FEMINISTA HISPANA.

In the act of naming ourselves we are born. Our lives are a constant struggle to be called by name. We have not gone any further than that. We name ourselves because we are, but others cannot even imagine that we exist and, therefore, refuse to call us by name. For me this constitutes the highest form of oppression: others so define you that they refuse to recognize the way you define yourself. And, it is the task of all peoples of good will to recognize evil, fight against it, hope for good and work to bring it about. This is what makes us human for love cannot exist without justice and, in our world today, justice does not exist without people.

In this article I explore the four worlds in which the life of *Feministas Hispanas* unfolds. This will provide a framework to

51

understand the invisible invisibility, the double burden of racial/ethnic diminishment and sexism that we endure, a burden which is often a triple one, for the feminization of poverty is a reality principally among racial/ethnic women.

However, before discussing these four worlds of the *Feminista Hispana*, I would like to propose that to understand what follows, the kind of understanding that leads to a conversion which precipitates action, there exist two prerequisites: commitment to truth and empathy.[1]

COMMITMENT TO TRUTH

In our world today there exists great awareness of justice and injustice. People are quick to claim their rights, to name their oppressors, to gather support and struggle for what is right. It is becoming increasingly hard to make someone understand that they are oppressors. It comes easy to claim we are oppressed, but we seldom bow our heads, accept the truth, and recognize our participation in oppressing others. We do not understand that being oppressed and being an oppressor are not mutually exclusive. Our commitment to justice makes it almost impossible for us to recognize our participation in systems that benefit us at the expense of someone else. Only our commitment to truth can help us to accept that the intricacies of our modern society often cause us to be

---

1 I would like to dedicate this article to so many people. Please know that if you are not mentioned by name it does not mean that it is not dedicated to you. First of all I wish to dedicate this to my mother, Nena. A woman of fierce spirit and unwavering determination, she taught me to demand much of myself and to struggle for what I believe. I also want to dedicate this to the four Hispanic women in the U.S.A. with whom I have shared in a significant way my struggle as *Feminista Hispana*. They are Yolanda Tarango, Margarita Castañada, Teresita Basso and Olga Villa-Parra. *Gracias, hermanas.* Thirdly, I want to remember five Anglo women who struggle unceasingly within the feminist movement against racism and with whom we can all count to have and exercise a preferential option for us Hispanic women: Mary Pellauer, Rosemary Radford Ruether, Rosalie Muschal-Reinhardt, Beverley Harrison and Marjorie Tuite. Finally I wish to acknowledge my debt of gratitude to two black feminists that have been true sisters to me and inspired me to better understand and to write about the struggle of the *Feminista Hispana:* Delores Williams and Katie Cannon. *VIVA LA HERMANDAD!*

oppressors while at the same time, without any doubt, being oppressed. Truth requires us to accept reality, while justice demands of us to struggle against oppression. One cannot exist without the other.

EMPATHY

Certain kinds of understanding require knowledge, intellectual comprehension, experiments, and even debates. The kind of understanding required for conversion necessitates more than anything else, empathy. Empathy is the ability of the heart to feel with the other person. It requires that we open ourselves not only at the intellectual level, but especially at the emotional level. To empathize is to risk, because it necessitates our being vulnerable.

Empathy does not ask that you feel the way I do, think the way I do, act the way I do. But empathy does demand that we listen with the heart. It is not only a matter of respecting what others say and do, who they are. Empathy asks that you seriously consider that what is true and good for others might well be true and good for you. That is the only way that new elements can enrich our society, our movement, for if not, those elements become mere appendages that can quietly and quickly be disposed of instead of becoming intrinsic parts of what is normative for all.

"YOU CAME HERE, YOU LEARN OUR LANGUAGE"

He politely listened to me and then, embarrassed, while continuing to empty trash cans into the dumpster, he sheepishly answered me, "Ay don espik inglish." When I repeated my question in Spanish, his eyes lit up, and after telling me he had no idea where the address I was looking for was, he said to me, *"Ven aca, chica, tu eres cubana?"* When he realized I was a Cuban like him, you would have thought we were long-time friends! And we were. In Cuba we might have never thought that but in a foreign land, both of us being Cubans made us friends!

There is no need for me to delineate here the multifaceted oppression that Hispanics suffer in this country. Our lack of ability to speak the language makes education, the golden ladder in this society up to now, a very difficult road to travel. Many of us arrive here without a financial base. Starting over is an everyday affair. To attain positions of power, economic well-being, and prestige are almost impossibilities for us, simply because we do not belong to the dominant culture.

There is a much more subtle oppression, however, that few understand or talk about. That is the oppression we suffer when those values, traditions, and customs that are intrinsic to being Hispanic are not valued, are not remembered, are not celebrated. In our attempt to fit in this society, we are constantly asked to become assimilated, to become Americanized. Do you know at what expense? To fit in this society means to accept the competitiveness intrinsic to this system which works directly against and to the detriment of our sense of community. To become Americanized means to adopt a "keeping up with the Joneses" mentality that requires a high degree of individualization. But we Hispanics value the person—the person, however, understood as a member of a family, of a community! To make it in this country we have to hide our emotions, and as we do, we die a thousand deaths. To be accepted as an American means having to give up our hyperbole and emotional binges, thus subscribing to an even flow of living which little by little kills our spirits.

We Hispanics feel oppressed in this society when we hear ourselves defined in negative terms: nondominant culture, minority, marginalized people. The oppression we suffer does not even have a name. We are included under the term racism, a word that only applies to us by extension: racism is oppression based on skin color and only lately has it come to mean also the systemic oppression of those belonging to a culture other than the dominant one. The oppression we Hispanics suffer has to do with struggling to explain what you mean only to realize that they will not understand because your patterns of conceptualization, your points of reference, your value system and loyalties are more foreign to them than the language your mother taught you—which they do not value enough to learn. "You came here, you learn our language," they say, so easily shrugging off the responsibility for the economic and political situations in our countries which obliged us to become refugees, for which they are at least partially responsible. And we then suffer the frustration not only of not being understood, but of not being able to influence actions.

Our oppression, our invisible invisibility as Hispanics is that sense you begin to have after you are here a short while that this society deals with you the way they do with a circus: they love our *mariachis, salsa, arroz con pollo, bacaladitos, margaritas*–we can really entertain them. With the oppressed of ancient times we say:

> Beside the streams of Babylon
> we sat and wept
> at the memory of Zion,
> leaving our harps
> hanging on the poplars there.
> For we had been asked
> to sing to our captors,
> to entertain those who had carried us off:
> "Sing," they said
> "Some hymns of Zion."
>
> How could we sing
> one of Yahweh's hymns
> in a pagan country? . . .
> —(Psalm 137)

The oppression and the invisible invisibility that are our lot as Hispanics in this country are the result of having the dominant culture's prejudices as the accepted and imposed societal norm.

For us *Feministas Hispanas,* to work against oppression is to work for liberation. We do not seek equal opportunities, we do not seek for success within the societal structures of this system. This system, and most probably the same can be said of the societal systems from which we come, functions in such a way that for us or for any group to be successful, other groups have to be oppressed. Because we believe that no one can be free until everyone is free, what we *Feministas Hispanas* seek is to participate in the community of struggle against all oppressive systems. This all-encompassing sense of liberation for which we struggle is a significant contribution that we *Feministas Hispanas* make to our own Hispanic people and to this society.

HORIZONTAL VIOLENCE

The Anglo culture even sets up our bouts: we fight the blacks, we fight the indigenous people, we fight the Asians and Pacific people in America. Horizontal violence becomes intrinsic to survival and in the end, the winner is the loser; the only winner is the dominant culture which keeps us alive for its own benefit. If when you win you sense you have lost, then you know what invisible invisibility is all about.

Our black sisters and brothers have long struggled for justice for themselves. In the women's movement *Feministas Hispanas* often join hands with our black sisters in the struggle for inclusivity at all levels. But in the movement as well as in society at large, we are often pitted against each other. "Minority representation" often means either a black or a Hispanic. The term racism, as I already mentioned, further contributes to the invisibility of Hispanics. Limited funds for "participation of minorities" puts us in a position of vying against each other.

Compared to us Hispanics, and comparisons are always extremely limited and limiting, our black sisters are ahead of us in the struggle. Because they have been here longer than we have, consciousness of the oppression they suffer is more common in society than under-standing what we Hispanics have to struggle against. Though indeed the advances made towards civil rights in this country are nothing to brag about, awareness of racism is at least a first step which has cost the black community long years of suffering, organizing, struggling, and dying.

Oppressed people need to know as much as possible about their oppressors in order to survive. Because the black women have been dealing with the dominant culture and race in this country longer than we have, they know their way around the streets of survival much better than we do. This is true not only in such areas as the welfare system of this country. Black women also have an under-standing of how to deal with a racist mentality. For us Hispanic women, many of whom have come here and not been born here, many of whom have not experienced ethnic prejudice until the ages of eighteen, twenty-five, forty—whenever we moved here—to come to understand why we are being discriminated against takes a long time. To learn how to deal with it takes even longer.

Third, Hispanic women have the extra difficulty of not being fluent in the English language. Many of us who have studied and acquired a degree are still handicapped linguistically, especially when it comes to writing. Though most probably it is as difficult for black women to be published as it is for us Hispanic women, at least the black woman has a certain competency in writing English that we Hispanic women lack. And the same is true regarding our fluency in speaking English. Though the majority of us are bilingual, our fluency in both languages tends to be limited. In any meeting others will easily express themselves more precisely than we will and, therefore, will be more easily understood.

Finally, there are certain characteristics in our Hispanic culture that place us at a disadvantage in our dealings with black women as much as with Anglo women. To point out just two of them: in our culture, when attacked in public, we do not defend ourselves. Our concept of honor is a most important factor in our behavior. If you attack me, you have blemished my honor. My attitude will tend to be not to respond to you—whoever attacks me is not worthy of a response. Since duels are a thing of the past, my attitude will be to delete from my life anyone who has offended my honor by attacking me. Our silence is many times taken as timidity or maybe even acceptance. Our silence is instead our way of saying that, faithful to who we are, we do not believe it honorable to engage the person attacking us.

Another cultural trait which many times works against us is our indirect, circuitous way of dealing with people and problems. Two things are operative in this trait: first, by not dealing in such a direct way you allow the other person a way out. Though "saving face" is not as strong a cultural trait of Hispanics as it is of other cultures, it is more operative for us than it seems to be for both Anglos and blacks. Second, because emotions are such an important element of our understanding and behavior, we need more time to explain, to talk about things. We cannot go to the heart of the matter in one big jump, because the emotional element tends to make circumstances more complex, and therefore, I believe, more human.

Though undoubtedly Hispanics also have differences with other cultural/ethnic groups, up to now the majority of the so-called minority women that I have dealt with in the feminist movement have been black women. *Feministas Hispanas* have to understand what is at work in our dealings with our black sisters. Black women also have to realize and respect that we are different, that we wish our differences to be recognized and respected, and that we want to represent ourselves, to speak for ourselves and not to be included under the term racism as an afterthought, not to be referred to as women of color for many of us are white with a tinge of olive-brownness and a twist in our tongues that makes us Hispanic. Only we, women who suffer the day-to-day oppression of racism, ethnic prejudice, classism, and sexism, can negate victory to the dominant culture by refusing to engage in a horizontal violence which makes losers of all of us.

FEMINISTAS HISPANAS
AND WHITE FEMINISTS

You sit at a meeting with women friends, with feminists who are quick to call you sister, and you sense the tension mounting every time you mention Hispanics, or ask, "What about the Hispanics?" You go home with a sense that you are crazy: they invited you to be a Hispanic presence and voice at their meetings, yet any time you bring up and insist on the particularity and specificity of *Mujer Hispana,* tensions rise. Those of you who have been present at a meeting but not visible, you know what invisible invisibility is, what it feels like. And you cringe when, with a sincerity that could move mountains, they turn to you and say, "How can we integrate Hispanic women in the feminist movement?" How do you, one of you among many of them, tell them that that question is wrong, that it increases your invisibility? Will they ever understand that it is not a matter of baking a cake? *Feminismo Hispano* is not one more ingredient to add. *Feminismo Hispano* is to be there as a motivating force, at the level of conceptualization, understanding, definition, planning, or the feminist movement in the U.S.A. will continuously betray itself.

Of course white feminists know oppression and their sufferings often parallel those of *Feministas Hispanas.* We are not trying by any means to engage here in a dispute of which kind of oppression is more oppressive. That is exactly the mind-set that leads to horizontal violence. But without negating their oppression, white feminists have to seriously consider three facts: the possibility of their personal ethnic prejudices and racism; the definition of goals and strategies of the feminist movement, which in seeking for equality rather than for liberation, necessitates an oppressed group which will indeed be the ethnic/racial groups; finally, the lack of ability of the movement up to now to attract ethnic/racial groups is possibly due to the sense we have that white feminists want us to join their movement, instead of asking us to participate in redefining the movement so we could indeed call it ours.

Concretely, *Feministas Hispanas* ask of white feminists:[2]

—to assume responsibility for the systematic analysis of ethnic prejudice and racism, instead of depending on us to raise the issue and aggressively pursue it.

—out of a sense of justice and commitment to the process of liberation, white feminists should have a preferential option for us and all ethnic women and women of color. Such a preferential option has to be translated into concrete actions such as facilitating our attendance at meetings, providing translations when necessary, creating an environment in which the culture and personality of Hispanic women can be fully expressed and valued.

—we urge white feminists to seriously pursue a study of Hispanic culture so that our dealings with each one can be characterized by a sense of mutual empowerment and enabling which can only be born out of knowing each other, mutual acceptance, admiration, and respect.

—finally, we beg of white feminists to understand that the double and triple oppression we live under demands of us to participate equally in the struggle against ethnic/racial prejudice as in the struggle against sexism. Furthermore, we ask for their support and solidarity at the level of action in combating racial and ethnic prejudice.

2 Yolanda Tarango and I worked together at drafting some of the following recommendations to white feminists in the summer of 1982.

Ada Maria Isasi-Diaz

HISPANIC AND FEMINIST: "SI SE PUEDE."

Invisible invisibility is what you feel when you sit among your own Hispanic people and, more and more, you feel like a stranger because they think of you as a threat. The male controlled and defined Hispanic movement in this country sees feminism and Hispanicness as mutually exclusive. Those of us *Feministas Hispanas* articulate enough to express our beliefs, values, concerns, are called and seen as traitors because we refuse to participate in the struggle from any perspective other than one both feminist and Hispanic. Years back a black woman shared with us what she tells her black brothers: "I am not going to fight now against the whites for my rights as a black and then down the road have to fight against you for my rights as a woman. No way, I'm doing it both at the same time." That is the message of the *Feminista Hispana* to the Hispanic males in this country.

I believe that the fear and mistrust Hispanic males have of us are due to the following: first, they are threatened by a feminist stance just like any other male of any other culture or any other racial group is. Second, males of oppressed groups tend to vent the frustration they feel due to the prejudice they suffer at work and in society at large by treating those who historically have been "under" them the same way they are treated by those who have power over them. Finally, I do believe that the ideology of the Hispanic movement in the U.S.A. is one of equality instead of liberation. Therefore, Hispanic men do not want structural changes, but rather access to the structures of power from which they are barred at present. The sense of liberation of *Feministas Hispanas* which demands structural changes is, therefore, a threat to their understanding of what would be good for them. Of course, they "know" that what is good for them "has to be" good for all Hispanics.

Our challenge as *Feministas Hispanas* is to continue to find ways of living out our commitment to our people without having to betray our feminist understandings. Meanwhile, we challenge Hispanic men to understand that their unwillingness to see the interconnections between racist/ethnic prejudice, classism, and sexism makes us, *Feministas Hispanas*, women without a people. It is with deep regret and pain that we *Feministas Hispanas* at times have to admit that we are more sisters to feminists of other races and cultures than we are sisters to Hispanic men. The injustice that Hispanic men do to us by repeatedly demanding us to choose will continue to work against the liberation of all Hispanic people. Unless both Hispanic males and *Feministas Hispanas* engage in serious dialogue, history will judge us harshly for having been unable to join strengths to fight oppression.

CONCLUSION

The inability to stop or diminish the oppressive structures of society which make of our living a mere surviving, the bewilderment of being pitted against other oppressed sisters and brothers, the pain of being rejected by those you, *Feministas Hispanas,* have birthed, nurtured, cared for, the demand from the Anglo feminist that you participate, but, oh! participate the way they want, when they want—that is what invisible invisibility, oppression, is all about.

Our situation as *Feministas Hispanas* is not an enviable one, but for centuries oppressed people have managed to merely survive in the eyes of the oppressors, while living quite fully within their communities. Our most urgent need, therefore, is the creation of community among ourselves, *Feministas Hispanas.* We have to create our own space to be, our own support network, our own viable means of holding each other accountable. Neither the white feminists nor the Hispanic males are going to freely offer us the opportunity to do it. We must grasp the moment at hand and create as Hispanic women have done throughout history a sense of *familia* among ourselves. Justice to ourselves demands it; the memory of the oppression and struggle for liberation of Hispanic women down the ages makes it our duty. But above all, the cry that touches our hearts is the cry of our Hispanic people here in the U.S.A. To negate our feminism or our Hispanicness is to betray the trust that our people have always had in us. As *Feministas Hispanas* let us continue to birth ourselves confident in the fullness of our womanhood and our deep-rootedness in our Hispanic culture and heritage.[3]

3 I realize that this article is incomplete without attempting to explain those dispositions and qualities of the *Feminista Hispana* which characterize her life and struggle. Such a study will be forthcoming.

5

Feminism and Peace

Rosemary Radford Ruether

The connections between feminism and peace are deep and long-standing. But these connections have been drawn more often by women's organizations expressing their commitment to peace as part of women's agenda than they have by peace groups. All too often, peace movements run by men have either excluded women from membership or from equal leadership, sometimes motivating women to form independent peace organizations. Almost all of the women's rights organizations of the late nineteenth and early twentieth centuries saw world peace as part of their vision for a new society.

One of the early peace groups to draw a connection between feminism and peace was the Garrisonian wing of the New England Non-Resistance Society in the 1830s, including among its members such prominent early abolitionist-feminists as Maria Weston Chapman, Lucretia Mott and William Lloyd Garrison himself. The group was also responsible for arranging the New England tour of the most prominent feminist abolitionists of the era, Sarah and Angelina Grimke. The Garrisonians based their view on a radical concept of nonresistance as conversion to perfection or holiness. They believed that conversion to radical Christian ideals entailed repudiation of all unjust structures of government, including those which subjugated women or which countenanced the enslavement of Negroes.

Christian perfection demands an immediate rejection of war and social injustice, they taught. There is no difference in this ideal of converted life for men or for women; both sexes are called to the

63

same life of perfection. Thus the Garrisonians both affirmed the connection between nonresistance and women's equality, and repudiated any special gender differences between men and women. Both men and women must be converted to this single ideal, they believed—men from their socialization in patterns of violence and women from their socialization in timidity and acquiescence to unjust social patterns.

The connection of many early pacifists and feminists with Quakerism is not accidental. The Society of Friends offered a congenial environment for both women's equality and nonviolence through a common understanding of a radical Christian ethic of love. The Shaker Society in nineteenth-century America also combined rejection of violence and war with the affirmation of women's equality. For the Shakers, this equality of woman was the revelation of the feminine side of God, or the feminine Christ, the revelation of divine Mother Wisdom. Through this revelation of God's female aspect, woman's full humanity is affirmed and she is able to take her rightful place in the church and in the order of redemption. The leading Shaker eldress of the Mount Lebanon community, Anna White, was an active worker in international peace organizations. She was the vice-president for the state of New York of the International Petition on Disarmament, which White presented to Theodore Roosevelt. For these radical Christians, love and peace were not specifically female qualities, but common ideals for both men and women.

For many nineteenth- and early twentieth-century women's rights and women's reform societies, the virtues of peace and love were linked particularly with women. These groups believed that men too must be converted to these ideals. But they accepted the current cultural identification of these virtues with women's nature and concluded that the vindication of peace would be linked with the ascendancy of women's influence in the public order. The Women's Christian Temperance Union promoted a department of Peace and Arbitration, headed for many years by Mary Woodbridge. In her oft-delivered speech on "Peace and Arbitration in National and International Affairs," Woodbridge saw the day of world peace hastening as women's influence in government grew. Women's influence in the establishment of peace would also hasten

Christ's reign as Prince of Peace over the world. Women around the world were seen as joining with American women in the establishment of arbitration as the alternative to settling international conflict through war.

The women's organizations of 1880–1915 generally accepted a close relationship between peace and women's suffrage. To be a suffragist was also to be antiwar. The progress of the human species demanded that war be replaced by arbitration and that there be general disarmament. However, in their view, the male had been socialized through his long association with war to seek violent means of resolving conflict. Male socialization thus preserved regressive and antisocial psychological traits. The enfranchisement of women would bring into political decision-making that half of the human race which had never participated in war as a direct protagonist and which, through its nurturing role, was innately against war. As women gained equal rights and were able to enter parliaments and decision-making bodies in equal numbers with men, their influence would be able to sway societies away from war and toward nonviolent political means of solving disputes.

The suffragists realized that most women throughout history had been the loyal supporters of their husbands' and sons' military activities, but they linked this female support for war with woman's unemancipated condition. As women were liberated from passive dependence on men, they would be able to direct their naturally pacific tendencies into the public arena as an independent force for peace and disarmament.

Suffragists and peace activists saw a connection between women's rights, peace, and a new concept of citizenship and nationalism. Jane Addams said in *Newer Ideals of Peace*, published in 1907, that the old concepts of citizenship were based on the society of males as warriors. Citizenship was related to the ability to bear arms in war; thus women, excluded from bearing arms, were also excluded from citizenship. Citizenship based on bearing arms fostered a hostile, competitive, chauvinistic concept of patriotism, which precluded international solidarity between national groups. The giving of citizenship to women would demand a new definition of citizenship based on nonviolent political methods of resolving conflict.

These links between feminism, peace and a new internationalism

were developed in the Women's Peace Party founded by Jane
Addams in 1915; the group later became what is still the oldest
women's peace organization, the Women's International League for
Peace and Freedom. The Women's International League, after its
founding congress in April 1915 in The Hague, soon gathered
national sections throughout western Europe and began to reach out
to found groups in eastern Europe, the Middle East and the Far
East. Much of that small but heroic generation of women who
entered their national parliaments or were sent as delegates to the
League of Nations in the 1920s and 1930s were members of the
Women's International League.

The league saw itself as modeling a new internationalism through
the relationship of its national sections to each other. National
sections of the league were expected to transcend a chauvinist
concept of nationalism. Instead, each national group was expected to
be the foremost in criticizing the unjust and war-making tendencies
of its own national government. American women would take the
lead in criticizing the American govenment, etc. A model of arbitration was set up in which the women from warring sides of a
conflict would arbitrate the dispute, with the women from the
aggrieved nation defining the situation, while the women from the
aggressor nation would accept and announce this criticism of their
own government.

The league hoped to present to male statesmen and parliamen-
tarians a new model of arbitration devoted to the international good
of the human community, rather than to the narrow advantage of
nations at the expense of the whole. Although this model of internationalism became increasingly difficult to practice with the rise of
the ideological movements of fascism and communism, even during
the darkest days of World War II and the pressures of the cold war,
the league has sought to maintain a model of friendly communication and solidarity across national divisions.

Although the Women's International League maintained the
Victorian cultural relationship between women's mothering nature
and world peace, the group discarded the identification of this goal
with the victory of Christianity or the establishment of the reign of
Christ that had been an intrinsic part of this idea in the nineteenth
century. This loss of the predication of feminism and peace on

Christian virtue both broadened and narrowed these movements. On the one hand, it allowed these women's groups to shake off what could only be regarded by non-Christians as an expression of religious imperialism. The establishment of a new international order of world peace based on justice was argued on humanitarian grounds, rather than in the language of religious sectarianism. People of all religious persuasions, as well as those inspired by secular humanistic philosophies, could join together in solidarity, while Catholics, Jews, and secularists could only be alarmed by the close link which groups such as the Women's Christian Temperance Union made between women's influence, world peace, and such specifically Christian agendas as prayer in the public schools and Sabbath blue laws. Interestingly enough, these conservative Christian agendas of the WCTU today are espoused by Christian groups that are antifeminist and prowar, while the WCTU linked women's rights in politics and economics with the establishment of Christian perfection in the public order.

The secularization of the values of peacemaking left groups such as the Women's Peace Party and the Women's International League with only a quasibiological link between these values and women's influence, however. It was presumed that women sought peace because their biological roles as mothers inclined them to biophilic activities. By contrast, males were thought to have fewer loving and peaceful impulses. Thus the women's peace movement was left with an implied doctrine of split natures and split ethics between men and women. Women were urged to gain power and influence in the world in order to counteract the male tendency toward aggression, but there was no longer a basis for a common ethic of peacemaking to which both men and women were called. By contrast, the forms of pacifism based on radical Christianity had not started out with a presumed ethical split between male and female genders. However much those forms recognized that males were socialized more toward war than were women, they featured an ethic of peacemaking based on Christian conversion to God's will for peace on earth that was directed to men and women equally.

With the rise of the new feminist movements of the late 1960s, new rifts appeared in the earlier connections between feminism and peace. The feminist movements of the 1970s could no longer make the connection which many feminists of the nineteenth century made between women's rights and Christianity. They found their nineteenth-century forebears in those anticlerical and even anti-Christian feminists such as Elizabeth Cady Stanton or Matilda Joselyn Gage, who suspected that Christianity was basically a religious agent of patriarchy and thus intrinsically hostile to feminism.

In addition, contemporary feminists have grown much less sure about the connections between feminism and peace. Although many feminists continue to believe that males tend toward hostility and violence, they are no longer sure that women's mothering role inclines women to nonviolence. Further, they are not sure that women should pursue a peacemaking ethic as an expression of their true or emancipated humanity as women. Rather, they suspect that women have become pacified through this ideology of woman's pacific nature and thus socialized into being passive victims of male violence. Women must learn to oppose male violence, to fight back by violent means, if necessary. With this assertion of a counter-violence of women against men in self-defense, the last strands in the fabric of the relationship of feminism and peace threaten to become unraveled.

Against this background of militant feminism, which did not hesitate to advocate counterviolence—at least in self-defense—to male violence against women, pacifists in the women's movement were made to feel isolated and defensive. Women who advocated nonviolence as the superior social ethic for dealing with conflict felt the need to defend themselves against the charge of antifeminism by the militants. They had to defend and redefine the links between feminism and nonviolence against a new assumption that female nonviolence promoted their passivity and victimization. Thus Kate Millet in her book *Flying* (Knopf, 1974) describes herself as approaching the podium with great trepidation during a panel at a 1971 women's conference on "Violence in the Women's Movement." Most of the other speakers—such as Florynce Kennedy, Gloria Steinem, Myra Lamb, Robin Morgan and Ti-Grace Atkinson—as well as most of the audience—seemed either to favor female violence or else to look at it with analytical detachment. With fear and trembling, Millet declared that she was about to "come out" as something far less acceptable than a lesbian in the women's movement. She was about to come out as a pacifist. "I wait wondering how they will take it. The word is so hated in the Left. To the hecklers 'all I can do is to ask you to be human to me. To listen.' Finally I have said it. . . . 'I want to speak in favor of and as an advocate of non-violence.'"

Although the links of an earlier feminism between women and peace seemed totally broken in such a gathering of militant feminists of the 1970s, in fact bits and pieces of the old assumptions still survive today in feminist ideology. The connection between patriarchy, violence and war which were first explored by feminist pacifists in the first decades of the twentieth century have been revived today. Although contemporary feminists may champion women's self-defense, few are anxious for women to engage in aggressive violence or to emulate male war-making as a way of proving women's equality. Underneath the rhetoric of militance there still survive presumptions about women's moral superiority— although it is no longer clear on what basis women claim to stand for a superior nature or ethic.

This question of the morality of violence or nonviolence was complicated by the desire of feminism to be in solidarity with Third World women. Both black and Third World liberation movements had repudiated nonviolent methods of social change in the 1970s in favor of violent revolution, if necessary. Third World and black women felt their first loyalty was to the black and Third World liberation struggles. First World feminists, in an effort to forge links between feminism and Third World women, wished to demonstrate the connections between the capitalist and racist systems of domination and patriarchy. But this seemed to suggest that the struggle against both patriarchy and war might involve something like methods of guerrilla warfare. The female guerrillas who had fought side-by-side with men in Nicaragua and other such areas were touted as models of militant womanhood. The peace movement was equally conflicted, since it also wanted to oppose American militarism in Third World liberation struggles. This put the movement in the contradictory position of assailing American militarism while advocating revolutionary violence for Third World peoples.

In a recent volume of essays, *Reweaving the Web of Life: Feminism and Non-Violence*, edited by Pam McAlister (New

Society, 1982), feminists in the peace movement struggle to find a higher synthesis among the denunciation of patriarchal violence, the advocacy of feminist militancy, and a vision of a new humanism that could shape a world without war. For many women in the peace movements of the sixties, feminist consciousness was sparked by increasing recognition of the sexism of the male leadership in the peace movement itself. Women in peace organizations began to recognize that traditional patriarchal assumptions about male and female roles still prevailed in these groups. Women were expected to do the rote work of typing and filing; men, to have the ideas and make the decisions.

One of the most extreme cases was the antidraft movement. Since only males could be drafted, the ritual act of resistance to war, turning in or burning one's draft card, was an exclusively male event. The draft resistance movement cultivated a macho image to counteract the image of the dominant society of draft resisters as cowards. One slogan of the movement, "Girls say yes to men who say no," revealed the sexist insensitivity of the male leadership of the movement. It was assumed that women working in the movement were simply molls of the male resisters. Consciousness of sexism in the peace movement caused women to form networks and caucuses among themselves; many women split with these peace organizations and joined the feminist movement.

Feminists who wished to maintain their connection with older peace organizations struggled to sensitize male leadership to sexist attitudes and to bring about more shared leadership between women and men. One way of drawing the connection between feminism and peace for many of these women was to demonstrate the continuity between male violence toward women in the home or in the streets, and war. For many men, violence in Vietnam was serious and important, whereas violence toward women was merely private and trivial. Feminists argued that both were expressions of the same mentality of patriarchy. The socialization of women to be victims and men to be aggressors is the training ground for the culminating expression of male violence in warfare, they said.

The exaltation of war in male culture has typically been accompanied by a strident sexism. The slogan of the Italian fascist writer Filippo Marinetti in the 1930s, "We are out to glorify war, the only health-giver of the world, militarism, patriotism, ideas that kill, contempt for women," vividly illustrates the emotional and ideological connections between supermasculinity, violence and negation of women or the "feminine." In macho mythology, women stand for a feared weakness, passivity, and vulnerability which must be purged and exorcised from the male psyche through the rituals of war. Feminists have pointed out the close connection between military indoctrination and sexism typical of the U.S. Army's basic training. A key element in the rhetoric of basic training is the putdown of women, and, by implication, all that might be "womanish" in the recruit who is being trained. The recruit is shamed by being called a "girl" or a "faggot," thereby inculcating a terror of his own feelings and sensitivities. Through his assault on his fears of weakness, a psychic numbing takes place which is then intended to be turned into aggressiveness toward a dehumanized "enemy."

The emotional identification of the male sexual organ and the gun is a recurring theme in basic training rhetoric. The U.S. Army training jingle, "This is my rifle [slapping rifle]; this is my gun [slapping crotch]. The one is for killing; the other's for fun," makes the psychological connection between violence and sexual dehumanization of women clear. The role of rape or the capture of women as part of the spoils of war can be illustrated by virtually every war in recorded history, not the least of which was the Winter Soldier Investigation of combined rape and violence toward captured Vietnamese women in the war in Southeast Asia. Patriarchy turns the sexual relationship into a power relationship, a relationship of conquest and domination. Women are the currency of male prowess, to be protected and displayed on the one hand; to be ravished and "blown away" on the other. The linking of male sexuality to aggression is the root of both patriarchy and war.

For many contemporary feminists, the response of women to male violence cannot simply be a contrary assertion of feminine values of love and nurture. These qualities themselves have become distorted in female socialization into timidity and vulnerability. Women are not so much peacemakers within the present order as they are repressed into passive "kept women." They acquiesce to male violence in the home and accept it in society. The first step for women, therefore, is to throw off these shackles of fear and lack of self-confidence. Feminists have pointed out that, although most women are of slighter build than most men, physique does not mean that women need be passive victims to every random male assault. Training in martial arts could equip women to defend themselves in many situations. Women who have gone through such training find that the greatest gain is a new sense of self-esteem. They no longer feel helpless before the possibility of attack. In the very way they now carry themselves, they signal to the male world that they are no longer an easy prey.

Although feminists wish to achieve a new sense of self-esteem that can fend off male violence, few want to move the whole way toward an emulation of male aggressive violence. Rather, they seek a new mode of human selfhood that could transcend both aggressive dehumanization of others and timid acquiescence or support of individual or collective violence. For some feminists this idea suggests a new appropriation of the ideal of nonviolence itself, not as passivity but as a courageous resistance to violence and injustice which reaches out to affirm rather than to negate the humanity of the other person.

True nonviolence must be based, first of all, on a secure sense of one's own value as a human being. Violence toward others, far from being an expression of self-worth, is based on a repression of one's sense of vulnerability which then translates into hostility toward others. The most violent men are those with the deepest fears of their own impotence. Training in nonviolence must be based on spiritual or personal development and empowerment of the self. An empowered self will not accept its own degradation, or that of others.

At this point, it becomes possible to forge new links between feminism and peace. Feminism fundamentally rejects the power principle of domination and subjugation. It rejects the concept of power which says that one side's victory must be the other side's defeat. Feminism must question social structures based on this principle at every level, from the competition of men and women in personal relationships to the competition of the nations of the globe, including the U.S. and the U.S.S.R. We seek an alternative power principle of empowerment in community rather than power over and disabling of others. Such enabling in community is based on a recognition of the fundamental interconnectedness of life, of men and women, blacks and whites, Americans and Nicaraguans, Americans and Russians, humans and the nonhuman community of animals, plants, air, and water. Nobody wins unless all win. Warmaking has reached such a level of destructiveness that the defeat of one side means the defeat of all, the destruction of the Earth itself. Feminism today sees its links with the cause of human survival and the survival of the planet itself.

Biophilic values, therefore, cannot remain the preserve of women or women's supposed special "nature" or ethics. As historic victims of violence and repression, as well as those socialized to cultivate supportive roles—but in a disempowered sphere—women may have a particular vantage point on the issue. But they are not immune to expressions of hostility, chauvinism, racism, or warmongering, even if their role has more often been to be the backup force for the main fighters. Conversion to a new sense of self that wills the good of others in a community of life must transform traditional women as well as traditional men.

Both feminism and peacemaking need to be grounded in an alternative vision of the authentic self and human community that was once provided by radical Christianity. This alternative vision must be clear that we are children of one mother, the Earth, part of one interdependent community of life. On this basis we must oppose all social systems that create wealth and privilege for some by impoverishing, degrading, or eliminating other people, whether they be the systems of domination that repress or assault women, or the systems that plan nuclear annihilation in a futile search for security based on competitive world power. Only on the basis of such an alternative vision can men and women join together to rebuild the earth.

BIBLIOGRAPHY

Addams, Jane. *New Ideals of Peace.* Chautauqua, NY: Chautauqua Press, 1907.
Bussy, Gertrude and Margaret Tims. *Pioneers for Peace: The Women's International League for Peace and Freedom: 1915–1965.* Oxford: Aldin Press, 1980.

Cooke, Blanche Wiesen, ed. *Crystal Eastman on Women and Revolution.* New York: Oxford University Press, 1978.

Degan, Marie Louise. *The History of the Woman's Peace Party.* Baltimore, MD: Johns Hopkins Press, 1939.

Key, Ellen. *War, Peace and the Future.* New York: G. P. Putnam's Sons, 1916.

McAllister, Pam, ed. *Reweaving the Web of Life: Feminism and Non-Violence.* Philadelphia: New Society Publishers, 1982.

6

Anti-Semitism

THE UNACKNOWLEDGED RACISM

Judith Plaskow

The subject of anti-Semitism frightens me. It does so not simply because anti-Semitism frightens me but because even discussion of it threatens to separate me from other women. It reminds me of our differences rather than our similarities. It reminds me that the women's movement, in appealing to women as women, frequently erases important cultural differences among us. It reminds me that sisterhood, while powerful, is not powerful enough to eradicate deeply-seated prejudice. The very process of trying to write this paper reminds me that I belong to different communities. As a feminist addressing other feminists, I want to be honest about the contradictions I see in Judaism and Jewishness. As a Jew, I do not want to be misheard or provide ammunition to the anti-Semite in my Christian feminist sisters.

Perhaps these conflicts are appropriate to my subject: complexity. As feminists, we are learning to acknowledge the complexity of oppression. We are becoming aware that race, class, and sex oppression are interstructured in the lives of many women.[1] They interlock not in an additive way, so that one is oppressed as a woman *and* a black, for example, but in an integral way which alters the total

1 Rosemary Radford Ruether uses the concept of "interstructuring." See, e.g., her *New Woman/New Earth* (New York: The Seabury Press, 1975), particularly Part Two.

75

experience of oppression.[2] We are forced to recognize that the complexity of oppression makes it possible for the same person to be both oppressed and oppressor and that as American feminists, we are many of us in both categories. But these insights, which are easier to assent to than fully to integrate into our analysis and practice, perhaps become particularly clear in the situation of the Jewish woman. To be a Jewish woman in America is to experience many aspects of the complexity of oppression, only a few of which I can discuss here.

It is necessary to admit at the outset that Jews hardly appear oppressed in the United States today. Anti-Semitism in the U.S., never as virulent as in Europe, declined in the decades after World War II to the point where many were predicting its complete disappearance.[3] Such discrimination as there was did not, in any event, prevent the economic integration of Jews into American life. While contrary to all the stereotypes, there are many poor and working-class Jews, the majority of American Jewry is comfortably ensconced in the middle class. Indeed, one might say Jews are exhibit A for the upward mobility of American society. Many an immigrant toiling in poverty on New York's East Side had the privilege of seeing children or grandchildren go to college and enter the professions—a fact that has occasionally been used against other minority groups.[4]

Moreover, since the vast majority of American Jews are white, we share white-skin privilege and have assimilated racism along with other American values. The disproportionately high percentage of Jews involved in the 1960s civil rights movement never represented a majority of American Jewry. Most Jews' attitudes toward blacks are probably indistinguishable from the attitudes of other Americans.[5] More concretely, in the last fifteen years, the Jewish and black communities have come into conflict on a number of specific

2 Elizabeth (Vicki) Spelman, "Theories of Race and Gender: The Erasure of Black Women," *Quest: A Feminist Quarterly* 4, 42–46.

3 Maurice D. Atkin, "United States of America," *Encyclopedia Judaica*, 15:1636.

4 Robert Weisbord and Arthur Stein, *Bittersweet Encounter* (New York: Schocken Books, 1972), 15.

5 Weisbord and Stein stress this point.

issues. The fact that Jews have sometimes been the last group out of an area before blacks move in has meant that in certain black neighborhoods, a disproportionate number of storekeepers and landlords are Jews. This makes Jews the buffer group, the representatives of the exploitative white community to the black community. In New York City, the underlying tensions created by this situation were exacerbated by the school crisis of 1968. In the fall of that year, a struggle between the largely black Ocean Hill school board and the United Federation of Teachers quickly acquired racial overtones. Jews who had "made it" in American society through the school system perceived black insistence on community control of assignment of teachers as a threat to their livelihood and place in society. For many blacks, on the other hand, the teachers' strike seemed to mark the Jewish community's backing away from commitment to quality education for blacks and thus to racial justice. General ill feelings were fanned by President Carter in the Young affair[6] and aggravated by Jewish/black tension over Jesse Jackson's presidential candidacy.[7] They were also reinforced by the recent and ongoing role of a number of major Jewish organizations in opposing affirmative action. The fact that this last turn of events is deeply disturbing to many Jewish feminists who clearly perceive the importance of affirmative action to Jewish *women* only illustrates the complexity of our situation. Whatever we may feel, in all these cases, the Jewish community appears as oppressor, not as oppressed.

Yet to be a Jew in the United States is to know that there are forms of oppression other than economic oppression. It is to be aware of the fact that acceptance comes in many shades. It is to know from a fairly early age that while Jews can and have entered the professions in this country, they are closed off from the avenues of real power. Again contrary to the stereotypes, Jews are not the bankers in

6 In August of 1979, a furor over a secret meeting he had had with a PLO official led UN ambassador Andrew Young to resign his post. There were many issues involved in the resignation, Carter's acceptance of it, and the Jewish community's reaction, but the incident left many blacks feeling that pressure from Jewish organizations had forced the resignation of a prominent black leader.

7 Jewish opposition to Jackson stemmed initially from his stance on the Middle East but greatly increased when, among other incidents, he referred to New York as "Hymietown." The press played an important role in heightening tensions in both this and the Young affair. One might ask: to what end and to whose benefit?

America nor are they the corporation heads. There has never been a Jewish president, and there are not very many Jews in Congress. To be a Jew in the United States is perhaps to have the money that would enable you to live in certain parts of town or to join certain clubs, and yet not be permitted to live there or join anyway. It is to have a cousin or uncle or sister who went to an inferior medical school or did not get to go at all because of anti-Jewish discrimination. It is to be aware that in the name of what is now euphemistically called "geographic distribution," certain colleges are still concerned not to admit too many whites from New York City lest the school have too many Jews.

Such forms of discrimination, while less than life-threatening, take a psychic toll. I recall as a child being taught never to ask people their religion, the hidden message being that they might ask me mine in return! While I would never deny my Jewishness, I was uncomfortable acknowledging it. I was aware quite early that it was not the preferred thing to be. This feeling is certainly related to the unwillingness of many Jews to press their own Jewish concerns and to the more subtle forms of self-contempt that come with not living up to particular standards of beauty, manners, or discretion. Such concerns and self-censoring are signs of internalized oppression, the process through which oppressed groups adopt the standards of the dominant culture and turn them against themselves.

While there are many ways internalized oppression works on Jews indiscriminately, there are also ways it takes special forms in Jewish women. Other Jewish feminists have written of attempts to iron their dark, kinky hair so different from the American blonde ideal, or to stop being "pushy" or shooting off their big mouths.[8] The epithet "pushy" need not be explicitly accompanied by "Jew" for the message to be conveyed that Jewish ethnic mannerisms do not conform to American norms, particularly norms of femininity. This message is proclaimed most clearly through a range of popular "Jewish woman" stereotypes, especially the image of the powerful, intrusive, devouring Jewish mother. She who epitomizes all that the culture fears in women, also represents all that Jewish women fear to

8 Letty Cottin Pogrebin, "Anti-Semitism in the Women's Movement," *Ms.* (June 1982), 68, 69. Evelyn Torten Beck, ed., *Nice Jewish Girls* (Watertown, MA: Persephone Press, 1982), particularly the Introduction and first section.

be. When this stereotype, and others—the spoiled, whining "JAP" (Jewish American Princess), the overbearing "equal," the sexual neurotic—are perpetuated and popularized by Jewish men, one sees their own self-hatred being projected onto and turned against Jewish women. Jewish women then bear the double burden of nonconformity to the rules of the wider culture and the contempt of Jewish men who have internalized the culture's norms.

The broader and more profound determinants of the American Jewish experience, however, fall on men and women more equally. To be a Jew in the United States is to live in an overwhelmingly and often unselfconsciously Christian country. It is to have one's school vacations scheduled around Christian holidays, to learn Christian carols and participate in Easter egg hunts, all the while being assured that these customs and holidays are not really Christian but American, "that they belong to everybody." When I lived in Wichita, Kansas, the local newspaper had a big picture of a sunrise on its cover one Easter with a caption remarking on how the coming of Easter brings a smile to the face of everyone, whether or not they are Christian. Such blithe cultural imperialism masks not only the indifference of most of the world toward Easter but also the Jewish historical experience of Easter as a time of fear, a time when Christians could be expected to take revenge on their Jewish neighbors for the death of Christ. This cultural imperialism is part of a broader phenomenon that shapes the experience of every oppressed group: the oppressed must know about the oppressor's culture, but the oppressor need know nothing about the oppressed.[9] Ironic as this is given the Jewish roots of Christianity, American Jews necessarily acquire a surface knowledge of major Christian beliefs and celebrations, while particularly outside of New York City, Christians are often totally ignorant of Jewish holy days and their meaning.

It is hardly surprising, given this Christian dominance, that to be a Jew in America is to meet anti-Semitism in its particularly Christian formulations. It is to learn that one is a Christ-killer, and perhaps to be beaten for being one, at a time when, without being sure who Christ is, one knows quite well one never killed anybody. I remem-

9 Ann Wilson Shaef makes this point for female and male culture in *Women's Reality* (Minneapolis: Winston Press, 1981), Chapter One.

ber standing on opposite sides of the street from the Catholic children on my block throwing bluestones back and forth while they yelled, "You're going to burn in hell." I did not know why I was going to burn in hell, but I recognized an insult when I heard one! A more subtle form of Christian anti-Judaism, one which ties in with the issue of cultural imperialism, is Christian perception of the essence of Judaism as rejection of Christ. From the Jewish perspective, this makes almost as little sense as the idea that the essence of Buddhism is rejection of Christ. Judaism has nothing to do with Christ. It is an independent tradition which did not end with the Old Testament, but which, in its mainstream rabbinic form, *began* in the same period that Christianity did.[10] This fundamental misunderstanding of Judaism denies its integrity and legitimacy as a living religion at the same time it supports a Christian interpretation of reality.

On another theme, to be a Jew in the United States is to know as a fundamental part of one's identity that in this century, a third of world Jewry was exterminated simply because they were Jews. Hitler's war against the Jews was not part of the wider war effort; in fact, it may even have lost him the war.[11] But anyone who had one Jewish grandparent, even if the family had been Christian for two generations, was exterminated as vermin. To be a Jew in the United States is to know that one *is* a Jew in the United States because parents and grandparents came here fleeing pogroms at the turn of the century. Had they not come fleeing other persecutions, they would have been part of the statistics of the Holocaust. Therefore, to be a Jew in the United States is to be a survivor. Jews are sometimes accused of seeing anti-Semitism where it does not exist and bringing it into being by their expectations. I do not doubt that this is sometimes true. But it is all too easy for non-Jews to discount or tire of the scars that come with knowing even thirdhand the impassioned hate directed at one's people within or almost within one's lifetime.

10 The destruction of the Temple in Jerusalem in 70 C.E. necessitated a profound reorientation of Jewish religious life, a reorientation carried out under the auspices of the rabbis beginning at Jabneh around 70.
11 Lucy Dawidowicz, *The War Against the Jews 1933–1945* (New York and Philadelphia: Holt, Rinehart, and Winston and Jewish Publication Society of America, 1975), 140–47.

This is all just background, however, to what many Jews perceive as a new escalation of anti-Semitism in this country as part of the right-wing backlash of the last few years. Reports of anti-Semitic incidents such as vandalism and cross-burnings have recently risen dramatically. And whether this is new or not, the women's movement has had its share of anti-Semitic incidents and feeling. Indeed, it is ironic that women who had abandoned their Judaism because it was sexist, seeking community in the women's movement, are now being forced back to Judaism because of feminist anti-Semitism.[12] As Sartre said in his book *Anti-Semite and Jew*, "The Jew is one whom other men [sic] consider a Jew."[13] Jewish women are learning the truth of this in a very painful way.

Certain forms of Christian cultural and linguistic imperialism in the women's movement cannot really be called anti-Semitism. While it would be nice if feminists were immune to attitudes that pervade the culture, there is no reason to expect they will be. Thus when feminist events are scheduled on Jewish holidays or when the supposedly interreligious Feminist Theological Institute is initially called the Institute for Theology and Ministry (ministry being a thoroughly Christian term), or when one of its organizers speaks of "giving birth to this baby (i.e., the Institute) and baptising her," these things can be understood simply as everyday thoughtlessness.

Other reports coming out of the women's movement are more disturbing, however. Jewish feminists have reported having to listen to anti-Semitic jokes. Their concerns have been trivialized and treated as "Jewish paranoia" in contexts where every other form of oppression is taken seriously. Anti-Semitic stereotypes have been used to silence or discount feminist Jews: she's just a Princess/Jewish intellectual/rich Jew/pushy Jew/cunning Jew, etc.[14] Most upsetting are stories about the women's conference at Copenhagen where American delegates found the anti-Semitism overt and intense. Novelist Esther Broner, for example, had a UN staffperson remark to her, "Denmark is wonderful, but the Germans take it over in the

---

12 Both Pogrebin and Beck discuss this phenomenon.

13 Jean-Paul Sartre, *Anti-Semite and Jew* (New York: Schocken Books, 1965), 69.

14 Pogrebin, "Anti-Semitism in the Women's Movement," 66 and *Nice Jewish Girls*, particularly the Introduction and first section.

summer, and I hate them. They only did one thing right: they killed the Jews." When Esther started to choke, the woman said to her, "Oh, did I hurt your feelings? Are you German?"[15]

Little in an American Jewish upbringing prepares one to deal with such remarks. In 1982, in the *New York Times Magazine,* Jewish historian Lucy Dawidowich had an article on American Jewry's response to World War II.[16] She argued that, contrary to the dominant view, American Jews did everything they could to try to save European Jewry; they simply lacked the power to be effective. In the following weeks, there were several letters to the *Times* heatedly disputing her interpretation of events. I do not know who is right. But it strikes me that it is easier for the Jewish community to beat its collective breast saying it did not do enough than to accept the fact of powerlessness. As an American white middle-class woman, that powerlessness terrifies me.

Nowhere do diaspora Jews experience this powerlessness more strongly than in relation to Israel. An important element in the anti-Semitism at Copenhagen, and in the American feminist movement, is anti-Semitism in its new and acceptable form of anti-Zionism. I do not consider criticism of the Israeli government anti-Semitism. The war in Lebanon horrifies me, and I deplore Israel's West Bank policies as strongly as anyone. But when the Jewish people are denied the right to decide *for ourselves* whether we are a nation, how to define ourselves, and how to shape our destiny, that is anti-Semitism whatever other names one chooses to put on it. Jews can raise their voices against Israeli policy and still ask themselves why, when other peoples kill, lie, maim, or steal, the world closes its eyes or legitimates their deeds in the name of self-defense or national liberation. When the Jews behave as a "normal" nation, however, the moral outrage of the world is focused upon them. From this I can only conclude that the world wants to see the Jews remain victims. In that status, we *may* be allowed a place among the world's

15 Pogrebin, "Anti-Semitism in the Women's Movement," 49. A fuller, pseudonymous report on Copenhagen, "Copenhagen: One Year Later," appears in *Lilith* no. 8: 30–35.

16 Lucy Dawidowicz, "American Jews and the Holocaust," *The New York Times Magazine* (18 April 1982), 46ff.

people, but for us to seek to determine our own future is unacceptable.

But I learn something else from Israel which brings me back to my initial point: to be oppressed does not protect one from being an oppressor. The bodies of Sabra and Shatila proclaim that to be a Jew and not a Nazi is, in a sense, a moral privilege, but it guarantees nothing about who the Jew will be when s/he comes to power.

A number of years ago, I wrote an article on anti-Judaism in Christian feminist treatments of Jesus.[17] In it, I discussed a problem which had disturbed and angered me for some time and which I felt Christian feminists had an obligation to address. Several months after I wrote the piece, I read an article by Alice Walker on racism in white feminist writing.[18] Essentially, she was saying about white feminists exactly what I had said about Christian feminists, and every point she made applied to me. The article frightened me because it made me wonder whether we are all locked into our own experience of oppression, wanting other people to hear and know us, but unwilling to undertake the difficult process of trying to know others. How can we use our experience of oppression, I wondered, not to wall ourselves in but to build bridges to one another?[19]

Thinking about this question sends me back to a basic affirmation of the Jewish tradition, its insistence on remembering that "we were slaves in the land of Egypt." Every Passover, the telling of the story of the Jewish people begins here. Several years ago, in the context of an anthology on Jewish feminism, Esther Ticktin suggested that the knowledge that we were slaves in the land of Egypt should become the basis of a new Jewish law governing the relationships between Jewish women and men. Just as Jews have the right to expect that a

17 "Christian Feminism and Anti-Judaism," *Cross Currents* (Fall, 1978), 306–9. Reprinted in *Lilith* no. 7: 11 and *Nice Jewish Girls*, 250–54 as "Blaming Jews for the Birth of Patriarchy."

18 Alice Walker, "One Child of One's Own: An Essay on Creativity," *Ms.* (August, 1979); reprinted in Alice Walker, *In Search of Our Mother's Gardens* (New York: Harcourt, Brace, Jovanovich, 1983), 361–83.

19 Since I wrote these words, I was privileged to hear a panel on "Racism and Anti-Semitism in the Women's Movement" at the 1983 annual meeting of the National Women's Studies Association. The four presenters, speaking out of their own oppression in ways which acknowledged the experience of others, began a genuine dialogue. Such moments, which, despite the continuing deep problems, are happening in many places, are a sign of hope for the future.

decent Gentile will not join a club that excludes Jews, so Jewish women have the right to expect that decent Jewish men will not participate in any Jewish institution or ritual which excludes Jewish women.[20]

But as women from many different backgrounds, each of us in her own way has been a stranger or slave in the land of Egypt. Could not Esther's sensitizing and consciousness-raising device become the basis for our ethical dealings with each other? As Cherrie Moraga put it, "We don't have to be the same to have a movement, but we *do* have to be accountable for our ignorance. In the end, finally, we must refuse to give up on each other."[21] Can we learn to listen to each other in our complexity? Can we learn to value our differences instead of being threatened by them? Isn't this part of what it should mean to be a feminist? Isn't this part of what it should mean to be a Jew?

20 Esther Ticktin, "A Modest Beginning," *Response* (Summer, 1973), 83–88.
21 Quoted by Evelyn Torton Beck in *Nice Jewish Girls* (Watertown, MA: Persephone Press, 1982), xxi.

7

On Healing
the Nature/History Split
in Feminist Thought

Joan L. Griscom

As I have considered the increasing discussion of the relation between women and nature, two important trends stand out, trends which appear to me strangely and seriously contradictory. This essay is an effort to help in healing this split in our thought.

The first trend involves the perception that there are four major systems of oppression in our patriarchal world: not only the domination of nature and women, but also domination by race and class. All four are thematically and historically interwoven. Sheila Collins echoed other feminist theorists when she wrote: "Racism, sexism, class exploitation, and ecological destruction are four interlocking pillars upon which the structure of the patriarchal rests."[1] Feminists are now exploring the nature of this interlocking, or, as Rosemary Ruether calls it, interstructuring.[2] What are the similarities and differences between these four forms of oppression? To what extent are they the same?

I pause for a note on terminology. *Sexism* and *racism* are fairly clear: each consists in regarding a group—for example, males or

1 Sheila D. Collins, *A Different Heaven and Earth* (Valley Forge: Judson Press, 1974), 161.
2 Rosemary Radford Ruether, *New Woman/New Earth: Sexist Ideologies and Human Liberation* (New York: Seabury, 1975).

whites—as superior to another group—females or nonwhites—on the basis of sex or race. *Classism* makes the same distinction on the basis of socioeconomic level; it operates nationally and, as in the relationship between the so-called developed and underdeveloped nations, globally. There is no one word that expresses the oppression of nature, but in accordance with these other terms, I would propose *naturism:* regarding humanity, one's own group, on the basis of nature, as superior to other groups, nonhuman nature. Admittedly, *nature* is a confusing word with many meanings. By *naturism,* I refer to humanity's domination of nature, which has resulted in the ecological crisis. It includes *speciesism,* the belief that humans are superior to other animals. There are other, subtler manifestations. For example, since *mind* is associated with human superiority and since *body* is associated with *animal,* naturism includes the belief that mind is superior to body.

The second trend which concerns me contradicts the first one. While feminists mostly agree that these four forms of oppression are analogous expressions of the patriarchy, there is a severe split between feminists who are primarily concerned with nonhuman nature and those who are primarily concerned with human history (race, class, sex). This seems to me a fundamental issue underlying what has been described as the split between "spiritual" (or "cultural" or "countercultural") and "political" or "political/economic" feminists.[3] So I use the terms *nature feminists* and *social feminists.* Nature feminists customarily derive their norms from nature, whereas social feminists derive them from history. Celebrating the close connections between women and nature, nature feminists affirm their biology; social feminists, intent on exploring social interconnections, are often deeply suspicious of biological explanations. Nature feminists, on the other hand, pay limited attention to social structures. At best, they are profoundly aware of racism and classism, and Third World and working-class women are part of the sisterhood, but nevertheless their journals normally lack analysis of such matters as race and class. Similarly, social feminists have paid

---

3 Charlotte Bunch, "Beyond Either/Or Feminist Options," *Quest* 3 (1976), 2–17; and Hallie Iglehart, "Unnatural Divorce of Spirituality and Politics," *Quest* 4 (1978), 12–24.

limited attention to nature. For example, while they may discuss the ecological crisis, few incorporate it into their full social analysis, and some do not discuss it at all.

In general, the two groups have been far more hostile to each other than their common concerns might suggest. Social feminists may accuse nature feminists of avoiding resistance to the dominant culture and pulling together for comfort in a way that lacks political rewards. In their abhorrence of patriarchal social structures, many nature feminists assume a separatist lifestyle. In defense, some respond that they are not simply involved in personal liberation, that it is necessary to change the symbol system of a society as well as to develop social/political strategies for change.[4] Those working to further a religion of ecology, such as feminist Wicca, are seeking symbols that can transform our consciousness and thus our culture. Social feminists point out that conditions of survival in other countries are worsening, and to siphon energy away from direct action to work on transformation of consciousness may bypass the need for human liberation.

The condescension implicit and often explicit in such attacks does not assuage feelings. The nature feminist seeks to preserve the planet as well as the species in the face of destructive naturism and calls on women's power to further the struggle. Elizabeth Dodson Gray refers to naturism as "the most 'ruthless' mastering of all,"[5] for if the planetary ecology is destroyed, all sexes, races, and classes will also be destroyed. The historical bias of the social feminist all too often bypasses this fundamental consideration. Social feminists are clear that a historical materialism which omits the oppression of women is defective. But similarly, a social ethic which does not fully include nature in its analysis is defective.

As I observe this split between social and nature feminists, I find that each has hold of something the other lacks. Social feminists emphasize history and often disregard nature and biology; nature feminists emphasize nature and often disregard history and social structures. This is the nature/history split; and it is, of course, a false

---

4 Starhawk, *The Spiral Dance: A Rebirth of the Ancient Religion of the Great Goddess* (San Francisco: Harper and Row, 1979).

5 Elizabeth Dodson Gray, *Why the Green Nigger? Remything Genesis* (Wellesley, MA: Round Table Press, 1979), 6.

split, a false dualism. In actuality, one can derive norms from history and still include nature, for our relation to nature is *part of* our history. And one can derive norms from nature and still include history, for human history is *part of* nature.

One reason for this split is the traditional separation, observable in many disciplines, between history (human society) and nature (anything other than human). It seems especially acute within the behavioral sciences.[6] This is a type of subject/object split that considerably antedates Descartes; the relation of humanity and nature is perhaps the central question of .all western philosophy.[7] One problem is the puzzling fact that we are at once part of nature and yet somehow separate. On the one hand, humanity is part of the total ecology, the total interlocking systems of the planet, and beyond; and, on the other hand, we are able to use and exploit our environment, to mold and shape its systems to our own purposes. In some sense, our biology and our culture are in conflict with each other; but, paradoxically, without our biology, we would have no culture.

In the rest of this essay, I will set out steps that seem necessary if feminists are to heal this split in our theory. We need to build conceptual connections between the four forms of oppression, and it is particularly important to build them between sexism, racism, classism—the three modes of human oppression—and naturism. I will then sketch some special insights which nature and social feminists offer each other, and briefly discuss as important issues: whether women are closer to nature than men.

THE CONNECTIONS BETWEEN THE FOUR MODES OF OPPRESSION

The philosophical roots of this oppression are found in the western version of dualism, a mode of thought that divides reality, or aspects of reality, in halves. Patriarchal western thought is pervaded with

6 History itself, as commonly taught and written, is chiefly human history. Rare indeed are books which set human history in an ecological context, such as Edward Hyams' *Soil and Civilization* (New York: Harper and Row, 1976).

7 Thomas B. Colwell, Jr., "Some Implications of the Ecological Revolution for the Construction of Value," *Human Values and Natural Science,* ed. E. Laszlo and J. B. Wilbur (New York: Gordon, 1970), 245–58.

"hierarchical dualism,"[8] the tendency not only to divide reality but to assign higher value to one half. Simone de Beauvoir traces this to be the primordial duality of Self and Other;[9] she shares Hegel's view that every consciousness is fundamentally hostile to another consciousness, a curiously individual and ahistorical perception for so social a feminist. Many others argue that dualistic thought develops out of sexism; some assign it to social domination in general. Whatever its source, it is the most powerful conceptual link between the four modes of oppression.[10]

In this value hierarchy, the first half of the dualism understands itself as intrinsically better than the second. Women have been seen as defective males throughout history, e.g., in Christian thought and psychological theory. Treatises are still written to defend the proposition that blacks are biologically inferior to whites. Human neocortical development, and the culture it enables, is understood as a clear sign of human superiority to animals. Since the first group is seen as intrinsically better, it is entitled to a larger share of whatever is divided. The higher socioeconomic classes are entitled to a greater share of wealth; and the myth persists that the poor are poor because they are either lazy or stupid. On a global basis, better food is reserved for men, for they are considered more valuable than women, and malnutrition is appreciably higher for Third World women. Nature is seen as so inferior to humanity that we have freely despoiled the environment for centuries.

Thus the superior half is entitled to more power than the inferior—power over, needless to say, not power for. The inferior groups become utilitarian objects, resources to be exploited and possessions to be enjoyed, a vast resource of profit and pleasure. Profit is reaped from the cheap labor of women segregated in pink-collar work or unpaid housework and child-rearing: pleasure is provided by woman as sexual object. Nature is also a convenient resource to be exploited for profit, as a source of energy or raw materials, or for pleasure, as a source of recreation. Since some humans think it

8 Ruether, *New Woman/New Earth*.

9 Simone de Beauvoir, *The Second Sex*, ed. and trans. H. M. Parshley (New York: Knopf, 1953; original publication 1949).

10 Most social feminists critique this dualism from a dialectical point of view, whereas many nature feminists are monist.

unethical to conduct medical experimentation on themselves, they displace the inconvenience and pain onto animals.

Interestingly, the lower part of each social dualism is associated with nature and regarded as somehow more "physical" than the higher part. Women are seen as physically weaker, more vulnerable to their physiology, and dangerously sexual, seducing men from higher pursuits. Actually, women, blacks, and the lower classes all appear more sexual. The lower classes supposedly have less sexual control and hence have more children. The myth of the sexual "Negro" has caused great violence between the races in American history. Nature herself, sheer physicality, personified as woman, must be transcended through culture, personified as male.[11] Elizabeth Dodson Gray, whose insistence on the centrality of nature sometimes gives her special insights, notes that nature is in turn demeaned by its association with women.[12] Environmentalism reflects sentimental femininity, whereas anti-environmental politics are seen as masculine, realistic, efficient, and tough.

One difficulty with sketching parallels between the four modes of oppression is the inadvertent suggestion that they are identical. It is important to be aware that, while there are fundamental similarities, there are also all kinds of intermediate contradictions; they are interstructured in complex ways, both as historical and contemporary processes. As Rosemary Ruether says:

> . . . they have not been exactly parallel. Rather, we should recognize them as interstructural elements of oppression within the overarching system of white male domination. . . . This intermediate interstructuring of oppression by sex, race, and also class creates intermediate tensions and alienations.[13]

Among these intermediate alienations are tensions between non-white and white working-class persons, between black women and black men, between working-class and middle-class women, etc. Historically, the black liberation movement has been male-dominated; until recently the tension between female and male has been suppressed. Similarly, feminism has been basically a white middle-

11 Sherry B. Ortner, "Is Female to Male as Nature Is to Culture?" *Woman, Culture and Society,* ed. Michelle Zimbalist Rosaldo and Louise Lamphere (Stanford: Stanford University Press, 1974), 67–87.
12 Gray, *Why the Green Nigger?*
13 Ruether, *New Woman/New Earth,* 116.

class movement and has denied or suppressed the experience of poor, nonwhite women, both in the nineteenth and twentieth centuries. Each liberation movement, it seems, has tended to gloss over the particular type of oppression within its own ranks. Thus we have the spectacle of a black movement that has been sexist and a feminist movement that has been both racist and classist.

THE INTERSTRUCTURING OF NATURISM
AND THE THREE MODES OF SOCIAL OPPRESSION

This interstructuring is equally complex. Social and ecological domination are inextricably fused not only in theory but also in practice, as William Leiss had made clear; the exploitation of the earth is used to enhance the power of the already powerful.[14] While Leiss speaks solely in terms of classism, the same points hold true for racism and sexism. In general, the oppression of nature has gained resources for the ruling class so that they have been able to perpetuate their exploitation of women, nonwhites, the poor and the Third World in general. And similarly, of course, the exploitation of persons enables greater exploitation of resources; the four oppressions feed off each other to benefit those on top. Naturism flourishes in a context of social injustice.

However, the ecological movement, supposedly the antithesis of naturism, is itself a movement associated with the oppressors. The attack on naturism is frequently perceived by the oppressed as simply another means of preserving the elite's status and affluence. Many in the Third World perceive environmentalism as a conspiracy to deprive them of the technology they need so desperately for development; pollution controls, for example, both impede development and cost them money. Closer to home, the global problem is mirrored small in controversies like that around the Kaiparowitz project in Utah. To conservationists, the project meant pollution and infringement on precious wilderness; to local people, it meant jobs and survival, and the Sierra Club became their enemy. Bumper stickers which proclaim "Eat an Environmentalist" suggest great anger and alienation.

14 William Leiss, *The Domination of Nature* (New York: Braziller, 1972).

It is quite possible for ecology to be thoroughly co-opted by industrial capitalism, in the short run if not in the long run. This is part of Andre Gorz's thesis in *Ecology and Politics*.[15] As he explains, problems such as pollution and limited resources may be seen simply as technical constraints on capitalism. Technology can adapt; ecological costs can be absorbed; and the process of exploitation can continue unchecked. Gorz describes chillingly how, under western capitalism, world leaders willing to use hunger as a weapon in the service of sociopolitical domination are developing a kind of eco-fascism. Such weaponry was proposed by Secretary of Agriculture John Block in his first public statement.

Nevertheless, ecology, although co-optable, remains a potentially subversive science. Its conceptual underpinnings of interdependence and balance clearly confront the hierarchical dualism underlying the systems of oppression. At a social level, it provides a critique of the greed and waste implicit in industrial progress and the dangers of unlimited growth. But it has to make common cause with feminists and those seeking to liberate us from the oppressions of race and class. As Rosemary Ruether says: "The ethic of reconciliation with the earth has yet to break out of its snug corners of affluence and find meaningful cohesion with the revolutions of insurgent people."[16] Some social feminists and various science-for-the-people groups have been working together on economic systems that can simultaneously benefit all persons and care for the earth. Both social and nature feminists have been working on the development of appropriate or alternative technology. Such cooperations are altogether vital if we are to avoid the catastrophic scene envisioned by Gorz.

WHAT DO SOCIAL FEMINISTS HAVE TO TEACH US?

The question of what the four modes of oppression have in common includes the question of what societal mechanisms or structures keep

---

15 Andre Gorz, *Ecology and Politics*, trans. P. Vigderman and J. Cloud (Boston: South End Press, 1980; original publication 1975).

16 Rosemary Radford Ruether, "Motherearth and the Megamachine," *Womanspirit Rising: A Feminist Reader in Religion*, ed. Carol P. Christ and Judith Plaskow (San Francisco: Harper and Row, 1970), 43–52.

them going. This is the kind of discussion lacking in works by nature feminists, such as Susan Griffin's passionate book *Woman and Nature*,[17] and it is a discussion to which social feminists have much to contribute. Social structures are, after all, just as imprisoning as individual consciousness. To a large extent, social structures condition our individual consciousness, and the transformation of consciousness is mediated by them. Nature feminists, of course, do not deny their existence, but in general they restrict their social analysis to sexism.

Social feminists teach us to add analyses of classism and racism to our attack on sexism. While it is possible to discuss women and nature without reference to class and race, such discussion risks remaining white and elite. Too much of the suffragist movement of the last century became a struggle of white women for white privileges. And nowadays, what do discussions of women and nature mean to working-class women whose daily necessities include welfare reform, abortion, daycare, decent working conditions, and the like? To study sexism without reference to racism or classism is really the privilege of white women in higher socioeconomic classes. Only for this group is sexism the only problem.[18]

Gorz's analysis of the potential co-optation of ecology by capitalism suggests the need for women to make common cause with other oppressed groups and incorporate those experiences into their analyses and strategies. He suggests the possibility that before naturism destroys planetary ecology, and humanity with it, human suffering may increase greatly beyond its present dimensions. In the face of such an enemy, human liberation movements need to work together.

WHAT DO NATURE FEMINISTS HAVE TO TEACH US?

In poetry, art, dance, and ritual, as well as in expository prose, nature feminists repeatedly remind us that we are part of the Earth and the universe, part of a great interdependent community of both

17 Susan Griffin, *Woman and Nature: The Roaring inside Her* (New York: Harper and Row, 1978).
18 Ruether, *New Woman/New Earth.*

animate and inanimate beings. Mary Daly invites us to rediscover "the cosmic covenant, the deep harmony in the community of being in which we participate."[19] In 1978, at a feminist conference on social ethics, a substantial number of participants—persons very sensitive to modes of social oppression—nevertheless took for granted that nonhuman nature is here for our use. In general, social feminists have been slow to perceive the parallels of naturism with the social dominations. To understand nature as a utilitarian object not only ignores the fact that we are part of nature but also sets up a false dichotomy between human and nonhuman nature. The ecological symbol of the Goddess, advanced primarily by nature feminists, has become a powerful symbol of the community of being for many feminists of different persuasions.[20] At best, rather than returning to pretechnological primitivism, nature feminists can assist us to live within ecological limits, regulating our wasteful consumption and not polluting our resources.

In addition, nature feminists can teach us to celebrate our bodies. It is only very recently that social feminists have started to say much about the body; and concepts are sadly lacking to help us link our individual embodiment with our social relations. Alice Rossi is the sociologist most responsible for introducing biology into her field,[21] and her pioneering efforts have been more attacked than facilitated. Traditionally, social feminists have been very suspicious of biology, in part because it has been used in reactionary ways against blacks and women. Further, our biology is in large part the reason we have been confined to the domestic sphere throughout history.[22] "Anatomy is destiny" are fighting words in the sisterhood. Nevertheless, in our efforts to reclaim our bodies and affirm our sexuality, there is room for bridge-building.

Nature feminists could help to save social feminists from certain excesses. Some have responded to the misuse of biology by denying its realities: the final chapter of Shulamith Firestone's *The Dialectic*

19 Mary Daly, *Beyond God the Father: Toward a Philosophy of Women's Liberation* (Boston: Beacon, 1973), 177.

20 Starhawk, *The Spiral Dance.*

21 Alice Rossi, "A Biosocial Perspective on Parenting," *Daedalus* 106 (1977), 3–24.

22 Ortner, "Is Female to Male as Nature Is to Culture?"

of Sex is an extreme example. She asserts flatly that we must "free humanity from the tyranny of its biology."

> Humanity can no longer afford to remain in the transitional stage between simple animal existence and *full control of nature*. And we are much closer to a major evolutionary jump, indeed, to direction of our own evolution, than we are to a return to the animal kingdom from which we came.[23]

So instead of succumbing to the "tyranny" of our biology, we will overthrow it and take total control. While Firestone traces most social domination to sexism, she does not extend this model to the relation of humanity and nature; indeed, she reverses it. In high contrast is Mary Daly's statement that we need to move "from a culture of rapism to a culture of reciprocity" with nature.[24]

ARE WOMEN CLOSER TO NATURE THAN MEN?

In a seminal article, Sherry Ortner argues that the universal devaluation of women (trans-historical and cross-cultural) has resulted from the association of women and nature.[25] Men, on the other hand, are customarily associated with culture. Nature feminists are now reversing the logic and invoking women's closeness to nature in order to heighten our value. A powerful theme in their work is the idea that women are closer to nature than men. It is a short step, though not all take it, to the affirmation that women are therefore in important ways superior to men.

The topic deserves an article in itself. It is both deeply complex and deeply emotional, and it may well be one of the greatest stumbling blocks to an alliance between social and nature feminists. So I shall simply sketch out a few issues. Much depends on the meaning of the word "closer," whether it applies to biological or social-psychological matters.

Those who believe that women's biology allies us more closely with nature cite processes such as menstruation and childbirth.

23 Shulamith Firestone, *The Dialectic of Sex: The Case for Feminist Revolution* (New York: Morrow, 1970), 193. Italics mine.
24 Daly, *Beyond God the Father*, 178.
25 Ortner, "Is Female to Male as Nature Is to Culture?"

These relate us to Mother or Sister Earth, the rhythms and processes of life, the flow of future generations, in a way that men's biology cannot replicate. Some argue that menstruation brings women a knowledge of our limits early in life, which may assist us to live within ecological limits. Others take the whole argument further and say that the very possession of a penis—an organ they perceive as intrinsically dominating and patriarchal—limits male perceptions and capacities.

I have several difficulties with such arguments. First, simply because women are *able* to bear children does not mean that doing so is *essential* to our nature. Contraception clarifies this distinction: the ability to give birth can now be suppressed, and there are powerful ecological pressures in favor of this. In this context, it is important that our biology *not* be our destiny. Second, I find it difficult to assert that men are "further" from nature because they neither menstruate nor bear children. They also eat, breathe, excrete, sleep, and die; and all of these, like menstruation, are experiences of bodily limits. Like any organism, they are involved in constant biological exchange with their environment and they have built-in biological clocks complete with cycles. They also play a role in childbearing; I do not share the perception that the removal of semen from a man's body and its implantation in a woman's some-how turns fatherhood into an adjunct role. In reproduction, men's genes are as important as women's.

I find that Elizabeth Dodson Gray's argument for the limitations of "penis-bound bodily experience" is a contradiction of her central theme, her powerful affirmation of ecological interconnectedness. Consider her beautiful description of body-in-connection-with-the-world: " ... who-we-are is rooted in our kinship with the natural. The water of life flows through our tissues, and we are nourished, watered, fed, sustained, and ultimately return everything in our bodies to the world around us."[26] Surely this is as true of men as of women. Besides, her vision of the penis as intrinsically dominating is contradicted by her own moving description of heterosexual inter-course, which indicates that a penis can be an organ of profound

26 Gray, "Why the Green Nigger?" 83.

interconnection.[27] A culture may indeed condition men to use their penises as organs of domination, but they are not innately bound to do so.

There is a serious problem in freezing biological differences into a theory of two natures in which women are relatively "good" (closer to nature) and men relatively "bad" (farther from nature). This sets up a new hierarchical dualism, as much the reverse of male sexism as Firestone's analysis. Since black is beautiful, white must be bad? Since Aryans are pure, Jews must be a danger to the race? Ultimately, the problem is ecological. In a true ecological vision, all participate equally, rocks as much as persons, males as much as females. All are part of the great community of being.

If the question is social-psychological, there may be more truth in the assertion that women are "closer" to nature: we may be potentially more sensitive to it. Certainly our social roles have largely been defined in terms of bodily functions, and differing sex roles and psychologies have developed. Conditioned to greater emotionality and nurturance, possibly we are more likely than men to respond to the idea of sisterhood with nonhuman nature.

But finally, and most importantly, the question itself is flawed. Only the nature/history split allows us even to formulate the question of whether women are closer to nature than men. The very idea of one group of persons being "closer to nature" than another is a "construct of culture," as Ortner puts it.[28] Since we are all part of nature, and since all of us, biology and culture alike, is part of nature, the question ultimately makes no sense.

CONCLUSION

As I contemplate the nature/history split, as it is manifested in the division and struggle between nature and social feminists, it becomes a Zen koan. Suddenly it becomes clear that our history is inseparably part of our nature, our social structures are inseparably part of our biology. As William Leiss wrote: " . . . once the illusion of the separation between nature and society is abandoned, the true

27 Gray, "Why the Green Nigger?" 97.
28 Ortner, "Is Female to Male as Nature Is to Culture?"

character of social development as a series of increasingly complex states of nature becomes apparent."[29] These are strange paradoxes, these seeming divisions between nature and culture, which dissolve into nothingness when one tries to take hold of them.

As has long been recognized, such either/or choices, such false divisions, are the curse of our patriarchal culture. When nature feminists assert that women are biologically superior to men, I think they are setting up a false split between men and women. When social feminists say that nature feminists are siphoning energy away from direct action if they choose to work on transforming consciousness, I think they are setting up a false either/or. A good ecological rule, when confronted wih such a choice, is to ask if both/and is a possible response. This is in keeping with the ecological ethical imperative: "Maximize interconnectedness."

Certainly there is little point in choosing up sides between nature and social feminists since, as I have tried to show, we have much to give each other. I therefore share Charlotte Bunch's wish for a "non-aligned feminism" which refuses to attach automatically to an either/or choice.[30] The feminist ethic spurs us to seek the truths in each other's positions rather than to assail each other's errors. This is easier said than done, of course, for we are all corrupted by the patriarchy; and *ad feminem* attacks, to coin a phrase, will remain in our literature. When such violence occurs between sisters it is doubtless well to look closely, for the issues that arouse the deepest emotions may be the most fertile to explore.

Social and nature feminists are part of each other. We have only just begun to study out the interstructuring of sex, race, and class. We need to work on understanding the interstructuring of naturism with the three modes of social domination. In working to heal the nature/history split, we may yet turn back the tide of ecofascism and advance our revolution.

29 Leiss, *The Domination of Nature*, xii.
30 Bunch, "Beyond Either/Or Feminist Options."

Mapping Paths
and Dreaming Dreams

RETRIEVING NORMS FROM EXPERIENCE

Part Two

8

Our Right to Choose

THE MORALITY OF PROCREATIVE CHOICE

Beverly Wildung Harrison

If women are to undertake the collective task of revisioning the morality of procreative choice, and of legal abortion as a dimension of that choice, we need both the clarity of a critical feminist analysis concerning procreative choice and the constructive wisdom gained from values learned in childrearing. In spite of some good reasons to be cautious about moral entanglements, moral legitimacy needs to be wrested from those who oppose procreative choice. Those who press moral claims while ignoring the concrete well-being of people do not deserve to control the definition of "morality." Nor do those who dismiss or make light of women's need for emancipation deserve the sanction or legitimacy of either religion or morality. It is far too late for anyone to deny the truthfulness of protests against antiwoman bias in established religious and moral traditions, especially as these traditions have shaped views of sexuality, procreation, and abortion.

THE BASIC MORAL ARGUMENTS
FOR PROCREATIVE CHOICE

Dispelling the myth of moral superiority on the so-called pro-life side of the abortion debate commits us to develop our moral arguments more compellingly and also to evaluate critically existing moral theory and moral theology as they bear on the abortion controversy. I must repeat that unless procreative choice is understood as a desirable historical possibility substantively conducive to every woman's well-being, all debate regarding abortion is morally skewed from the outset. Yet no question is more neglected in moral evaluation of abortion than the prior question of whether women should have procreative choice. To say that this is the prior issue is to fly fiercely in the face of the precedent set by earlier discussions of the morality of abortion. Unbelievable as it may seem, many Christian ethicists, *including* proponents of legal abortion, would prefer to ignore or even suppress the fact that abortion is a birth control method. Others imply precisely that women should be condemned for using abortion as a means of birth control.[1] Only when we begin to perceive the importance of procreative choice in women's lives and to face the limitations of other contraception do we have a full context for realizing what it means to deny women access to legal abortion. We can then also better understand why the issue of abortion must never be separated morally from other issues related to the morality of procreative choice, including sterilization abuse, too-ready resort to unnecessary hysterectomies,[2] and broader issues of women's health care and social well-being. That efforts to deny women access to abortion are widely interpreted as acts of moral sanctity while widespread patterns of sterilization abuse go unnoticed[3] bespeaks the ease with which our society distorts the reality of women's lives.

1 That abortion is being used as a means of birth control is often hurled at women as a "charge." See Germain C. Grisez, *Abortion: The Myth, the Realities and the Arguments* (Washington, DC: Corpus Books, 1969).

2 The American Medical Association has acknowledged the widespread resort to unnecessary hysterectomies as a problem. Community health organizations have protested that poor women are subject to hysterectomies in training hospitals in order that residents may gain surgical experience. According to Jane Brody's "AMA Report on Incompetent Doctors," *New York Times* (27 January 1976), some 260,000 women undergo needless hysterectomies each year due to "errors of judgment."

3 The problem of sterilization abuse is widespread and takes many forms, among them using tubal ligations or hysterectomies to prevent further conceptions and requiring sterilization to prevent conception among welfare recipients or emotionally retarded women. Sterilization abuse of welfare recipients has been documented in several states. See Rosalind Pollack Petchesky, "Reproduction, Ethics, and Public Policy: The Federal Sterilization Regulations," *Hastings*

Any evaluation of a human act that misrepresents its full meaning in human life deserves to be faulted as moral abstractionism. Yet few moralists even recognize that with respect to abortion women do not, in the first instance, choose it at all. Rather, mature women choose to shape their own procreative power within a meaningful life plan. The decision for or against abortion arises either from a failure in such rational life planning owing to circumstances outside a woman's control or from a failure to take responsibility for contraception. Abstractionism in relation to the concrete reality of women's lives is characteristic of much western intellectual life but is overcome when the dilemmas that characterize men's lives are the focus of moral reasoning. Over the centuries, for example, Christian moral theologians have wrestled with the question of the use of violence in war—the so-called just-war issue—and in the process they have demonstrated a remarkable capacity for empathy toward the dilemmas of choice that rulers face in war.[4] They demonstrate no such empathetic casuistry in relation to women's options in the abortion dilemma, which is why I insist that ignoring the life circumstances out of which a woman confronts an abortion dilemma is inherently antifemale, regardless of whether the reasoner intends such gender-negative consequences.

Human pregnancy is in some respects *sui generis* as a human experience. To say that is to acknowledge that pregnancy is not precisely analogous to other human experiences either culturally or

Center Report 9 (1979), 29–42. See also *Women Under Attack: Abortion, Sterilization Abuse and Reproductive Freedom* (New York: Committee for Abortion Rights and Against Sterilization Abuse [CARASA], 1979). The American College of Obstetricians and Gynecologists has relaxed various professional constraints on the use of sterilization in recent years. See "Sterilization: Women Fit to Be Tied," in *Health Policy*, Advisory Center Bulletin 62 (January/February 1975), 4. See also Karen Lebacqz, "Sterilization: Ethical Aspects," and Jane Friedman, "Sterilization: Legal Aspects," in *Encyclopedia of Biomedical Ethics* 4 (Washington, DC: Georgetown University Press, 1978), 1606–17.

4 The contrast between Christian theological reasoning in relation to participation in war and reasoning on the morality of abortion requires further exploration. The surface distinctions are striking, however. The entire tradition of just-war reflection after Augustine turned to elaborating criteria to *justify* Christian participation in war. See Frederick R. Russell, *The Just War in the Middle Ages* (London: Cambridge University Press, 1975). By contrast, discussion of abortion riveted on the question of when in the course of pregnancy the prohibition of abortion was to apply.

biologically.[5] It is a long, complex biological process that, over time, produces a human life. In the process, a woman's body becomes the mediative vehicle for the emergence of that new life. This biological process requires a woman's cooperation. She must adjust her activities, take special care with her diet and her health, and in myriad other ways alter her lifestyle to bring the pregnancy to a successful outcome. There is always genuine physical risk involved and, in some cases, actual physical danger to the pregnant woman, but we must recognize that women bear not only the biological risks but also the cultural, social, and economic consequences of pregnancy and childbearing.

As a result, the misrepresentation of abortion at the level of women's personal lives turns out to be only a minor part of the problem. The distortion in the way the individual dilemma is interpreted is repeated and reinforced at the collective, historical level. Very little written about abortion incorporates a recognition of the distinctive character of the human reproductive process, not merely as a biological reality but also as a historical and cultural one. I have never read a word of moral discussion on abortion that recognizes the complex history of women's efforts to control and shape their own power of reproduction. That few moral philosophers or moral theologians have paid attention to the role of the "politics of reproduction" in human history is not surprising given the unacknowledged depth of antifemale bias in the dominant intellectual tradition. However male moralists respond on this matter, we must underscore the fatefulness for our lives of this failure to set the act of abortion in its proper human context.

There are, of course, no uncontestable grounds for moral claims, just as there are many ways to frame this call for procreative choice so integral to the global "rising of women." I believe, however, that the strongest possible moral argument will focus in the two directions already identified. On the one hand, we should take a cue from our European feminist sisters, especially committed Italian women,

5 There is an important technical issue at stake in contending that abortion is a *sui generis* biological experience. In ethics, an evaluation of an act frequently hinges on its analogous relationship to other approved or disapproved acts. With respect to abortion, the *sui generis* claim means that most analogies are rendered ineffective.

who comprehend the importance of appealing to foundational social justice considerations in seeking legal abortion.[6] To rest a claim morally on social justice criteria means that the matter at hand is arguably a part of the basic conditions needed for a good society because they are foundational for the well-being of people. Learning from the wisdom of their Catholic heritage, these European women recognized that the strongest moral grounding for legal abortion rests in the claim that any society has a positive moral obligation to support the conditions for women's well-being. That the basic conditions needed to pursue our own life plans are moral requirements of the just society has been widely recognized in religious ethics and moral philosophy. There is *nothing controversial* about this claim that a good society is one that promotes conditions for this enhancement.

The inability of many people to see that procreative choice is conditional to women's social well-being reflects a failure of moral imagination and empathy. Many simply cannot "take the role of the other"[7] when this involves identifying positively with women's lives. Happily, a few moralists have seen the moral importance of non-coercion in childbearing. Their hypothesis is that if we all had general knowledge of the nature of childbearing prior to awareness of who *we* would be in society, we would choose to reject social coercion in procreation as a condition for women's lives. It is important to emphasize that pondering the conditions for a good society along these lines helps us see that anyone who faced life with the prospect of childbearing would choose rules accordingly and elect procreative choice. Jewish moral philosopher Ronald Green has contended rightly that men and women alike would opt for a policy of procreative choice as the basis of childbearing if they had to determine the rules for a good society without knowing whether they would be female or male in that society.[8]

6 Rosemary Radford Ruether, "Italy's 'Third Way' on Abortion Faces a Test," *Christianity and Crisis* 41:8 (11 May 1981), 130, 141–43.

7 The importance to personal development of "taking the role of the other" was explored initially by sociologists Charles H. Cooley and George Herbert Mead. Both sensed its importance for moral development. Charles H. Cooley, *Human Nature and Social Order* (New York: Schocken, 1902); George Herbert Mead, *Mind, Self, and Society* (Chicago: University of Chicago Press, 1934).

8 Ronald Green, "Conferred Rights and the Fetus," *Journal of Religious*

Green's sort of contractualist argument for determining the rules for a good society has high standing among philosophical moralists today. The basic notion underlying this approach is that one way to clarify the criteria for social justice is to return ourselves in our imagination to an "original position" in which together we choose rules for society without foreknowledge of what our own concrete situation in that society would be. This paradigm of moral reasoning has been advanced by the work of moral philosopher John Rawls, especially in his much-heralded *Theory of Justice.*[9] This view that rational moral choice should conform to principles we would agree to disinterestedly—in an "original position," free of privilege, under conditions uncorrupted by concrete or specific self-interest—is now widely accepted in moral theory. I share the view that envisaging moral rules for a good society without specific knowledge of who we might be in that society is *one* good way to clarify our sense of foundational moral requirements—that is, our criteria for social justice. It is important to recognize that under the best available conception of disinterestedness in ethics, procreative choice makes sense as a foundational social justice claim. It is a moral ideal that stands the test of current notions of moral rationality.

We need not embrace the current certitude of much moral philosophy that disinterestedness is the most important ingredient or characteristic of moral reason to grasp the importance of such "original position" arguments. In fact, a more adequate perspective on moral reason enables us to see that the greatest value of such arguments is that they do not detach us from specific interest or elevate disinterestedness *per se.* Rather, they invite our interest in positive moral value, that is, our investment in a fair society in which nobody would be trapped at an irrevocable disadvantage. Rawls and other contractualists like Green who seek to liberate us from the bias of individual self-interest have in fact helped us revision the *common* good. They propose a creative method that encourages us to think together about what a fair or just society would entail and that requires an empathy too few of us attempt in

Ethics 2 (Spring 1974), 55–74.
9 John Rawls, *A Theory of Justice* (Cambridge: Belknap Press, Harvard University Press, 1971).

evaluating actions. Proceeding this way in considering procreative choice forces men and women alike to enter sympathetically into the life situation of one faced with unwanted pregnancy, to feel as she feels, and to face what she faces. It was just such basic social justice or good society arguments that enabled our Italian sisters, facing the implacable opposition of their church, to nevertheless advance claims for procreative choice persuasively and to convince a clear majority of Italians that they, not the Roman hierarchy, had moral right on their side.

In spite of the strength of original position appeals, however, it is critical not to let our moral case for abortion rest exclusively on abstract, contractualist claims about principles or views of rational choice limited to norms of disinterestedness.[10] Our other line of reasoning must be a strong utilitarian argument emphasizing the actual social vulnerability of women, one rooted in a concrete history of subjugation. This reality also makes the availability of abortion absolutely critical morally. No concern for social justice is genuine if it does not lie close to concrete historical consequences. To enhance the "quality of life" of a society by adopting policies whose consequences deteriorate the life conditions of "the fifty-one percent minority"[11] is bizarre. Regardless of whether people concur that procreative choice falls within the rubric of a good society, we need to challenge them to apprehend the concrete reality of women's historical oppression, especially in relation to childbearing.

As I have already observed, in this nation, and especially elsewhere on the planet Earth, the conditions for procreative choice are hardly available. In the United States, the defeat of the ERA should serve as a continuous reminder that not even formal legal equality between men and women is desired by the powers that be. And formal legal considerations aside, the economic and political inequality between men and women is marked; many recent gains by women are being reversed rapidly. The reality of most women's lives everywhere is constrained by severe economic inequity and by

10 For a critique of this view of moral reason, see Daniel Maguire, *The Moral Choice* (New York: Doubleday, 1978).

11 The phrase reverses Deborah S. David and Robert Brannon, ed., *The Forty-Nine Percent Majority: The Male Sex Role* (Reading, MA: Addison-Wesley, 1976).

the strong cultural pressures reinforcing inferiority. Given contemporary society's operative values and social dynamics, more and more children born today are very likely to be dependent solely on their mother's emotional and economic support. We need to stress this *de facto* reality, which includes the fact that most women already live under strong and often coercive pressures either for or against childbearing. It is also surely time to reject the innuendo that most women currently make quick decisions about abortion and casually elect abortion in a morally irresponsible fashion. Such claims really deserve branding as arrogant moralism, especially in light of the contrasting track records of men and of women in relation to moral values and moral concerns overall.

While a majority of people in American society favor some degree of "choice" for women in childbearing, apparently far fewer recognize the precariousness of the social conditions necessary to undergird genuine choice or the breadth and depth of subtle coercive factors, whether for or against choice. My earlier discussion should have made it obvious that many women choose abortion reluctantly in situations of marginal desperation, recognizing realistically that they cannot maintain conditions for their own and a dependent child's survival given the social and economic constraints governing their lives. Some women are overtly pressured, or indirectly lured, into choosing sterilization as a nonreversible means of birth control.[12] Still other women bear children they do not want, or only half-desire, because in a community hostile to any other fate for them, the stigma of abortion would be greater than they could bear. And others choose abortion as a birth control method of last resort

12 In Puerto Rico, owing to a variety of factors, sterilization came to be used widely in public health facilities and in Protestant mission hospitals. No one disputes that by now at least thirty percent of Puerto Rican women of childbearing age have been sterilized. Naturally, this situation has engendered pervasive resentment among Puerto Rican people. See especially Dr. Helen Rodriguez, "Population Control: The U.S. and Puerto Rico," in *Theology in the Americas*, Detroit II Conference Papers, ed. Cornel West, Caridad Guidote, and Margaret Coakley (Maryknoll, NY: Orbis Books, Probe Edition, 1982), 34–39. Puerto Rican and other Third World women have been used also as "guinea pigs" in experiments involving other means of contraception. See Mary Forell Davis, "Contraceptive Research: U.S. Policies and the Third World," unpublished manuscript, Union Theological Seminary, 1976. See also Dr. Helen Rodriguez, "The Social Politics of Technology," *Women's Rights Law Reporter* 7:5 (1983).

because, in a society still contemptuous of women's rights to contraception and to active sexuality, they do not have access to safer, more reliable means of contraception. Still others, especially young women, legitimately fear familial and social reprisals or psychological abuse for seeking contraception at all.

Those who continue to claim that feminist argument is morally irrelevant demonstrate contempt for women's lives. A wise ethic protests the moral myopia of any ethical theory incapable of integrating world historical data into its analysis. Of course these lines of argument make sense only to those whose moral sensibilities encompass a concrete refusal of the ancient trivialization of women's lives. Frequently we reach the limits of moral argument precisely because social pressures invite us to relinquish the task of transforming and deepening moral value. And yet it is the confrontation with perpetual moral insensibility that pushes people "beyond morality" into pragmatic and morally cynical politics. Understandably, then, the present political conflict over abortion tempts us to a political stance of "win at any cost." Even as we pursue a vigorous and well-organized strategy for procreative choice, we need to probe continuously the implications of our moral stance for our politics and to increase our sensitivity to the strengths and limits of the ideologies at work in the political arena.

THE MORAL DIMENSIONS
OF PRO-CHOICE POLITICAL CLAIMS

The still widely-held view that anti-abortion proponents have a monopoly on the moral factors in the abortion controversy remains not merely a substantive moral problem but a strategic one as well. To be sure, part of the "moral legitimacy" adhering to the anti-abortion position rests simply in the way that any appeal to established moral tradition resounds. Such appeals are designed to trigger and restore our confidence in a certain moral weight foundational to established traditions and born of the power of social convention. Ruling ideologies invariably are expressed in an array of religio-moral terminology. An adequate sociology of knowledge discloses[13]

13 A sociology of knowledge perspective attends to the total configuration of

that at the outset of any moral conflict, legitimacy invariably appears to reside with the dictates of propriety set by dominant groups within a society.

Gaining perspective on the centuries of ideology generated by male-dominated institutions is not easy. Even many women still believe at a subconscious level that unless women's lives are constrained by unquestioned and unquarreling assent to our so-called natural destiny—that is, our biological role as childbearers—we will become in some way "defective" as women. These male-generated theories claiming that our procreative power is literally our "essence" or "nature" have become very much a part of who *we* feel we ought to be.

Clarifying the connection between our socio-moral vision and the so-called pro-choice political position is especially urgent, precisely because feminist moral values—those that affirm and respect women's well-being—have deep implications for all of our lives. As a result, most women sense that a pro-choice political agenda cannot be one-issue politics. Equally urgent is that more women come to appreciate that the considerable power of feminism in the lives of contemporary women is rooted not, as some have claimed, in women's growing selfishness, preoccupation with self, or even narcissism[14] but in women's growing self-respect. This self-respect has been generated over against the many women-negating values, which also and simultaneously bespeak antihuman values long expressed in the dominant society. Women, especially feminists, are the ones rightly demanding a more integrated approach to all of human life, seeking social policies that place humane values and personal worth at the center of both our interpersonal relations and public life. The slogan "The personal is the political" has meant,

social interests in which ideas are embedded. The sociology of knowledge is not, as some have claimed, a discrete methodology or discipline. Rather, it is a conceptual sensibility relevant to any mode of inquiry. See *The Sociology of Knowledge: A Reader*, ed. James E. Curtis and John W. Petras (New York: Praeger, 1970).

14 Christopher Lasch, *The Culture of Narcissism: American Life in an Age of Diminishing Expectations* (New York: Warner Books, 1979). For an analysis of Lasch's assumptions about women, see Berenice M. Fisher, "The Wise Old Men and the New Women: Christopher Lasch Besieged," in *History of Education Quarterly* 19:1 (1978), 125–41.

among other things, that we need to seek our social and political ends in a way consistent with the personal values we espouse; it also means that nothing can be good for society that concretely negates people.

Because our "moral intuitions" have implications not only for how we develop our ethics but also for how we struggle for procreative choice, it is well to observe how deeply feminist conviction runs counter to prevailing political "wisdom." It is deeply ingrained in the ethos of this society that good politics permit or even require moral posturing, but when push comes to shove one should fight for one's political goals on any terms, giving no quarter to moral considerations. I join many other feminists in identifying this split between politics and morality as a symptom of patriarchal consciousness. Many of us believe, probably correctly, that women's lives historically have been less relationally brutal than men's because women as a group have not yet capitulated to such deep, value-denying dualism. Many women would forgo politics rather than be implicated in this separation.

Some adherents of procreative choice, especially men accepting the political "realist" line, have resorted to morally dubious arguments in support of a pro-choice position. These crass utilitarian arguments take the form, for example, of urging that the availability of legal abortion is desirable because it lowers welfare costs and lightens taxpayers' burdens in caring for the poor or because it reduces illegitimacy. There is surely some political mileage to be gained from the use of such covert racist appeals or appeals to class privilege. Those who are morally serious about the struggle for human liberation, however, are wise to assume that such arguments turn out, in the long run, to be bad politics. Gaining support for abortion by reinforcing race and class hostility is costly to our sense of polis and community, and it further injures many of the very women most desperately in need of conditions for procreative choice. Furthermore, even if crass utilitarian arguments prove effective in the short run, we need to remember that at the moment the other side controls the moral momentum on the issue; it is this reality, not permeable by such arguments, that must shift. Procreative choice is a morally right position because it creates conditions essential to the well-being of over half the human species, not because it allows any of us to live free of social obligation to provide for the common welfare, especially that of less advantaged people.

The fact remains that political pragmatism—that is, appeal to whatever arguments "work" in political debate—will always characterize good politics for dominant groups in a society. But this sort of short-term expediency is never an option for marginalized, disenfranchised, and disadvantaged citizens in any society; moral power is one of the deepest resources available to subjugated and oppressed people. Women are collectively the most disadvantaged people *within* their own communities and social groups, and their moral courage, often unnoticed, has been decisive for their communities' very survival. We need to make a political case that interrelates the need for legal abortion and the concrete pressures of racial-ethnic and all poor women's lives. The double and triple jeopardy of gender, race, and class must be central to our approach.[15] Our political goal will be genuinely secure only when more people grasp that we cannot prohibit legal, elective, surgical abortions without further violating the well-being of the vast majority of women and the children they bear, especially those most socially vulnerable because of other historic patterns of oppression.

IDEOLOGICAL PITFALLS
IN FEMINIST POLITICAL ARGUMENT

One reason our political arguments about abortion fail to cohere to the outlines of a social-justice moral argument such as the one I have sketched is that politically involved women, like most men in political debate, adopt certain ideological assumptions of male-generated political theory without sufficient critical scrutiny. Liberal or mainstream feminism has not struggled deeply enough with the moral implications of dominant political rhetoric.

A look at the political and legal context of the discussion quickly reveals that the debate around abortion is shaped, obviously enough, by terminology appropriate to the nation's political and legal traditions. We need to be aware, however, that the forms of rhetoric

15 Frances M. Beal, "Double Jeopardy: To Be Black and Female," in Robin Morgan, ed., *Sisterhood Is Powerful* (New York: Vintage, 1970), 340–53.

appropriate to politics, law, and morals are not, to say the least, always perfectly coordinated. Many people believe that the state should desist from exercising jurisdiction over abortion, relying on the right of privacy held to be implicit in several constitutional amendments. *Privacy* in legal parlance literally means "resting outside the spheres of government control." In the discourse of recent politics and much social theory, however, the term *private* has taken on a somewhat different connotation, stemming from the individualistic assumptions of the reigning social theory. Claiming that something is a "private" matter has come to mean that it is "unrelated to social reality," or that it affects an individual alone and should not be a shared reality. Although it is a fiction that at any point reality is *not* social, our liberal political rhetoric is saturated with such antisocial implications.

When we shift to moral discourse the complexity deepens. In moral terms, anything "private" should be construed as "standing outside the sphere of morality." If anything is private, it is a matter of utter indifference morally. Obviously, then, appeals to abortion as a "private matter" can be and frequently are heard as claims that abortion is "beyond morality." Pro-choice proponents sometimes conflate legal appeals to privacy and moral claims, misleading both sides on this point.

Furthermore, our appeals to "choice" in pro-choice politics some-times exhibit a similar ambiguity. Our statements are received as an appeal to some abstract value, *choice for choice's sake*, rather than to *procreative choice as a substantive moral good*. Furthermore, whenever we speak casually of choice without sufficiently ground-ing our language, we seem to imply that governmental noninter-ference is a good in itself, apart from social consequences. This sort of celebration of abstract choice betrays the heavy hand of the antisocial individualism of nineteenth-century liberalism (today's laissez-faire conservatism). Such political theory makes liberty, rather than justice, the be-all and end-all of the good life. Appeals to liberty often actually mask our desire to prevent others from con-straining *our* economic activity so that we may be free from accountability for the effects of our activity on our common life.

Real moral choice is, of course, never abstract. The moral right to procreative choice, including the legal or moral option of abortion, is much more basic than "mere liberty" defined as noninterference or lack of any constraint. Nor are our appeals for choice ever really merely for choice's sake. To claim procreative choice as a right means that it is a foundational condition for our well-being in society. Because there can be no real freedom without such substantive conditions, moral claims are more basic than claims to liberty. To put the point another way, morally we all deserve as much liberty as is consistent with not violating others' basic life conditions. The reason choice or liberty came to be seen as an end or value in itself in early liberal political theory was that the images of the human being and human nature underlying laissez-faire ideology were antisocial. A person or self was conceived of as an isolated monad, a "lone ranger"[16] who can, if he or she will, live free of social entanglements or "contract" into society at whim.

Zillah Eisenstein has documented that even the best liberal political theory cannot accommodate the full agenda of women's historical liberation, arguing that even a moderate feminist political stance must necessarily carry feminists beyond political liberalism and its individualistic assumptions.[17] Eisenstein's claims about political theory and strategy are even more applicable to feminist moral theory and argument concerning procreative choice and abortion. Morality is, intrinsically, about our social relations, including our social relations to ourselves. The tendency of liberal political theory to image human beings as isolated and discrete entities who may, *if they choose,* enter into society flies in the face of most women's experience. Such libertarian assumptions reflect social privilege, power, and wealth. Women know, especially through childbearing and childrearing, that our social interrelations are basic even to our biological survival and are not now, nor have they ever been, entirely optional.

For a moral point of view the idea that abortion is and should be a

16 John R. Wikse, *About Possession: The Self as Private Property* (University Park: Pennsylvania State University Press, 1977), 13ff. To reject liberty as a key category for conceptualizing rights is to break with dominant liberal politial theory. In my view, "rights" are basic shares of the conditions of well-being a society can provide its members.

17 Zillah Eisenstein, *The Radical Future of Liberal Feminism* (New York: Longman, 1981). See also Susan Moller Okin's excellent *Women in Western Political Thought* (Princeton: Princeton University Press, 1979).

strictly "private" matter does not deserve standing. It implies that childbearing is a purely individual concern, separable from our own and others' well-being, from all our interpersonal obligations, and from the common good. The effect of liberal rhetoric on some mainstream feminist argument is noticeable in the implication that individualism is a more basic value than genuine community. This is simply untrue; when the conditions of community collapse, "individual" centeredness is also threatened. A few proponents of procreative choice may even seem to suggest that women should be able to live free of any accountability in the use of their procreative power. Such libertarianism no doubt appeals to more privileged groups who have every reason to welcome laissez-faire doctrine in social and economic relations, but it is simply not consistent with social reality. Women, like men, have accountability to others for the overall well-being of our common life, no more and no less. To be sure, part of our present moral conflict is due to that fact that, by virtue of women's procreative power, females have been expected to take *more* responsibility for creating and sustaining basic humane conditions than men. Simultaneously, women have been expected *not* to seek or express genuine moral freedom, especially, as I have observed, when it comes to their unparalleled power of procreation.

Even as we recognize the moral inadequacy of treating abortion merely as a private matter, many will continue to make legal claims based on presumed constitutional provisions for "the right to privacy." We need to recognize, however, that grounds for this and other legal appeals are murky. Though many believe that matters involving intimacy and family and domestic relations ought to be protected by the right to privacy provisions that some construe to be implicit, especially in the Ninth and Fourteenth Amendments, the courts have been erratic in sustaining such claims. Nor is misogyny a stranger in the history of our legal provisions relevant to women. Even such critical constitutional provisions as the due process and equal protection clauses of the Fifth and Fourteenth Amendments frequently have been rendered irrelevant whenever woman's "nature" could be invoked to justify differing treatment.[18] In any

18 For a discussion of some of the "exemptions" of women under the equal protection clauses of the Constitution, see Jeanne Mager Stellman, *Women's*

115

case, I have made it clear that legal appeals to privacy do not
encompass optimal moral concerns directly. To help people who
care about social justice hear us more accurately we need to be
aware that such legal claims to abortion are not equivalent to our
best moral arguments.

From a moral point of view it is appropriate to recognize that our
legal claims are somewhat precarious because important basic,
foundational moral conditions of life were not recognized as critical
by the socially elite men who penned—and later interpreted—the
Constitution.[19] Our analysis must not absolutize the U.S. Constitution, which is a somewhat more limited vehicle for grounding
human rights than our political rhetoric usually acknowledges. The
authors of the Constitution were eager, of course, to guarantee
conditions for the *political* participation and social liberty *vis-à-vis*
the state for men like themselves; in the process they secured formal
provisions for a number of rights that are genuinely foundational to
human well-being. What a feminist analysis must stress, however, is
that no direct constitutional provision was made for that most basic
foundational requirement on which women's existence as the "social
other" of intimacy relations pivots—the right to bodily integrity,
including the noninvasion or nonvoluntary manipulation of our
bodies by others.[20] While, as we will see, there are common law
precedents against bodily invasion, they have never been applied to
women as childbearers. The critical need for foundational moral
recognition of body-right was surely not apparent to slave-owning

Work, Women's Health: Myths and Realities (New York: Pantheon, 1977), 188ff.
Recent Supreme Court decisions on abortion have rejected the view that
indigency is relevant to the issue of equal protection. Hence the decision that the
Hyde Amendment, prohibiting the use of public monies to finance abortions, does
not violate the principles established in *Roe v. Wade.*

19 For the text and legal interpretations that have developed, see Thomas
James Norton, *The Constitution of the United States: Its Sources and Its
Application* (New York: Committee for Constitutional Government, November
1962 edition).

20 For a compelling analysis of the problems of individualism in feminist
reflection on abortion, and a fine statement of what is at issue in terms of
women's control of their reproductive capacity, see Rosalind Pollack Petchesky,
"Reproductive Freedom: Beyond a Woman's Right to Choose," *Signs* 5:4
(Summer 1980), 661–85. Petchesky's work in this area has led her to a conclusion
very similar to my own.

white males at a point in history when both slaves and wives were legally their property, but it must be apparent to anyone who cares about social justice in the twentieth century. I elaborate this moral argument elsewhere, but here it is important not to overlook the fact that our liberal political heritage puts no great emphasis on this most concrete moral right.

It is also important to examine a related and equally critical point about legal arguments in relation to abortion. The shifting reasoning of the U.S. courts in recent abortion decisions demonstrates that the present legal grounds for procreative choice are far from secure.[21] In the original Supreme Court decision legalizing abortion, *Roe v. Wade*, Justice Harry Blackmun gave women's well-being some centrality in his argument. He claimed the state has a legitimate interest in women's well-being and linked this interest with justification for procreative choice. Since the *Roe-Wade* decision, concern for women's well-being has hardly been mentioned in the Court's reasoning. Furthermore, the state's interest in promoting child-bearing has emerged in the discussion. No woman should rest easy when this sort of legal thinking characterizes the judiciary. Given these developments, legal claims to "right to privacy" may be pressed with even greater force. Those who appeal to privacy should be prepared to reject criticism that their appeals imply a lack of moral sensibility on the part of pro-choice proponents. Some of our critics encouraged the confusion between our legal claims and our moral ones, and we can predict that they will continue to try to heighten that confusion.

To recognize the moral limits of political liberalism is not, of course, to reject this society's liberal heritage *in toto*. My own affinities with theological liberalism should be clear enough already. "Liberalism" has a complex and shifting history, but its current limits are set by its abstract individualism. I am persuaded that the survival of liberalism's best insights is contingent on a total break with laissez-faire ideology and on the integration of substantive social justice concerns, including economic democracy, in the liberal

21 See Kristen Booth Glen, "Abortion in the Courts: A Laywoman's Historical Guide to the New Disaster Area," *Feminist Studies* (February 1978), 1–26.

arguments. The "individual as central sensibility,"[22] liberalism's deepest moral fruit, may yet survive if such shifts occur. The deep moral wisdom that people are to be treated as ends, never merely as means,[23] when it is not taken to deny that we are social, interdependent beings, is too precious to lose. Liberal ideology goes astray not because of its concern for people but because of its portrayal of people as individual monads and the overwhelming tendency of liberals, now often among the affluent and privileged, to assume that guarantees for individual welfare are already embodied in our political-social structure. The truth is that in this society one's "individuality" is respected in direct proportion to one's wealth, social standing, race, gender, and age. Even wealth may not give access to social power if one is neither white nor male. Speaking of the morality of abortion as if women were abstract individuals for whom procreation is largely a simple matter or an asocial, nonrelational decision is absurd. And it is this same mystified individualism that motivates some people to perpetuate the serious illustion that genuine procreative choice for women will be ensured merely by securing the legality of abortion. Here, as elsewhere, liberals persistently misperceive and misrepresent the extent and nature of social constraint and control. Freedom *from* political, economic, or legal constraints is held to be a sufficient foundation condition for the actual exercise of human freedom. The *de jure* or legal freedoms of liberal political constitutions are a sufficient condition for *de facto* freedom *only if one has access* to the various forms of social, political, economic, and personal power.

Disentangling our moral case for procreative choice from assumptions of individualistic liberalism will pave the way for establishing common ground with some of our opponents who also rightly reject such liberalism on moral grounds and out of fear that this "superficial" moral theory, with its dualistic "public" and "private" split between morals and politics, is eroding concern for social justice. To

22 The term is Michael Lewis's. See *The Culture of Inequality* (Amherst: University of Massachusetts Press, 1978), Part 1.

23 This maxim is most often associated with the moral theory of Immanuel Kant. In interpretations of Kant's ethics, his "teleology of ends" is often ignored. See Jeffrie G. Murphy, *Kant: The Philosophy of Right* (London: Macmillan, 1970).

ultimately unite with our opponents over concern for the common good is possible, I believe, precisely because of the moral and religious vision underlying a feminist commitment at the center. Many critics of feminism have branded feminists as rigid and uncompromising in our abortion politics. Yet, given our moral concerns, we exhibit more genuine sympathy for our opponents than those who merely believe that all abortion politics are too zealous and unseemly.

In our present situation many women's almost intuitive recognition of the zero-sum nature of the personal abortion dilemma mitigates efforts to develop strong politics of procreative choice. In spite of the persistent diatribe from the radical Right, most women are only too well aware that, given the life-affirming value they celebrate and wish to exemplify in their own lives, abortion is not only an agonizing dilemma but one that defies simplistic moral definition. If women trust their power of self-interpretation, their reluctance to impose their own convictions on others can be transformed into a positive resource not only for moral reason but for the new sensibilities this nation requires in its political life. Deeply felt and deeply registered awareness of the complexity of life can be a source of both moral and political wisdom.

In insisting that the power of procreative choice be ours, we are necessarily seeking a considerable shift in the distribution of power in society. Far from being a matter of social indifference or a "private affair," procreative choice will alter the dynamics of social power considerably. Our opponents know this, and it is the reason they fight us. Some women, too, find the idea of appropriating our rightful social power threatening, so conditioned have they become to social powerlessness. But such fears cannot be permitted to obscure the issues at hand. With social power comes a necessary social accountability. It is obvious that much of the hysteria generated by the abortion controversy stems from the fear of some people that women cannot be competent historical agents. Though women's moral record historically is probably superior to men's, the irony is that women's ability to exercise social power is perceived as less trustworthy than men's, precisely because of women's historical social disadvantage. If my thesis is correct that procreative choice involves a major historical shift and that it is a great moral good uniquely foundational to women's well-being, then the success of present anti-abortion politics would be a moral disaster for the whole society. It would extend the dubious moral reality of female subjugation and male supremacy. To subvert the conditions for procreative choice is simultaneously to set back women's long struggle to gain all of the other conditions of human dignity that the wisest men, through their moral theories and theologies, have argued constitute human well-being. The institutions of male supremacy have been perhaps fifteen thousand years in the making. The social conditions for the end of this supremacy are only now at hand. We are still far from incorporating them in a way relevant to most women's lives. A society over half of whose members lack the basic conditions for the exercise of rational choice when such conditions are available could not, by any moral standards, be counted as a good society. Not until this simple point also becomes obvious will "the longest revolution" be won.[24]

24 The phrase is Juliet Mitchell's, "The Longest Revolution," *The New Left Review* 40 (November–December 1966), 11–37.

9

While Love Is Unfashionable

ETHICAL IMPLICATIONS
OF BLACK SPIRITUALITY AND SEXUALITY

Toinette M. Eugene

For you there shall be no longing, for you
    shall be fulfillment to each other;
For you there shall be no harm, for you
    shall be a shield for each other;
For you there shall be no falling, for you
    shall be support to each other;
For you there shall be no sorrow, for you
    shall be comfort to each other;
For you there shall be no loneliness, for you
    shall be company to each other;
For you there shall be no discord, for you
    shall be peace to each other;
And for you there shall be no searching,
    for you shall be an end to each other.
—Kawaida Marriage Commitment

INTRODUCTION

Black spirituality and black sexuality, properly understood as aspects of the holistic life-style of Afro-American women and men, are a closer fit than hand and glove. Nonetheless, taken together these issues also represent two of the most serious ethical challenges that the contemporary black church must address. While we may affirm

121

the covenantal poetry above which is based on an African worldview and value system, we must also acknowledge another Afro-American reality which sorely lacks the spiritual and sexual fidelity expressed in the poem.

One of the most neglected ministries in the black church has been the holistic integration of sexuality and life. Although the black church has been one of the key supportive institutions for upbuilding family life and values,[1] the need to address issues and attitudes dealing with sexuality, with mutuality in male/female relationships, and with the more recent impact of black feminism has never been greater than today.

This essay investigates the relationships between black spirituality and sexuality in the quest for mutuality among black women and black men. I will examine these issues with particular reference to the unifying factor of black love. The focus is holistic, that is, it illuminates black spirituality and sexuality as they are experientially related. The assumptions of this approach are incarnational. Consequently, a theology of black male/female friendship which is mutual, community seeking, as well as other-directed, is a central, incarnational, and liberational premise for this work in an era in which any effort at committed love appears unfashionable.

SPIRITUALITY AND SEXUALITY AS RELIGIOUS ASPECTS OF THE CONTEMPORARY BLACK EXPERIENCE

We must acknowledge at the outset a widespread and well-known experience within the black community. Michelle Wallace, among others, agrees that experience of distrust has driven a wedge between black women and black men:

> For perhaps the last fifty years there has been a growing distrust, even hatred between black men and black women. It has been nursed along, not

1 For an excellent theological treatment of the unique relationship between the two institutions of the black family and the black church, see J. Deotis Roberts, *Roots of a Black Future: Family and Church* (Philadelphia: Westminster Press, 1980). See also Andrew Billingsley, *Black Families in White America* (Englewood Cliffs, NJ: Prentice-Hall, 1968) and Herbert G. Gutman, *The Black Family in Slavery and Freedom, 1750–1925* (New York: Pantheon, 1976) for extensive documentary examinations of this issue.

only by racism on the part of whites, but by an almost deliberate ignorance on the part of blacks about the sexual politics of their experience in this country.[2]

This basic distrust between black women and black men accounts for the inability of the black community to mobilize as it once could and did. The religious aspect of *black sexuality*, by which I mean the basic dimension of our self-understanding and way of being in the world as black male and female persons, has been distorted into a form of black sexism. Because of this basic distrust, the beauty of black sexuality, which also includes our sex-role understandings, our affectional orientations, physiological arousal and genital activity, and our capacity for sensuousness, has become debilitated. The power of black sexuality to contribute to our liberating mission to change our oppressive condition has been weakened. This basic distrust disables and distracts us as we strive to bring about the reign of God, which is a theological, as well as a political reality, for black women and black men.[3]

Theologian Jacquelyn Grant adds another significant aspect of the nexus between black spirituality and black sexuality: the effects of sexism on the kerygmatic and proclamatory mission of the black church. She insists:

> If the liberation of women is not proclaimed, the church's proclamation cannot be about divine liberation. If the church does not share in the liberation struggle of Black women, its liberation struggle is not authentic. If women are oppressed, the church cannot possibly be "a visible manifestation that the gospel is a reality"—for the gospel cannot be real in that context. One can see contradictions between the church's language or proclamation of liberation and its action by looking both at the status of Black women in the church as laity and Black women in the ordained ministry of the church.[4]

The holistic expression of black spirituality is a central part of what

2 Michelle Wallace, *Black Macho and The Myth of Superwoman* (New York: Dial Press, 1979), 13.

3 See J. Deotis Roberts, *A Black Political Theology* (Philadelphia: Westminster Press, 1974), for further explanation of the reign of God as both a theological and political reality.

4 Jacquelyn Grant, "Black Theology and the Black Woman," in *Black Theology: A Documentary History, 1966-1979*, ed. Gayraud Wilmore and James

is at stake in liberating relationships between black women and men in the church and society.

Spirituality is no longer identified simply with asceticism, mysticism, the practice of virtue, and methods of prayer. Spirituality, i.e., the human capacity to be self-transcending, relational, and freely committed, encompasses all of life, including our human sexuality.

Specifically, Christian spirituality involves the actualization of this human transcendence through the experience of God, in Jesus the Christ, through the gift of the Spirit. Because God, Jesus, and the Spirit are experienced through body-community-history, a black Christian spirituality includes every dimension of black life. We must begin to re-employ the power of black spirituality as a personal and collective response of black women and black men to the gracious presence of the God who lives and loves within us, calling us to liberating relationships with one another and with all people on Earth.

BLACK LOVE AS FOUNDATIONAL FOR THE EXPRESSION OF BLACK SPIRITUALITY AND SEXUALITY

A black liberating love must serve as the linchpin to link black spirituality and sexuality. Black love is the agent of gospel liberation as well as the strongest asset of the black and believing community. Black love, expressed through the faithful witness of our spirituality and sexuality creates awareness of the living God who is in every place. Black love sustains our own ability to choose and to discern, and nurtures the sense of the bonding and *esprit d'corps* which allows black women and men to be distinctive in the style of our self-acceptance. Black love confirms and affirms our affection for God, self, and others, especially those who have also been oppressed.

Historically, black love enabled the incredibly crushed spirits of enslaved black women and men to look beyond their immediate, undeserved suffering to a God who would never forsake them in their hour of anguish and despair. Historically, it has been the religious aspect of black love which enabled black Christians to

Cone (Maryknoll: Orbis, 1979), 423.

believe always in the worth of each human life: born and unborn; legitimate and "illegitimate"; single and several-times married; young and old; unemployed and inexperienced.

Any major misunderstandings or doubt about the ability of black love to link and liberate the power of spirituality and sexuality can be traced to the effects of our enslavement experiences. Historically, it was criminal for blacks to express extended love for one another or to establish lasting relationships of social interdependence and care. Blacks were wrenched from our African societies in which sexual behavior was orderly and under firm family and community controls. Under the system of slavery black people were bred like animals; white men were allowed to sexually coerce and abuse black women; black families were frequently broken up and legal marriage was often prohibited. Sexual instability was forced upon the Afro-American community.[5]

Racist myths and stereotypes perpetuated these distortions to this day, falsely detailing black hypersexual activity and an inability to maintain and nurture marital commitments. Racists also repeat ubiquitous rumors about violent relationships among black men and their women or wives. It is impossible for the many white Americans reared on this pathological mythology to think, speak, or write with historical accuracy or ethical understanding about the integrity of black love and relationships.

Despite these assaults, black love has continuously flowed between black people, almost like breath (the *nepesh*, the *ruah* or the *pneuma*, which scriptural studies tell us is like the breath of God), breathing life into dead or desperate situations. This death-defying capacity of black women and men to go on giving and receiving love has been incredibly preserved within a hostile and racist American environment. Such tenacious black love had its spiritual genesis in African soil where it developed unencumbered, at least in its beginnings, by the prejudices of American puritanical Christianity. We must hold on to this strong inheritance from our African past if there is to be any hope for nurturance, growth, and fruitfulness in black male/female relationships in our black church and society.

5 See Wade Nobles' "African-American Family Life," in *Black Families*, ed. Harriet Pipes McAdoo (Beverly Hills, CA: Sage Publications, 1981), 77–86.

Racist assumptions and myths perpetuate the lie of a "black love deficiency." Black persons educated in the black religious experience have recognized that if black people today are to be liberated, we must continue to conceive of and model ourselves as a morally creative and spiritually generative race of women and men who choose to act out of our own positive *ethos*. We must continue to create and articulate our own positive expressions and standards of excellence rather than continue to be confined and defined by the negative images of a dominant social, sexual, cultural, and political system which does not value blackness as inherently good.

Black love ought always to serve as an essential normative and descriptive referent for the relationship found in black spirituality and sexuality. I arrive at this ethical "ought" or injunction for our future based on results which are verifiable in our brutal and painful past history as a people in this country. It may be historically demonstrated that in times past whenever black women and men consciously and consistently dared to express black love through an integration of their spirituality and sexuality, they became a source for liberating social transformation in both the black community and in the white world around them. The abolitionist and feminist Sojourner Truth, through her involvment in redressing the racist and sexist oppression of her times, is an excellent example of the way in which the integration of personal spirituality and sexuality may come to fruition in a prophetic paradigm for the sake of the reign of God. (I shall return to examine the religious experience of Sojourner Truth as a model for our theme.)

In the days gone by, black love expressed between black women and men was at worst illegal or at least highly unprofitable in every way for those trying to survive in impossible situations. Nonetheless deliberate choices were made by our foreparents which: 1) enabled Afro-American peoples to create and perform under great duress their own wedding rituals such as the slave marriage custom of "jumping the broomstick" or the practice of "marrying in blankets";[6]

6 See Gutman's *The Black Family in Slavery and Freedom, 1750–1925*, 273–84 for fuller discussion of black slave marriage rituals. "Jumping the broomstick" served as the most common practice to transform a "free" slave union into a legitimate and respected slave marriage. "Marrying in blankets" referred to the ritual by which a slave woman brought her blanket or bedroll to place beside that

2) promoted an internal sexual ethic in the slave communities which safeguarded marriages, secured the welfare of children and forbade indiscriminate or irresponsible sexual relations; 3) prompted hundreds of former slaves to search endlessly for a reunion with their spouses, children, and relatives after the Emancipation Proclamation of Lincoln.

These realities are foundational for an understanding that black love expresses a sacramental statement about the relationship of black spirituality to sexuality. Without a realistic assessment of the innumerable ways black women and men have endeavored to hold fast to each other, and to cherish one another, it is easy to generate theological premises and sociological strategies based on false foundations. For example, it is true that urban life-styles and escalating unemployment have contributed greatly to the breakdown of many black marriages and families. However, it is equally critical to assert the historical fact that until the third decade of the twentieth century, the majority of black marriages and families were thriving and stable.[7]

This practical understanding of black integrity, fidelity, as well as familial stability, enables a clearer assessment of the pathologies of racism and sexism which affect black male/female relationships in church and society. Racism and sexism continue to hinder us from expressing the depths of black spirituality and sexuality as epitomized in black love.

RACISM AND SEXISM AS CRITICAL FACTORS
AFFECTING THE BLACK QUEST FOR MUTUALITY

Racism and sexism, operative in our midst, are the two primary negative factors which affect black male/female relationships. Any ethical reflection on the issue of sexism in relation to racism requires

of her intended husband to signify their intent to share life and love together as a committed couple. In a note Gutman records that this simply symbolic action so disturbed Yankee missionaries that they even imposed "severe strictures" on South Carolina slaves "marrying in blankets."

7 See Herbert G. Gutman as cited in Edward P. Wimberly, *Pastoral Counseling and Spiritual Values: A Black Point of View* (Nashville: Abingdon, 1982), 62.

a coming to terms with the suffering and oppression which have marked past pathological relationships between black women and black men. Honest reflection on the issue of sexism in relation to racism may also highlight positive aspects of the challenge and conversion available to black and believing women and men who want to deal with their own spirituality and sexuality as a means of coming to terms with a new life in God.

Jacquelyn Grant explains the effects of sexual dualism on the self-image of black people. "Racism and sexism are interrelated," she says, "just as all forms of oppression are interrelated."[8] Racism and sexism have provided a theological problem within the Christian community composed of both black women and men who theoretically are *equally* concerned about the presence of freedom and justice for all. "Sexism, however, has a reality and significance of its own because it represents that peculiar form of oppression suffered by Black women at the hands of Black men. It is important to examine this reality of sexism as it operated in both the Black Community and the Black Church."[9]

A careful diagnosis of the sickness and the sin of sexism within the black church calls forth a challenge to ministers and laity alike. The failure of the black church and of black theology itself to proclaim explicitly the liberation of black women indicates, according to this assessment, that neither theology nor the church can claim to be agents of divine liberation or of the God whom the evangelist describes as the Author and Exemplar of black love. If black theology, like the black church, has no word for black women, then its conception of liberation is inauthentic and dysfunctional.

There are two basic forms which such sexism takes in black male/female relationships: sexist and spiritualistic splits or divisions within reality.

Sexist dualism refers to the systematic subordination of women in church and society, within interpersonal relationships between males and females, as well as within linguistic patterns and thought formulations by which women are dominated.[10] Hence the term

8 Grant, "Black Theology and The Black Woman," 422.
9 Grant, "Black Theology and The Black Woman," 422.
10 James B. Nelson has made extensive use of the concepts of "sexist and

"patriarchal dualism" may be also appropriate, or more simply, the contemporary designation of "sexism," may be used. *Spiritualistic dualism* has its roots in the body-spirit dichotomy abounding in white western philosophy and culture introduced at the beginning of the Christian era. Hence, the term "Hellenistic dualism" may also be appropriate. It must be noted in offering these descriptive distinctions about sexual and spiritual dualisms that African philosophy and culture was and still is significantly different from these white western conceptualizations.[11] It is this African worldview which has given rise to the holistic potentiality residing in authentic expressions of Afro-American spirituality and sexuality today.

Sexist dualism has pathologically scarred not only the white community from which it originated but has also had its negative effect within the black religious community.[12] Sexist dualism, which has been organized along racial lines, refers to "schizophrenic" male attitudes toward women in general who are imaged as either the virgin or the whore—the polemical Mary or Eve archetype represented by the female gender. The prevailing model of beauty in the white, male-dominated American society has been the "long-haired blond" with all that accompanies this mystique. Because of this worldview, black women have had an additional problem with this pseudo-ideal as they encounter black men who have appropriated this norm as their own.

Sexist as well as racist dualisms have elevated the image of the white woman in accordance with the requirements of a white worldview into becoming the respected symbol of femininity and purity, while the black woman must represent an animality which can be ruthlessly exploited for both sex and labor. Similarly the sexist dualism present within pseudo-biblical teaching argues that *woman* is responsible for the fall of "*man*kind," and is, consequently the

spiritualistic dualism" in *Embodiment: An Approach to Sexuality and Christian Theology* (New York: Pilgrim Press, 1976). See especially Chapter Three. I have attempted to turn his categories into explicit reflection on black sexual experience.

11 See John Mbiti, *The Prayers of African Religion* (New York: Orbis, 1975) and *Concepts of God in Africa* (London: SPCK, 1970) for further connections made on the nexus between black spirituality and an integral worldview.

12 See Rosemary Radford Ruether, *New Women, New Earth: Sexist Ideologies and Human Liberation* (New York: Seabury, 1975), Chapter Five.

source of sexual evil. This dualistic doctrine has had its doubly detrimental effect in the experience of many black women.[13]

The self-image and self-respect of many black women is dealt a double blow by both black religion and black society. Thus, black women are made to believe or at least accept on the surface that they are evil, ugly, insignificant, and the underlying source of trouble, especially when the sense of intimacy begins to break down in black love relationships.

This dualistic doctrine has nurtured a kind of compensatory black male chauvinism (as evidenced in typical black church patterns and black nationalism movements) in order to restore the "manliness" of the one who had traditionally been humiliated by being deprived (according to a white patriarchal model) of being the primary protector for his family. In such manner, sexist dualism has been a central limitation in the development of a black love which at its zenith is the most authentic expression we have of the unity of black spirituality and sexuality.

A disembodied spirituality has also been a central limitation in the development of black love. Spiritualistic dualism has been a central factor in persistent efforts to portray faithful black love as an unfashionable and hopelessly anachronistic way of establishing black liberation and black material success and achievement. Eldridge Cleaver obviously recognized the racism and sexism in this spiritualistic form of dualism. Cleaver readily identified bodily scapegoating as an aspect of the sickness within racist/sexist relationships: "Only when the white man comes to respect his own body, to accept it as part of himself will he be able to accept the black man's mind and treat him as something other than the living symbol of what he has rejected in himself."[14] Bodily scapegoating implies a discomfort with our own bodies which leads us to discredit any human body-person which differs too much in appearance and similarity from our own. This scapegoating is particularly evident in racist, white-black relationships. But it is equally obvious in the revealing and discrediting attitudes of some men, white and black,

13 Grant, "Black Theology and The Black Woman," 422.
14 Eldridge Cleaver, as quoted by Robert Bellah in *The Broken Covenant: American Civil Religion in Time of Trial* (New York: Seabury, 1975), 105.

about the assumed menstrual "uncleanliness" of women, or the intrinsic "repulsiveness" of the pregnant female form.

Because blackness has long been understood as a symbol for filth as well as evil, a spiritualistic dualism prevalent in the worldview of many white persons has allowed them the racist option of projecting onto black persons any dirty or disgusting bodily feelings which they may harbor within themselves. Because of the fertility potential symbolized by the female menstrual and pregnancy cycles, a spiritualistic and sexist dualism has also been created and sustained by white and black males which has allowed them to act out their own latent anxieties and hostilities by sexually depreciating the value and worth of the black female person.

As long as we feel insecure as human beings about our bodies, we will very likely be anxious or hostile about other body-persons obviously racially or sexually different from our own embodied selves. Thus, the most dehumanizing spoken expressions of hostility or overt violence within racist and/or sexist experiences are often linked with depreciating the body or body functions of someone else. Worse yet, though, the greatest dehumanization or violence that actually can occur in racist and/or sexist situations happens when persons of the rejected racial- or gender-specific group begin to internalize the judgments made by others and become convinced of their own personal inferiority. Obviously, the most affected and thus dehumanized victims of this experience are black women.

Racism and sexism diminish the ability of black women and men to establish relationships of mutuality, integrity, and trust. Racism and sexism undermine the black communities in which we live, pray, and work out our salvation in the sight of God and one another. However, in coming to terms with racism and sexism as oppressions affecting us all, the black church does have access to the black community in ways that many other institutions do not. The black church has a greater potential to achieve both liberation and reconciliation by attending carefully to the relationships which have been weakened between black males and females.

Because the black church has access, and is often indeed the presiding and official agent in the process of sexual socialization, it has a potentially unlimited opportunity to restore the ancient covenant of Scripture and tradition which upholds the beauty of black love in its most profound meaning. Wherever black love is discouraged or disparaged as an unfashionable or unattainable expression between black women and black men, the black church has an unparalleled option to model these gospel values of love and unconditional acceptance. By offering from its storehouse an authentic understanding of black spirituality and sexuality, the black church becomes paradigmatic of the reign of God materializing and entering into our midst.

I have referred to spirituality as a commitment and life style, as the growth and response of the human personality to the beauty and benevolence of a liberating God. For black Christians in particular, the praxis of spirituality is a conscious response to the call for discipleship by Jesus. It is intimately related to the moral and ethical conviction which moves us from the private, prayerful posture of bowed head and bent knee to the public, prophetic position of proclaiming before oppressor and oppressed alike: "Thus saith the Lord of Justice. . . ."

For black Christian women and men, the importance of the spiritual life cannot be overplayed. It is what unites those of African ancestry in the possession of a distinctive *ethos*. For black Christians, our African heritage allows us to comprehend spirituality as a *Lebenswelt*—as a life-experience—as well as a worldview. Our African heritage allows us to share in a collective mindset that recognizes yet does not rigidly separate the sacred from the secular, or insist on negative, polemic (i.e., Hellenistic) distinctions about the relative merits of the ideal and actual, the body and the spirit, or the profane and the pristine.[15]

Dualisms, sexist or spiritualistic, have no place within the seamless garment of authentic black religious experience. It is this integrative understanding implicit and inherent in the Afro-American religious *Lebenswelt* that allows spirituality and sexuality to be considered together and as aspects of a holistic religious experience for black women and men in the church and society. Whatever one decides in the historical debate surrounding the actual degree of African retentions in the New World, it is certain that the black church in

15 See John Mbiti, *African Religion and Philosophy* (Garden City, NY: Anchor Press, 1969), for additional emphasis on the integration of African lifestyles and value systems: epistemology and axiology.

America has thrived on the dynamic qualities of an African spirituality. History has evidenced a faith affirmation among black religionists that indicates "both the individual and community have a continuous involvement with the spirit world in the practical affairs of daily life."[16]

A striking description of African Christian spirituality provides in summary format a black perspective:

> [African Christian] spirituality is a dynamic and outgoing concept. . . . There is nothing cerebral or esoteric about spirituality; it is the core of the Christian experience, the encounter with God in real life and action. Spirituality is the same thing as continuous or experiential prayer—prayer as a living communion with God who is experienced as being personally present in the relationships of humanity. It is the mode of living, the essential disposition of the believer, and it imparts a new dimension to the believer's life. In other words, it is not only a new way of looking at human life, but a new way of living it. It is unnecessary, perhaps, to draw any sharp dividing line between theology and spirituality. Theology should be spiritual theology . . . it should not be merely speculative, but should encourage active commitment.[17]

Because of this overarching emphasis in black spirituality on human persons, relationships, and values, the black church is in a prime position to invite and reestablish in creative ways a dialogue between black women and black men. Because the black church is seen to be the driving force of the movement toward the recovery of a meaningful value system for the black community, it has tremendous potential for fostering constructive, instructive, and reconciling discussion on issues of mutuality, sexuality and spirituality for black women and men. It is obvious that the foundational theory and the theology are all in place to accomplish this dialogue, yet the praxis is still limited or lacking if we are at all honest in our reflection upon our lived experience. The recovery of a meaningful value system enriching the relationships between black women and men still remains underdeveloped, or at best only moderately achieved.

The tendency to opt for a spirituality which is unrelated to our

16 Gayraud S. Wilmore, *Black Religion and Black Racialism* (Garden City, NY: Anchor Press, 1973), 197.

17 Aylward Shorter, ed., *African Christian Spirituality* (Maryknoll: Orbis, 1978), 47.

black bodily existence or the temptation to become too heavily fixated at the level of the physical, material, or genital expressions of black love keeps us off balance and unintegrated in religiously real ways. Thus, relationships between black women and men in the black church and community still struggle to reveal that *imago Dei* of which Scripture speaks:

> Then God said, "Let us make man in our image, after *our likeness*" ... so God created ... Male *and* female ... (Gen 1:26f.)

> For as many of you as were baptised into Christ have put in Christ. There is neither slave nor free, there is neither male or female; for you are all one in Christ Jesus. (Gal 3:27f.)

It is impossible to adequately establish any Christian perspective on human sexuality without first returning to and affirming the value that God has forever made human flesh and "body-persons" the privileged place of the divine encounter with us. Perhaps, as we are able to deepen our understanding of black spirituality as an embodied, incarnational, holistic and earthy reality and gift given to us by the God who became enfleshed to dwell with us as a "body-person," we may become better at the praxis which this implies.

If God has so trusted and honored the human body by taking on a human form and accepting human sexuality as a way of entering into relationship with all humanity, how much more must we strive to imitate the model of spirituality and sexuality offered to us by the Word-Made-Flesh. God freely chose to become a body-person as we are. I am persuaded to think that many of us are simply too afraid to take ourselves that seriously and act "freely mature with the fullness of Christ himself" (Eph 4:13).

In the process of exploring theologically how this ontological blackness points to the *imago Dei* in black humanity we are immediately referred back to the context of the feminist challenge. To theologically explore ontological blackness requires us to engage in open and nondefensive dialogue with others about creative use of sexually inclusive *language* for God as well as sexually inclusive *images* which serve to symbolize God. Although we may take great pride and satisfaction in the language and image of the phrase "God is Black," there is still a black feminist question which is appropriately raised for our consideration: "Have we simply shifted from imaging and thinking of God in white male terminology into conceiving and speaking of God as a black male figure?"

James Evans offers a straightforward reply to this concern in his article on "Black Theology and Black Feminism."

> If blackness is an ontological symbol [pointing out the *imago Dei* in humanity] then it means more than physical blackness and also more than maleness. . . . Blackness must mean the racism and liberation from it experienced by black men. It must also mean the racism/sexism and the liberation from them experienced by black women. If blackness as an ontological symbol refers to authentic humanity, then it cannot become simply a "living testament" to failure in white male/female relationships, but must point to new relationships.[18]

This consideration of new relationships between black women and black men and with a God whom we choose to image as black and as androgynous within our contemplation and conversation necessarily urges us onward in the ethical task of reintegrating and restoring the fullness of meaning to black spirituality and sexuality. The search for ways of expressing and experiencing an inclusive vision of God calls us to the task of offering and receiving black love which joins and sustains our spiritual and sexual lives in appropriate ways.

Through a deepening trust and mutuality in our relationships with God, self, and others, the expressions of black love which may seem so unfashionable or unsophisticated to the world may serve to bond black women and men even more closely together in our worst periods of trial and tribulation as well as in our best moments of joy and achievement.

FEMINISM AND FRIENDSHIP
AS EMBODIED EXAMPLES OF BLACK LOVE

There are hopeful signs on the horizon pointing to an increasing sense of mutuality and deepening of understanding in black male/female relationships. Black women who are feminists do want to deepen their exchange of experiences with black men, and to make

18 James H. Evans, Jr., "Black Theology and Black Feminism," *The Journal of Religious Thought* 38 (Spring–Summer, 1982), 52.

plans together for a future full of hope. As Jeanne Noble puts it: "Black women want to be involved. . . . Black women want to be partners, allies, sisters [with black men]! Before there is partnering and sharing with someone, however, there is the becoming of oneself. And the search and discovery of authentic selfhood on the part of black women has begun."[19] Black feminism as a concept is *not* meant to describe militant, manhating females who are strict separatists without sensitivity for anyone but themselves—a sort of chauvinism in reverse. Black feminism is defined as a self-acceptance, satisfaction, and security of black women within themselves. Similarly, in the case of black men who understand themselves as feminists, black feminism for them is an attitude of acceptance of black women as peers—an attitude which is verifiable in their behavior and efforts on behalf of and in solidarity with black women. Black feminism proceeds from the understanding, acceptance, and affirmation of black women as equal and mutual in relation to black men, to an increasing openness of mind and heart to be in solidarity with and in self-sacrificing compassion and action for others who have also been oppressed or marginal in society. This solidarity includes being in communion and consultation with all Third World peoples, and implies dialogue and discussion with white women's liberation actions as well as with gay liberation movements in this country.

As black men and women come to understand and to express this kind of black feminist perspective in relation to one another and for the sake of bringing about the reign of God into our world, this kind of black love is not always going to be fashionable or acceptable to everyone. However, by accepting the divine demand to struggle against both sexism and racism, black feminists (both men and women) can experience and express a black love that is both redemptive and refreshing. There are those who have been there in the struggle before us and can show us the way. A renowned example of black Christian feminism, and a model of the quest for mutuality between black women and men and all oppressed others, was the emancipated slave and celebrated mystic, Sojourner Truth.

19 Jeanne Noble, *Beautiful Are The Souls of My Black Sisters* (New York: Prentice-Hall, 1978), 343.

While Love Is Unfashionable

Born into slavery in upstate New York at the end of the eighteenth century, Isabelle Bomefree received a call to begin a new life in 1843. At the age of forty-six she took a new name that summed up her vocation and conviction to be a Sojourner or pilgrim of the Truth. She suddenly felt called to leave her employment in New York City and set out to do God's work in the world. For the next forty years she moved about the country lecturing, singing, and helping the cause of abolition of slavery. After the Civil War she worked tirelessly and selflessly for the betterment of the lot of freed slaves as well as for all women's rights. She knew well that black love expressed in black spirituality and sexuality was not always welcomed warmly as a means of liberation or reconciliation in the places where she was called to minister. As a black Christian feminist on a quest for mutuality among all peoples, she offers an embodied example for our consideration.

A tall, forceful woman with a booming voice, we are told she spoke plainly about prayer to God. In the autobiographical account of her life, which she dictated since she was unable to write, she recounted in *The Narrative of Sojourner Truth* this religious experience that she had when she was still a slave:

... (Sojourner) told Mrs. Van Wagener that her old Master Dumont would come that day, and that she should go home with him on his return ...

... before night, Mr. Dumont made his appearance. She informed him of her intention to accompany him home. He answered with a smile, "I shall not take you back again; you ran away from me." Thinking his manner contradicted his words, she did not feel repulsed, but made herself and child ready ... [to] go with him. ...

... But ere she reached the vehicle, she says that God revealed himself to her, with all the suddenness of a flash of lightning, showing her "in the twinkling of an eye, that he was *all over*"—that he pervaded the universe— "and that there was no place God was not." She became instantly conscious of her great sin of forgetting her Almighty Friend and "ever present help in time of trouble."

... She plainly saw that there was no place, not even in hell where he was not; and where could she flee? Another such "a look" as she expressed it, and she felt that she must be extinguished forever, even as one, with the breath of his mouth "blows out a lamp," so that no spark remains.

... When at last the second look came not, and her attention was once more called to outward things, she observed that her master had left, and exclaiming aloud, "Oh God, I did not know you were so big," [she] walked into the house.[20]

The rest of Sojourner's life was a long conversation with her "Almighty Friend," God. All who met her would always be struck by the calm self-possession of this stately black woman. The most characteristic aspect of her spirituality was the vivid sense of God's presence everywhere (a distinctively African worldview), and her simple manner of praying everywhere.

Sojourner's suffering was as direct a result of her blackness as it was a result of her ministry, and it was a significant element in her spiritual development. And, "because of this humility," according to Heb 5:7–8, "this prayer was heard." Daughter though she was, she learned obedience in the school of suffering, and once transformed, she became a model of liberation and of the quest for mutuality for us and for the encouragement of all who will learn from her example.

Through her intimate relationship with God, Sojourner Truth offers us a model for a theology of friendship which may serve to further our understanding of the quest for mutuality between black women and men as well as with all other persons. Sojourner Truth understood and related to God consistently and continuously as her dear and "Almighty Friend." The narrative of her life declares that, "she talked to God as familiarly as if he had been a creature like herself; and a thousand times more so, than if she had been in the presence of some earthly potentate."[21]

Relationships which are mutual, community-seeking, and other-directed are critical in the encouragement of any lasting commitments between black women and men. They are also critical for the development of friendships or intimacy between couples or groups who wish to embody the meaning of what has been defined as black love. It is these characteristics of mutuality, communality, and

20 Sojourner Truth, as quoted by Olive Gilbert in *Narrative of Sojourner Truth* (Chicago: Johnson Publishing Company, 1970), 46–48.

21 Gilbert, *Narrative of Sojourner Truth*, 43. The *Narrative* also relates Sojourner's affection for her friend Jesus in detail, pp. 48–52, 119–22, and elsewhere.

disinterestedness (in the best sense of its meaning as an unbiased personal interest or advantage in a relationship) that have the most potential to transform our culture and to create the preconditions necessary for the reign of God to take root and to grow in our midst.

Such a theology of friendship seems much more adequate than just a theology of sexuality standing alone, or just a simple rendition of spirituality offered for application in our times. A theology of friendship is more adequate and appropriate for us because it acknowledges that it is not sexuality or spirituality *per se*, but friendship which determines what the quality of a relational life can be with God and others.

When we can accept and relate to God as our "Almighty Friend," we are no longer left only with the limiting notions of God available to a patriarchal system—i.e., Father, Lord, and King. Nor are we stuck with the alternate prevailing terms of Mother Hen, or the recently reclaimed feminine Holy Spirit or Holy Wisdom which are often rolled out to balance the gender images of God. With Sojourner Truth as a witness we may discover the androgynous, unfettered notion of God as Friend—a notion which can serve to strengthen and encourage the quality of all of our intimate and personal relationships as well as our broader social connectedness.

Some characteristics which may prove useful for understanding God as Friend are mutuality, the urge toward community, and disinterestedness. Mutuality has been suggested by theologians and others who are concerned with how God is affected by humankind and *vice versa*. One feminist theologian describes it in this way:

> Mutuality is that quality of the otherness of God which is really God's oneness with us. To characterize otherness as mutuality is to say that God can only be understood in human terms, but that very understanding is affected by our belief in God. In short, mutuality means that our relationship with God is freely chosen on both sides (unlike family or government images like Father and Lord in which the relationships are not necessarily intentional and gratuitous).[22]

A related characteristic of mature friendships, i.e., a sense of and need for communality, is an essential quality of the Christian and

22 Mary E. Hunt, " ... A Feminist Theology of Friendship," in *A Challenge to Love,* ed. Robert Nugent (New York: Crossroads, 1983), 153.

triune God. The idea of the reign of God, the gathering of all that is into a harmonious community, is another way of describing the God-human cooperation which results in salvation and liberation. Jesus is the Force in Christianity, the Friend whose relationship with us is manifested in our being part of the Christian community of God. Our membership is authenticated, as it was in Sojourner Truth's case, by the works of love and justice which we embrace. This is not the pietistic, "What a friend I have in Jesus." Rather, it is the lived experience we have of a historical group of friends. Jesus' friendships with his immediate community of women and men disciples are a model for our contemporary Christian life. This is the community which derives its identity from the laying down of life for friends. We can conclude that the missionary vocation which springs forth from Christianity is in fact a call and an invitation for black women and men in particular to go forth in ministry and mutuality together to make friends with all people all over the world.

The sexist and spiritualistic dualisms previously discussed would have us believe that "the world, the flesh, and the devil" are a collective evil which militates against our enjoyment of any meaningful relationships. However, when we begin to recognize and respect one another as embodied persons with a body-soul unity, and when we begin to see the world not as some grimy abstraction but as the clean and earthly clay from which we were created, then a final characteristic of a theology of friendship can come into play. Other-centeredness, disinterestedness, or a willingness and desire to place others ahead of our own personal ambition, is the quality of relationality which is essential to making the love expressed between black women and men a reflection of God's love for us and others. In this world when a philosophy of "make way for me first" is so prevalent, other-directedness as an aspect of the theology of friendship can help us to see how the world is really oriented not just for our individual pleasure but for our collective future. The pleasure of a few cannot be allowed to determine the future of everyone, or it will soon become no future for anyone. While self-centeredness and narcissism remain the fashionable norm regulating the self and larger society (including our governmental policies and positions on nuclear disarmament, and over-involvement in Third World nations' political liberation decisions), we must work at expressing a currently unfashionable praxis of black love.

> While love is unfashionable
> let us live
> unfashionably.
> Seeing the world
> a complex ball
> in small hands;
> love our blackest garment.
> Let us be poor
> in all but truth, and courage
> handed down
> by the old
> Spirits.
> Let us be intimate with
> ancestral ghosts
> and music
> of the undead.
> While love is dangerous
> let us walk bareheaded
> beside the Great River.
> Let us gather blossoms
> under fire.[23]

23 Alice Walker, "While Love is Unfashionable," in *Revolutionary Petunias and Other Poems* (New York: Harcourt, Brace, Jovanovich, 1972), 68. In an interview the author indicates that this poem was written during the period of her marriage to a white man and while they lived in a southern state with laws against miscegenation. I have used the same poem to encapsulate the difficulties and devotion entailed in the love expressed by black women and men for each other. Although the applications of the poem may differ, the larger context in which Walker explains her black feminist freedom to love in her own fashion and with whom she chooses does not appear to be violated.

10

Discipleship and Patriarchy

EARLY CHRISTIAN ETHOS AND CHRISTIAN ETHICS
IN A FEMINIST THEOLOGICAL PERSPECTIVE

Elisabeth Schüssler Fiorenza

INTRODUCTION

The studies of ethics in the New Testament and its various themes and problems are vast, and the discussions on the use of the Bible in Christian moral theology are numerous.[1] To summarize the contents of the literature on biblical ethics and to discuss its theoretical-theological aspects adequately in a short paper would be presumptuous. To assume a relationship and interaction between Christian ethics and early Christian ethos, between contemporary moral theological reflection and first-century ethical instruction, is conven-

---

1 For a review and discussion of the hermeneutical and methodological issues involved see among others: E. LeRoy Long, Jr., "The Use of the Bible in Christian Ethics: A Look at Basic Options," *Interpretation* 9 (1965), 149–62; Charles Curran, "Dialogue with the Scriptures: The Role and Function of the Scriptures in Moral Deliberation and Justification," in *Catholic Moral Theology in Dialogue* (Notre Dame: Fides Publishers, 1972), 24–64; James M. Gustafson, "The Place of Scripture in Christian Ethics: A Methodological Study," *Interpretation* 24 (1970), 430–55; Allen Verhey, "The Use of Scripture in Ethics," *Religious Studies Review* 4 (1978), 28–39; James Childress, "Scripture and Christian Ethics: Some Reflections on the Role of Scripture in Moral Deliberation and Justification," *Interpretation* 34 (1980), 371–80; and the very useful book of Bruce C. Birch and Larry L. Rasmussen, *Bible and Ethics in the Christian Life* (Minneapolis: Augsburg Publishing House, 1976).

tional but nevertheless difficult to assess. The hermeneutic-methodological problems raised by the actual encounter of a predominantly philosophical-systematic mode of inquiry with a historical-critical mode of analysis are complex and far from being resolved. Nevertheless a scholarly consensus seems to have emerged that the common ground for the two disciplines is given in the church since the "community of Christian Scriptures" is also the "community of moral discourse." Not only do the Scriptures provide resources for the church's moral discourse and its systematic reflection in Christian ethics, but they also form and guide the Christian community as a people "who derive their identity from a book."[2] The moral authority of the Bible is grounded in a community that is capable of sustaining Scriptural authority in faithful remembrance, liturgical celebration, ecclesial governance and continual reinterpretation of its own biblical roots and traditions.

Situating the authority and significance of Scripture for Christian ethics in the community of faith[3] positively assimilates the results of biblical scholarship which has for a long time stressed that the community of Israel and of early Christianity is the *Sitz im Leben* of biblical writings. Biblical texts have to be read in their communal, social, and religious contexts and be understood as faith-responses to particular historical situations.[4] No systematization of biblical moral injunctions, therefore, seems possible. It is misleading to speak about a uniform biblical or New Testament ethics since the Bible is not a book but a "bookshelf," a collection of various literary texts that span almost a millenium of ancient history and culture. True, some similarities in themes or affinities in religious perspectives can be established. But such a systematization of themes and such a unifi-

2 Stanley Hauerwas, "The Moral Authority of Scripture: The Politics and Ethics of Remembering," *Interpretation* 34 (1980), 356–70, 367.

3 See, e.g., Bernhard Fraling, "Glaube und Ethos: Normfinding in der Gemeinschaft der Gläubigen," *Theologie und Glaube* 63 (1973), 81–105 and the diverse writings of James Barr, especially his contribution, "The Bible as Document of Believing Communities," in *The Bible as a Document of the University*, ed. Hans Dieter Betz (Chico: Scholars Press, 1981), 25–47.

4 For a discussion of different paradigms and heuristic models in biblical interpretation see my article "For the Sake of Our Salvation: Biblical Interpretation as Theological Task," in *Sin, Salvation, and the Spirit*, ed. Daniel Durken (Collegeville: Liturgical Press, 1979), 21–39.

cation of perspectives depends on the selective activity of the biblical interpreter, the systematic construction of the ethicist, or the one-sided selection of the church rather than on the unilateral and clear-cut authority of Scripture itself. Therefore neither the biblical nor the moral theologian can eschew hermeneutical reflection and critical evaluation of biblical traditions.

While the pluriformity of biblical ethos and ethics is long recognized and the concomitant quest for the "canon within the canon" is much debated in biblical scholarship,[5] the discussions among ethicists on the authority of the Bible and its use in moral discourse seem not to center on the need for a critical *evaluative* hermeneutics[6] of the Bible and Christian tradition. Remembrance can be nostalgic, and reinterpretation of oppressive traditions can serve to maintain the *status quo.* The history of the church and its appeal to the authority of Scripture shows that biblical traditions are not only life-giving but also death-dealing. The appeal to Scripture has authorized, for example, persecution of Jews, burning of witches, torture of heretics, national wars of Europe, the subhuman conditions of American slavery, and the antisocial politics of the Moral Majority.

The political appeal to the moral authority of the Bible can be dangerous if it is sustained by the "community of the forgiven" but not by the *ecclesia semper reformanda.* It can be dangerous, especially if the Christian community is shaped by the remembrance of "the historical winners" while abandoning the subversive memory of innocent suffering and of solidarity with the victims of history.[7] In short, the Bible and its subsequent interpretations are not only sources for liberation but also resources for oppression. It can be a resource not only for solving moral problems and generating moral

5 For a helpful review of the problem see Jean Charlot, *New Testament Disunity: Its Significance for Christianity Today* (New York: E. P. Dutton, 1970).

6 For the definition of ethics as "an evaluative hermeneutics of history" see Gibson Winter, *Elements for a Social Ethics: Scientific and Ethical Perspectives on Social Process* (New York: Macmillan, 1966) and Thomas W. Ogletree, "The Activity of Interpreting in Moral Judgment," *The Journal of Religious Ethics* 8 (1980), 1–25. Ogletree proposes an "historical style" in ethics as an "explication of meanings forming the life worlds of representative actors in concrete situations."

7 See Johann Baptist Metz, *Faith in History and Society: Toward a Practical Fundamental Theology,* trans. David Smith (New York: Crossroads Books, 1980), 88–118, 185–99.

challenges, but also for legitimizing dehumanization and violence. The moral character of its theological vision and the moral injunctions of its traditions must be assessed and adjudicated in critical theological discourse if Scripture is to function as revelation "given for the sake of our salvation."[8]

It is obvious by now that this caveat shares in the moral impetus and theoretical insights of political and liberation theologies which do not seek to use Scripture "as an ideology for justifying the demands of the oppressed"[9] but rather strive to rescue the biblical vision of liberation from the ideological distortions of those who have formulated, interpreted, and used the Bible against the cultural and ecclesial victims of the past and the present.

From its inception feminist interpretation and concern with Scripture has been generated by the fact that throughout Christian history the Bible has been used to halt the emancipation of slaves and of women, on the one hand, and to justify such emancipation, on the other hand. Elizabeth Cady Stanton has eloquently summed up the negative use of the Bible as a weapon against women's demand for political and ecclesial equality:

> From the inauguration of the movement for woman's emancipation the Bible has been used to hold her in the 'divinely ordained sphere' prescribed in the Old Testament and New Testament. The canon and civil law, church and state, priests and legislators, all political parties and religious denominations have alike taught that woman was made after man, of man, an inferior being, subject to man. Creeds, codes, Scriptures and statutes are all based on this idea.[10]

8 For this expression see "The Constitution on Divine Revelation of Vatican II," in *The Documents of Vatican II*, ed. Walter Abbott and Joseph Gallagher (New York: America Press, 1966), 119. Salvation must not be restricted to the salvation of the soul from sin, but must be understood as total human wholeness and liberation.

9 Stanley Hauerwas, "Moral Authority of Scripture," 356. Like Metz, Hauerwas uses as key interpretative categories memory and narrative/story, but neglects how Metz spells out their critical implications. Insofar as Hauerwas asserts that the church is the "community of the forgiven" without asking it to repent and to reject its oppressive traditions, he does not do justice to the memory of the innocent victims in history. Thus his theology has no room for a critical hermeneutics of liberation.

10 Elizabeth Cady Stanton, *The Original Feminist Attack on the Bible: The Woman's Bible*, intro. by Barbara Welter, reprint of 1895 ed. (New York: Arno

As in the last century so also today the Bible is used against the women's liberation movement in society and church. Whenever women protest against political discrimination, economic exploitation, social inequality, and secondary status in the churches, the Bible is invoked because it teaches the divinely ordained subordination of women and the creational differences between the sexes. Anti-ERA groups, the cultural Total Woman Movement, and the Moral Majority appeal to the teachings of the Bible on the family and Christian womanhood. These right-wing political movements, which defend the American family in the name of biblical Christianity,[11] do not hesitate to quote the Bible against shelters for battered women, for physical punishment of children, and against abortion, even in cases of rape or child-pregnancy.

Yet throughout the centuries the Bible has not only served to justify theologically the oppression of slaves and women. It has also provided authorization for Christian women and men who rejected slavery and patriarchal subjection as un-Christian. This dialectical use of the Bible in the moral-theological discourse of the church could be amply documented. A careful survey of the history of biblical interpretation would show that in the church's moral discourse on women's role and dignity, certain key passages have emerged and have had *formative* historical impact.[12] Such key passages are, e.g., Gal 3:28, the appeal to the women prophets of the Old and New Testaments and the gospel stories of Mary and Martha or of the Woman at the Well.

Key texts for the moral-theological justification of the patriarchal limitation and repression of women's leadership and roles include, e.g., Genesis 2–3 and especially the prescriptive New Testament trajectory of texts demanding the submission and silence of women in patriarchal marriage and church. No doubt, the church as the community of moral discourse is shaped by this scriptural trajectory

Press, 1974), 7.

11 See Linda Gordon and Allen Hunter, "Sex, Family, and the New Right: Anti-feminism as a Political Force," *Radical America* 11 (1978), 9–25; Charlene Spretnak, "The Christian Right's 'Holy War' Against Feminism," in *The Politics of Women's Spirituality* (New York: Anchor Books, 1982), 470-96.

12 See my article, "'You are not to be called Father': Early Christian History in a Feminist Perspective," *Cross Currents* 39 (1979), 301–23 for a methodological discussion of these dynamics.

of *Haustafeln* (household codes) and their faithful remembrance and reinterpretation. The church's dominant structures and articulations are patriarchal and until very recently its moral and theological leadership has been exclusively male. The ongoing formative power of these biblical texts has led to the silencing and marginalization of women in the church and legitimized our societal and ecclesial exploitation by patriarchal family and church structures. In contemporary democratic society the Bible and biblical religion serve often to strengthen politically antidemocratic elements and trends by reproducing ancient patriarchal structures of inequality and slavelike conditions in the family and the economy. The political alliance of anti-ERA and anti-abortion forces with conservative biblical religion becomes understandable in light of these scriptural texts.

At this point the objection could be raised that such an assessment of the "politics and ethics of biblical remembrance" not only seriously misconstrues the church's moral discourse on Scripture but also overestimates the political function of the Bible as historical-cultural formation. However, the political strength of such right-wing movements as the Moral Majority documents how certain biblical remembrances can be employed successfully in the contemporary political struggle. This continuing cultural-political influence of the Bible has been, in my opinion, largely overlooked by many in the contemporary feminist movement, who have written off both organized religion and traditional "family" rather than branding the patriarchal structures and elements within biblical religion and family. Such a feminist wholesale rejection of religion has played into the hands of the present conservative political backlash.

Finally, the contention that the political Right and Christian feminists equally misuse the Bible for their own purposes by resorting to proof-texting requires a scholarly historical and theological assessment of such proof-texts cited in the contemporary political struggle. In other words, public discussion needs to move from more generalized moral political discourse in church and society to disciplined theological scholarship if we are to assess the *political* function of biblical remembrance, i.e., if we are to judge the impact of biblical traditions and texts on the contemporary Christian community and on American culture that is still largely, if superficially, shaped by biblical religion. What I propose here is a development of biblical ethics that does not presuppose the apolitical character of Scripture and assume that *all* biblical tradition and texts have the authority of Scripture and promote the "common good" merely by reason of their inclusion in the canon.

I do not assume in such a disciplined discourse that the biblical exegete will provide only the historical cultural "data" for systematic reflection and moral theological evaluation, since such a division of labor would neglect the insights of the hermeneutical discussion itself. Instead I envision a disciplined dialogue between biblical scholars and moral theologians that enhances the critical-reflective competence of the whole Christian community. In what follows I will attempt such a discourse. I will first sketch the historical-critical assessment of one New Testament ethical tradition and its theological significance and meaning for today as asserted by biblical scholars. Then I will seek to *evaluate* such biblical theological interpretations from a feminist perspective and discuss the elements of a feminist critical *evaluative* hermeneutics.

Because of the contemporary political discussion, the so-called New Testament *Haustafeln* and their scholarly interpretation suggest themselves as a test-case of my proposal for the collaboration of biblical scholars and Christian ethicists in the service of the Christian community as a community of moral discourse. My critical exploration of the *Haustafel*-trajectory and its discussion in contemporary exegetical scholarship is meant, therefore, as an invitation to investigate methodologically the same biblical tradition from the scholarly perspective and with the theoretical tools of Christian ethics. The purpose is to develop biblical ethics as an "evaluative hermeneutics" of biblical traditions and of the Christian communities they have shaped and are still shaping.

EDITOR'S NOTE

Omitted here are Part I. Historical Critical Analyses of the *Haustafel*-Trajectory, and Part II. Biblical Theological Evaluation of the *Haustafel* Ethics. The *Haustafeln*—three pairs of reciprocal admonitions (to wife-husband, slave-master, and father-child)—are found in their complete form in Col 3:18–4:1 and Eph 5:22–6:9, incompletely often elsewhere. Central interest of the injunctions lies in the submission and obedience of the weaker group and the authority of the head of the household, the *paterfamilias*. Schüssler Fiorenza surveys literature regarding the philosophical-political underpinnings of the *Haustafel's* Christianizing of patriarchal social and ecclesial structures, and raises questions about assumptions concerning the structure of the house churches. In Part II she then criticizes from a feminist perspective three types of contemporary theological evaluations of the *Haustafel*-trajectory which justify as Christian this early pattern of patriarchal submission: the *Haustafel* as 1) adaptation to prevailing patriarchy as necessary for survival, 2) a social alternative to an unworldly ascetic ethos engendering flight from the world, and 3) as derived from Jesus' call to service insofar as they demand "revolutionary subordination."

III. A FEMINIST EVALUATIVE HERMENEUTICS OF THE BIBLE

Recognizing that androcentric language and patriarchal traditions have erased women from history and made them "non-beings," post-biblical feminists argue that biblical religion is not retrievable for feminists who are committed to the liberation of women. Biblical religion ignores women's experience, speaks of God in male language, and sustains women's positions of powerlessness by legitimizing women's societal and ecclesial subordination as well as male dominance and violence against women, especially against those caught in patriarchal marriage relationships. Therefore it is argued that feminists must leave behind biblical religion and reject the authority of the Bible because of its androcentric patriarchal character. Revisionist interpretations are at best a waste of time and at worst a further legitimization of the prevailing sexism of biblical religion. They are, therefore, a co-optation of women's energy and of the feminist movement. Feminist vision and praxis is rooted in the contemporary experience of women and does not derive its legitimacy from the Christian past and the Bible.

Although this post-biblical feminist critique of biblical religion must be taken seriously, it must also be pointed out that such a feminist strategy is in danger of too quickly conceding that women have no authentic history within biblical religion. It therefore too easily relinquishes women's feminist biblical heritage. Yet western feminists cannot afford to deny our biblical heritage if we do not want to strengthen the powers of oppression that deprive people of their own history and engender the reality-constructions of andro-centric texts and patriarchal scholarship. Moreover such a feminist strategy cannot sustain solidarity and commitment to *all* women whether they are "liberated" or not.[13] It cannot respect the positive self-identity and vision that women still derive from biblical reli-gion. Post-biblical feminism must either neglect the positive biblical influences on contemporary women or declare women's involve-ment with biblical religion as "false consciousness." However, any social and cultural feminist transformation in western society must deal constructively with biblical religion and its continuing impact on American culture. American women are not able to completely discard and forget our personal, cultural, and religious history. We will either transform biblical history and religion into a new libera-ting future or continue to be subject to its patriarchal tyranny.

Feminist Christian theologians have responded in different ways to the challenge of post-Christian feminism and have sought to develop different hermeneutical frameworks for spelling out theo-logically what it means to be a self-identified woman and a Christian. We have, therefore, developed different analyses and approaches to the interpretation and evaluation of biblical religion in general, and biblical texts in particular. In my own work I have attempted to formulate a feminist Christian theology as a "critical theology of liberation."[14] I have done so with reference to contem-

13 See, e.g., Mary Daly's feminist stance in *Beyond God the Father* (Boston: Beacon Press, 1973) which conceives of "sisterhood as anti-church" and in *Gyn/Ecology: The Metaethics of Radical Feminism* (Boston: Beacon Press, 1978) which redefines sisterhood in terms of "the bonding of the Selfs" who have "escaped" from patriarchal space as "the territory of non-being." This under-standing of "sisterhood" no longer can sustain feminist solidarity with all women because it does not understand the feminist movement as the "bonding of the oppressed" but as the gathering of the ideologically "pure," as "the network of Spinsters and Amazons."

14 Elisabeth Schüssler Fiorenza, "Feminist Theology as a Critical Theology of Liberation," *Theological Studies* 36 (1975), 605–26. Carol S. Robb, "A Frame-work for Feminist Ethics," infra, and especially the very helpful introduction to *Womanspirit Rising: A Feminist Reader in Religion*, ed. Carol Christ and Judith Plaskow (New York: Harper & Row, 1979).

porary oppression of women in society and church, especially my own church, as well as with respect to the Bible and early Christian history.

In the context of such a feminist theology I have sought to develop a feminist biblical hermeneutics as a critical evaluative hermeneutics.[15] Such a hermeneutics not only challenges androcentric constructions of biblical history in language but also critically analyzes androcentric texts in order: *first* to arrive at the lived ethos of early Christians that developed in interaction with its patriarchal cultural contexts; and *second* to critically determine and evaluate its continuing structures of alienation and liberation. Such an evaluative feminist hermeneutics uses the critical analytical methods of historical biblical scholarship on the one hand and the theological goals of liberation theologies on the other hand, but focuses on the historical struggles of women in patriarchal culture and religion.

First: Historical-critical scholarship has worked out the pluralism of biblical faith experience, ethos, and community. It has shown that biblical texts are embedded in the historical experiences of biblical people and that the Bible must be understood in the context of believing communities. It is therefore necessary to reconstruct as carefully as possible not only the structure of biblical texts but also the paradigms of biblical faith and biblical communities shaped by these faith-experiences. However, this interpretative paradigm of historical-critical scholarship often understands the Bible theologically as the prime model of Christian faith and community that defines and controls the contemporary community of faith.

A feminist critical hermeneutics of liberation seeks to read the Bible in the context of believing communities of women, of the "church of women." It realizes that a feminist re-vision and trans-

---

15 See my articles, "Interpreting Patriarchal Traditions," in *The Liberating Word: A Guide to Nonsexist Interpretation of the Bible,* ed. Letty Russell (Philadelphia: Westminster Press, 1976), 39–61 and "Toward a Feminist Biblical Hermeneutics: Biblical Interpretation and Liberation Theology," in *The Challenge of Liberation Theology: A First World Response,* ed. Brian Mahan and L. Dale Richesin (New York: Orbis Press, 1981), 91–112. See also Elizabeth Fox-Genovese, "For Feminist Interpretation," *Union Seminary Quarterly Review* 35 (1979/80), 5–14; Ernst Feil, "Konfessorische' Implikationen der Wissenschaft: Folgerungen für die theologische Ethik," *Herder Korrespondenz* 34 (1980), 28–37.

formation of biblical history and community can only be achieved in and through a critical evaluation of patriarchal biblical history and androcentric texts. It recognizes, as a hermeneutic feminist principle, that being woman and being Christian is a social, historical, and cultural ecclesial process. What it means to be a Christian woman is not defined by essential female nature or timeless biblical revelation but grows out of the concrete social structures and cultural-religious mechanisms of women's oppression as well as our struggles for liberation, selfhood, and transcendence. Feminist identity is not based on the understanding of women as defined by female biology or feminine gender differences and societal-ecclesial roles but on the common historical experience of women as an oppressed people,[16] collaborating with our oppression and at the same time struggling for our liberation in patriarchal biblical history and community. A feminist critical hermeneutics of the *Haustafel* texts has the aim, therefore, to become a "dangerous memory" that reclaims our foremothers' and foresisters' sufferings and struggles in and through the subversive power of the critically remembered past.

Such a critical feminist hermeneutics is distinct from a feminist hermeneutics that derives the "canon" of feminist Christian faith and ethos from the Bible and therefore isolates the "liberating" impulses of biblical vision from its oppressive aspects. Such a hermeneutics therefore seeks to distinguish between historically limited patriarchal traditions and the liberating biblical tradition,[17] between the liberative essence of the revealed text[18] and its historical patriarchal-cultural expression, between the liberating prophetic critique[19] and the Bible's historical-cultural deformations.

16 For a similar but distinct approach see Beverly Wildung Harrison, "The Power of Anger in the Work of Love: Christian Ethics for Woman and Other Strangers," *Union Seminary Quarterly Review* 36 (1981), 41–57; Eleanor Humes Haney, "What is Feminist Ethics? A Proposal for Continuing Discussion," *The Journal of Religious Ethics* 8 (1980), 115–24.

17 For this distinction see Letty Russell, *Human Liberation in a Feminist Perspective—A Theology* (Philadelphia: Westminster Press, 1974).

18 Phyllis Trible, *God and the Rhetoric of Sexuality* (Philadelphia: Fortress Press, 1978) uses the metaphor of the biblical text "wandering through history to merge past and present."

19 This position is succinctly stated by Rosemary Radford Ruether, "The Feminist Critique in Religious Studies," *Soundings* 64 (1981), 388–402. "Liberationists would use the prophetic tradition as the norm to critique the sexism of the

Such a feminist hermeneutics seems sometimes more concerned with establishing the revelatory authority of certain biblical texts or traditions than with carefully analyzing the particular roots and historical structures of women's oppression and struggles for liberation in patriarchal biblical history and religion. Such a hermeneutics is, as a result, in danger of formulating a feminist biblical apologetics instead of sufficiently acknowledging and exploring the oppressive function of patriarchal biblical texts in the past and in the present. It would be a serious and fatal mistake to relegate the *Haustafel*-trajectory, for example, to culturally conditioned biblical traditions no longer valid today and thereby overlook the authoritative-oppressive impact these texts still have in the lives of Christian women.

A *feminist* "politics and ethics of scriptural remembrance" that shapes the Christian community as a community of moral discourse must keep alive the sufferings and hopes of biblical women and other "subordinate" peoples[20] in order to change and transform the patriarchal structures and ideologies of the Christian churches shaped by the New Testament pattern of patriarchal submission and silence. In the final analysis a critical feminist hermeneutics of the Bible has to call patriarchal biblical religion to personal and structural *metanoia* of feminist praxis before it can proclaim that the communities shaped by the Scriptures are "the community of the forgiven." In the last analysis such an evaluative hermeneutics of liberation is not just geared to the liberation of women but also toward the emancipation of biblical religion from patriarchal structures and ideologies so that the "gospel" can again be recognized as "the power of God for salvation" (Rom 1:16).

Second: The critical evaluation of the *Haustafel*-trajectory and its scholarly interpretations has highlighted that its patriarchal ethics was asserted over and against an "egalitarian" Christian ethos. Biblical and moral theologians have labeled this ethos as unrealistic enthusiasm, gnostic spiritualism, ascetic emigration, or antinomian behavior that did not take seriously the given patriarchal structures

religious tradition. Biblical sexism is not denied, but it loses its authority. It must be denounced as a failure to measure up to the full vision of human liberation of the prophetic and gospel messages" (400).

20 See Elisabeth Schüssler Fiorenza, "Sexism and Conversion," *Network* 9 (1981), 12–22.

of its everyday life and world. Early Christian women and slaves who took the gospel of freedom seriously are thereby disqualified and their faith experience and praxis is rendered rationally or theologically suspect. Yet such a decision for the historical feasibility and theological orthodoxy of the biblical pattern of patriarchal submission over and against the "unworldliness" or "heresy" of the egalitarian ethos implies a historical-theological evaluation that is not derived from the New Testament itself. Such an evaluative interpretation acknowledges, however, that the New Testament testifies to such an early Christian ethos of coequal discipleship. Otherwise scholars could not disparage it.

A feminist critical hermeneutics that derives its canon from the struggle of women and other oppressed peoples for liberation from patriarchal structures must, therefore, call such scholarly interpretations and evaluations to accountability, and must carefully analyze their theological-political presuppositions and social-ecclesial interests. By making explicit its own evaluative feminist canons of liberation it can reclaim the early Christian ethos of the discipleship of equals as its own biblical roots and heritage. In doing so it engenders a paradigm shift in biblical ethics insofar as it does not appeal to the Bible as its primary source but begins with women's own experience and vision of liberation.

In such a feminist evaluative paradigm the Bible and biblical revelation no longer function as a timeless archetype but as a historical prototype open to feminist theological transformation.[21] The Bible is not the controlling and defining "court of appeals" for contemporary biblical feminist theology and community but its *formative* root-model. Only in such a way can biblical revelation become liberated from its imprisonment in androcentric language and cultural-historical patriarchy. Only in and through a critical evaluative process of feminist hermeneutics can Scripture be used as a resource in the liberation struggle of women and other "subordinated" people. The vision and praxis of our foresisters who heard the call to coequal discipleship and acted in the power of the Spirit must

---

21 For this distinction between archetype and prototype see Rachel Blau DuPlessis, "The Critique of Consciousness and Myth in Levertov, Rich, and Rukeyser," *Feminist Studies* 3 (1975), 199–221.

be allowed to become a transformative power that can open up a feminist future for biblical religion.

Third: Such a feminist biblical future depends not only on the faithful remembrance of the oppression and liberation of women in biblical history but also on the critical exploration of the continuing effects of the *Haustafel*-trajectory in our own time and democratic society. Such a feminist evaluative exploration is not only rooted in the personal experience of women but also utilizes feminist scholarship and scientific theoretical discussion. While feminist theology has severely criticized and challenged present-day patriarchal church structures, it has not sufficiently utilized the theoretical feminist critique of marriage and family as the place of women's patriarchal oppression. It has concentrated on the analysis of cultural dualisms, but not sufficiently explored their ideological roots in patriarchal societal structures.

Susan Moller Okin, a political philosopher, has shown that the Aristotelian political ethics of the *Haustafel* is still operative in contemporary American democratic society. Although the patriarchal family has been modified in the course of history, nevertheless political philosophy still works with the Aristotelian premise that the free propertied man is the full citizen, whereas

> all the other members of the population—slaves and artisans as well as women—exist in order to perform their respective function for the few free males who participate fully in citizenship. The "nature" of all these groups of people are defined in terms of their satisfactory performance of their conventional functions.[22]

However, whereas for the Greeks the private, secluded sphere of the household was important primarily as economic base, in modern times it is also crucial as a highly important aspect of affective life. Since the wife is responsible for the private sphere of the household, even a liberal philosopher such as John Stuart Mill asserts that she can only take on outside responsibilities after she has successfully taken care of *her* domestic responsibilities.

Even though liberalism is supposed to be based on individualism

---

22 Susan Moller Okin, *Women in Western Political Thought* (Princeton: University Press, 1979), 276.

and to understand society as constituted of "independent, auton-omous, units" it is clear, according to Moller Okin, that in spite of this individualistic rhetoric, the "family" and not the adult human individual is the basic political unit of liberal as of nonliberal philosophers. The adult members of a family are assumed to share all the same interests. Yet, whenever a conflict of interest occurs between husband and wife, the presumption in political and legal philosophy has been that such a conflict of interest must be decided by the male head of the household. Moreover, the public political sphere of "man's world" is defined by competition and self-interest but not by values of compassion, love, and altruism, since such values are relegated to the private sphere of the home as women's domain. To legally and politically recognize women as individual citizens in their own right would, therefore, entail a change of the family structure and of political philosophy. Moller Okin concludes: "If our aim is a truly democratic society, or a thoroughly democratic theory, we must acknowledge that anything but a democratic family with complete equality and mutual interdependence between the sexes will be a severe impediment to this aim."[23]

She also points out that the radical feminist critique of marriage and family has to be specified both as a critique of *patriarchal* household and societal relationships and an affirmation of inter-personal relationships of adult members who live in a "familial" community. Moreover, feminists have to recognize that woman's oppression is not constituted by her biological endowments but by her function in the patriarchal family as a cultural-political creation. "It is not the fact that women are the primary reproductive agents of society, in itself, that has led to their oppression, but rather that reproduction has taken place within a patriarchal power structure, has been considered a private rather than a social concern, and has been perceived as dictating women's entire lives, and as defining their very nature."[24]

Although Moller Okin did not analyze the political implications of the New Testament *Haustafel*-trajectory, she has documented that

23 Moller Okin, *Women in Western Political Thought*, 289. See also Nannerl O. Koehane, "Speaking from Silence: Women and the Science of Politics," *Soundings* 64 (1981), 422–36.
24 Moller Okin, *Women in Western Political Thought*, 296.

the Aristotelian political ethics of natural inequality has shaped western political philosophy and society. A truly democratic society therefore would necessarily presuppose not only a radical change of the patriarchal family but also a radical transformation of the patriarchal churches into communities of equality and mutual interdependence, since not only the family but also the Christian churches have an important socializing function in American society.

The early Christian ethos of coequal discipleship in community could provide a model for the "new family" as adult community of equality, mutuality, and responsibility for the home *and* for the "world." It could provide a model for the restructuring of the "patriarchal household of God" into a kinship community without clerical fathers and spiritual masters not patterned after the biological patriarchal family. A feminist critical hermeneutics of liberation seeks to reactivate this early Christian ethos for today so that it can become a transformative historical model for the ordering of interpersonal communities, society, and the churches.

Because early Christian writers introduced the prescriptive Aristotelian ethics of patriarchal submission and patristic writers advocated an ascetic rejection of marriage and women, they together prevented a Christian understanding of marriage and family committed to the radical discipleship of coequals.[25] Insofar as the patriarchal household and misogynist asceticism, but not the radical discipleship of women and men as equals, have become the structural models for the dominant institutional churches, Christian theology and communal praxis have not developed ecclesial structures capable of challenging the societal separation of the private sphere as the sphere of interpersonal love sustained by the self-sacrifice of women and the public sphere as a sphere of brutal self-interest and competition. It has, therefore, failed to develop communal structures capable of socializing children into the Christian values of coequality in community, *diakonia,* and discipleship,

---

25 See also Beverly Wildung Harrison, "Some Problems for Normative Christian Family Ethics," *Selected Papers, 1977. The American Society of Christian Ethics* (Waterloo, Ontario: The Council on the Study of Religion, 1977), 72–85; Barbara Hilkert Andolsen, "Agape in Feminist Ethics," *The Journal of Religious Ethics* 9 (1981), 69–81.

rather than into the cultural values and patriarchal roles of super-ordination and subordination, of masculinity and femininity.

Now that historical-critical scholarship has proven the New Testament *Haustafel* to be a Christianized form of Aristotelian ethics, and feminist critical analyses have shown its destructive impact on women and the community of coequal discipleship, the church as the community of moral discourse is clearly challenged anew to incarnate the early Christian vision and praxis of coequality in community. True, both the ethos of coequal discipleship and of the patriarchal pattern of submission can claim scriptural authority and canonicity. Both are expressions of believing communities in the first century and today. Insofar as the patriarchal pattern of sub-mission has decisively formed Christian tradition and communal structures it can claim even greater historical influence and institu-tional powers for its own vision of how to live as a Christian community.

Nevertheless feminist theology, as a critical theology of liberation, must reject the theological scriptural claims of this patriarchal pattern because of its oppressive effects on the life of women and other subordinated peoples. A feminist critical hermeneutics has as its own canon the liberation of *all* women from oppressive struc-tures, patriarchal institutions, and internalized values. It therefore interprets, retrieves and evaluates biblical texts and communal structures. It accepts and rejects them as well as their political-social functions in terms of its own canon of liberation. A feminist critical ethics that is committed to the liberation struggle of women and the whole church, therefore, insists that the ethos and praxis of coequal discipleship must transform the patriarchal *Haustafel* ethics and its institutional structures, if women and the Christian church are to have a feminist Christian future.

11

Female Friendship
and Feminist Ethics

Janice Raymond

One of the contributions that radical feminism has made to the women's movement has been its consistent emphasis on the primariness of woman-identification. Debates and discussions about the centrality of woman-identification and what manifestations it takes have focused on definitions of sisterhood and feminist communities, degrees and kinds of separatism, lesbianism, and the necessity for women to act collectively in the political arena. Few of these discussions have raised the issue of female friendship, and none of which I know have focused on friendship's moral and political aspects.

This essay argues that an imperative of feminist ethics is an analysis of female friendship. I contend that an adequate feminist ethics must not only take profound cognizance of female friendship but must also be based on it. And, further, that if ethics and politics are to be rejoined, a task to which feminist ethicists should be giving serious thought, female friendship may provide the grounding for such a reunification. Another task of feminist ethics is to restore vital meaning to the word and reality of friendship and to show how it relates to feminist action in the world. Friendship has become such a vacuous word. In modern times, it has lost its vitality and deep meaning content so that it has now become possible to speak of home cleaning products as a woman's "best friend."

The word and reality of friendship was not always so lacking in substance. In pre-Christian times, the tie of friendship was considered the highest form of communion between two persons, superseding the bonds of marriage.[1] However, such a friendship, as well as the classical ideals of friendship, described those relations which the philosophers of antiquity claimed were only possible between men. In short, friendship in these earlier times was what I have termed a *homo-relational* affair.[2] Christianity endowed marriage with the esteem that friendship had been given by the Greeks asserting that in doing so, it placed a higher value on women and married life.[3] This claim was true only within a very limited and limiting sphere. Neither classical friendship nor Christian marriage sanctified friendship or love relationships between two women.

Within the tradition of classical friendship, women were judged to be without the passion, sense of individuality, and presence of common world and worldliness that make friendship possible. Montaigne is a more modern representative of the Greek philosophical perspective that female friendships are shallow because women do not "appear to be endued with firmness of mind to endure the strain of so hard and durable a knot."[4] So impressed were the Greeks with the manliness of the passion of friendship, with its power to prompt men to high thought and heroic action, that the love of friendship was set above the love of man for woman.

1 See Edward Carpenter, *Iolaus: An Anthology of Friendship* (London: Swan Sonnenschein & Co., 1902), especially Chapter I and pp. 97–99. See also W. M. Rankin, "Friendship," *Hastings Encyclopaedia of Religion and Ethics*, VI:131–32. See also L. Lemme, "Friendship," *The New Schaff-Herzog Encyclopedia of Religious Knowledge*, 1952, IV:398.

2 The normative and real power of male homo-relations is disguised on all levels by the fact that such man-to-man rapport is institutionalized in every aspect of an apparently *hetero-relational* culture. I use the term hetero-relations to express the wide range of affective, social, and economic relations that are ordained between men and women by men. It is women who bear the burden of living out the hetero-relational imperative. Indeed, this is a male homo-relational society that is built on male-male relations, transactions, and bonding at all levels.

3 See, for example, W. M. Rankin, "Friendship," *Encyclopaedia of Religion and Ethics*, VI:131, 133. See also Lemme, "Friendship," IV:398.

4 "Of Friendship," in *The Complete Essays of Montaigne*, trans. Donald M. Frame (Stanford, CA: Stanford University Press, 1965), 138. Carpenter quotes J. A. Symonds on this same subject: " ... all the higher elements of spiritual and mental activity, and the conditions under which a generous passion was conceivable, had become the exclusive privileges of men" (47).

The classical tradition of homo-relational friendship was closely connected with thinking. Harnack points out that the "history of the Greek schools of philosophy is at the same time the history of friendship."[5] It was the philosophers of ancient Greece who gave an intellectual development to the idea of friendship. With Socrates, for example, friendship became both the condition and content of education and educated thought. The relation between student and teacher was a friendship bond while, at the same time, friendship was an object of education. It was subject to philosophical analysis, and its origin, nature, and development became the subjects of discourse.

The virile nature of friendship as defined by the Greeks was associated not only with high philosophical discourse but with war and the bonding between men on the battlefield. Some of the historical and literary examples of men who love each other with a love "beyond the love of women" are those of fighting men: Achilles and Patroclus from the *Iliad;* Hercules and his beloved Ioläus; and the famed Theban Band, of whom it was first said that "An army of lovers cannot fail."[6] However, this army of friends and lovers did fail, when they were annihilated by Philip of Macedonia who, as his army slew the "sacred" batallion of friends, wept mightily at such a destruction of brave and loving men. The Greeks have no monopoly on the link between male bonding and war. The communion of committed soldiers becomes the communion of committed revolutionaries, as exemplified by such figures as Mao and Che Guevara who had their own brand of glorifying violence and romanticizing it as that which joins men together.[7]

Friendship between men became an institution in Greek life. In Plato's time, it was probably *the* most important basis of statesmanship and of the formation of the *polis* itself. With the Greeks,

5 See Adolf Harnack, *The Mission and Expansion of Christianity in the First Three Centuries,* trans. and ed. James Moffatt (New York: G. P. Putnam's Sons, 1908), I: 420–21.

6 I will not discuss here the homosexual character of Greek friendship between men, nor the connections between male homosexuality and ideals of virility. I would refer the reader to an introductory discussion of these topics in Janice Raymond, "A Genealogy of Female Friendship," *Trivia* I (Fall, 1982), 5–26.

7 A. James Gregor, *The Fascist Persuasion in Radical Politics* (Princeton, NJ: Princeton University Press, 1974), see especially pp. 4–5, 255, 404–5.

politics was the business of friends. Friendship kept states together, and Aristotle maintained that friendship and justice were concerned with the same objects and exhibited by the same persons. However, the citizens of this *polis* were all male. Women had no civic status, and therefore friendship and politics were male prerogatives. Neither slaves nor women, who were considered to be like slaves in many ways, could be friends or holders of political office.

> ... friendship became a social distinction, a moral safety-valve, and an intellectual and religious inspiration. The citizen or politician who sought an escape from the hardness and corruption of society could say with Socrates, "I have a passion for friends" (Plato, *Lysis*, 211). Friendship, indeed, touched Greek life and morality with emotion, and acted with "the expulsive power of a new affection." Its exercise is a revelation of the Greek mind, and its history is the summary of Greek moral life.[8]

One lesson that the student of female friendship may learn from the classical philosophical tradition of friendship is its constant emphasis on the political nature of this relation. In any strong sense of the word friendship, feminists can also criticize the Greek reality of friendship for not measuring up to the philosophical ideal. Male citizen-friends often killed each other for power and objectified each other, especially young boys, for sexual gratification. However, as far as the Greek *ideal* of friendship is concerned, women can learn that the best feminist politics proceeds from a shared friendship.

FROM SISTERHOOD TO FEMALE FRIENDSHIP

Feminists have talked much about the ideals and realities of sisterly solidarity. The political virtue of solidarity, materialized in the early feminist slogan, "sisterhood is powerful," was extremely significant in catalyzing women to action in the beginning of this wave of feminism. The necessity for sisterhood arose out of the recognition that women were/are oppressed in all cultures and throughout all periods of patriarchal history. In the solidarity of sisterhood, feminists began to struggle against all forms of male tyranny against women: rape, pornography, battering, international sexual slavery,

---

8 Rankin, *Hastings Encyclopaedia of Religion and Ethics*, 132.

etc., and to realize in doing so that women had much in common. Sisterhood became a way of expressing the spirit of women's resistance to the common global reality of women's oppression. The saying, "sisterhood is powerful," signalled a coming together of women formerly separated from each other. Ideals of sisterhood became materialized in feminist literature, theory, and action. Different schools of feminism all stressed the necessity to build a strong political solidarity of sisterhood.

Over the past two decades, we have seen that indeed sisterhood is powerful. There have emerged rape crisis centers, battered women's shelters, feminist bookstores, women's health clinics, feminist journals and magazines, and university women's studies programs, to name but a few of the ventures that sisterhood has been able to institutionalize. All of these undertakings generated and were founded on a sisterly solidarity but, in my opinion, some of them failed because there was nothing to hold them together beyond what I would call the communion of resistance. Unfortunately, sisterhood that was created in the struggle against all forms of male tyranny did not mean that women became friends, i.e., that they shared a common world beyond the struggle. Sisterhood did not automatically create a private and public space where female friendship could occur.

Friendship has been viewed traditionally as an intimate and personal relationship. Thus it is difficult for many to understand that friendship is political, i.e., as the Greeks especially knew, it has power to affect the world and to change the distribution of power in the world. Friendship retains this power because it provides friends with a common world. Friendship confirms the presence of a world that women hold in common with other women who share similar attractions and values. This common world of friendship thus gives women a connection to the world so that they do not lose their bearing, especially in a world that is not only man-made but woman-hating as well. A sharing of personal friendship becomes, at the same time, a grounding for social and political existence. Female friendship is a political statement that women come together not by default (because men oppress women), but because there is an intrinsic vitality in our coming together. Female friendship infuses sisterhood with a vibrant source and force of affection.

Janice Raymond

GYN/AFFECTION

Affection is a carefully chosen word in my discussion of female friendship. The more commonly understood meaning of affection is a feeling, emotion, fondness, attachment, and love for another. There is an additional meaning of affection, however, that conveys more than the personal movement of person to person. Affection in this sense means the state of influencing, acting upon, moving, and impressing, and of being influenced, acted upon, moved, and impressed. I would maintain that women who *affect* other women stimulate response and action; bring about a change in living; stir and arouse emotion, ideas, and activities that defy dichotomies between the personal and political aspects of affection. And finally, I would suggest a new word, *Gyn/affection*, to encapsulate this personal and political movement of women toward each other. Gyn/affection is thus a synonym for female friendship, but it has a distinct meaning context of its own. The basic meaning of *Gyn/affection* is that women affect, move, stir, and arouse each other to full power through friendship. One task of feminism has been to show that "the personal is political." Female friendship gives integrity to that claim. The word Gyn/affection is meant to reunite the political and personal aspects of friendship.[9]

While it is true that certain kinds of political activity are and have to be possible between persons who are not friends, both politics and friendship are restored to a fuller meaning when they are brought together, i.e., when political activity proceeds from a shared affection, vision, and spirit, and when friendship has a more expansive political effect. We need to create a feminist politics based on friendship, and we need a philosophy of friendship that is realized in investing women with personal and socio-economic power. A genuine friendship goes beyond the world of the Self's relations with other Selves to the society in which the female Self is allowed to grow. Thus the active and dynamic expression of female friendship involves more than feeling. It means the sharing of a common life and participation in a common world.

9 See Raymond, "A Genealogy of Female Friendship," for a more extensive development of the concept of Gyn/affection.

More than most philosophers, Hannah Arendt has discussed the concept of *worldliness*. Arendt's notion of worldliness, although analyzed in the context of the history of the Jews and of Judaism, has much relevance for feminists and feminism today.[10] The concepts of worldliness and friendship must be intimately linked in the lives of women today who live with a basic *tension* that feminism presents—that of participating in the world as men have fabricated it, while yearning to go beyond it.

DISSOCIATION

Because women have been the eternal victims of male cruelty and injustice; because survival has been the key focus of female existence and feminist political thought; because women have almost everywhere lacked involvement in and control over the political world in which we have lived; and because the world is man-made, many women have developed a *worldlessness* or *dissociation* from the world. Women in general have assumed this worldlessness almost by default, i.e., by virtue of the passive positions most women have been forced into throughout history and in almost every culture. Other women, such as some feminist separatists, have made dissociation from the world a political ideal and reality. The difficulty in both cases is that when women make dissociation the basis for survival or for affinity, many come to conceive of their existence as independent from the rest of the world. Philosophically, this can make women narrow in vision; politically it can make them very vulnerable. Even radical and voluntary dissociation from the world, originally undertaken as a necessary and daring political stance, can culminate in women developing a worm's-eye view of the world and being more exposed to attack than ever before. The more women dissociate from the world, the further removed are women from a definite share of what should be a common world. This is the condition of any group within any diaspora, whether scattered there voluntarily or forcibly.

10 Among the works of Hannah Arendt that discuss the concepts of worldliness and worldlessness, see especially *The Jew as Pariah: Jewish Identity and Politics in the Modern Age,* ed. Ron H. Feldman (New York: Grove Press, 1978). See also Feldman's introduction to this work.

On the other hand, the dissociation from the world that is not chosen for consciously defined feminist reasons—in other words, that experienced by women in general whose apprehension of the world is derivative from husbands or other men—is reinforced by these women's lack of knowledge that they are a common people. In contrast to other oppressed groups, women do not possess the past of a cohesive and self-conscious community with its own political traditions, philosophical vitality, and history, or should I say that this past is one that most women know little about. The rootlessness of women in their own group identity contributes more than anything to the worldless, unrealistic, and unpolitical perception that many women have of the world.

Female friendship—not just any kind of friendship—but the Gyn/affection of which I have spoken, is one way to rootedness, to the grasp of reality that women need, and to the experience of our own history. Female friendship, of this nature, orients women to the world, not as persons but *as women*. To paraphrase Hannah Arendt, when one is oppressed as a woman, one must respond as a woman.[11] Female friendship cannot arise in a context where women have "the great privilege of being unburdened by care for the world,"[12] because Gyn/affection is a political virtue with a political effect.

Any strong and critical reality of female friendship cannot be created within a dissociated enclave of women who have little knowledge of or interest in the wider world. Female friendship is strongest and most effective when it takes shape *within an enclave of women who are located in the world* by virtue of their thinking and action and who do not dissociate from the world nor from each other. The feminist "reconstitution of the world," to use Adrienne Rich's phrase, can only come about in a worldly context and in struggle against the forces that threaten us. Reconstituting the world means reconstituting our lost bonds with our original Selves and with

---

11 Arendt's original words, as quoted in Elisabeth Young-Bruehl, *Hannah Arendt: For Love of the World* (New Haven: Yale University Press, 1982), were as follows: "When one is attacked as a Jew, one must defend oneself *as a Jew*" (109). Unfortunately, Arendt would not have applied these same words to feminist resistance. For evidence of this contradiction, see 272–73.

12 Hannah Arendt, "On Humanity in Dark Times: Thoughts About Lessing," in *Men in Dark Times* (New York: Harcourt, Brace & World, 1968), 14.

others like our Selves.[13] Strong friendships with strong women shape the world as women imagine it could be, while permitting women to move with worldly integrity in the world as men have made it.

ASSIMILATION

The opposite of dissociation is *assimilation* to the world. This is another posture that many women have assumed as a location in the world. Assimilation is the stance of a woman who desires to succeed in the world of men but who forgets, or constantly tries to ignore, the fact of her femaleness. The assimilationist strives to lose her female identity, or to go beyond it, or to be regarded *as a person* in a world that grants the status of persons only to men. Realism, survival, worldliness are all acquired by assimilation to the male-dominant world on its own terms.

Assimilation spells the end of any strong reality of female friendship even before it begins. For the assimilationist, men and/or male-defined structures are what counts. As women assimilate, they are accepted into the ranks of male society mainly as exceptions and insofar as they do not interfere with the homo-relational bonds that men have established. In order to become part of the male dominant society, women have to believe (or pretend) that they are both persons and women, in the ways that men have defined both *for women.* What is demanded of assimilationist women by the male-dominant world is that they behave in ways that distinguish them from ordinary women (e.g., they are encouraged to be bright, articulate, upwardly mobile professionals), but at the same time that they exhibit acceptable manners and modes of femininity (e.g., charming behavior, wearing feminine clothing or makeup). The complicated psychology demanded of the assimilationist woman is that she both *be* and *not be* a woman, or that she be the woman that men still recognize while avoiding the woman who recognizes her Self and other women who are Self-defined.

Assimilation fosters private solutions. Eveything reduces to per-

13 I use Mary Daly's device of capitalizing *Self* to distinguish between the man-made feminine self, "the imposed/internalized false 'self'" of women, and the authentic Self which women are re-creating.

169

sonal self-propulsion. It is a forward self-propulsion that does not depend on authentic Self-definition, Self-movement, and certainly not on Gyn/affection. Thus it locates women in an isolated sphere of action that is built upon a pseudo-individualism. For the assimilationist, the world becomes anywhere that is accessible to any "rational" woman without questioning the boundaries of the terrain or one's location within them. This world becomes an inauthentic one for women, not by virtue of the *fact* that it is man-made but because that fact is not doubted and defied.

In a society that is not only hostile to women, but pervaded by what Andrea Dworkin has named woman-hating, it is possible to assimilate only by assimilation to anti-feminism also. Explicitly or implicitly, assimilationists disidentify with other women, whether they are in the company of men or women, or both. The irony of this is that both men and women will always perceive them first and foremost as women. It is unfortunate that assimilationists do not recognize, or ignore, this basic fact, wishing it would go away, when it never will.

The road to assimilation is the road to conformism, conformism very often to new stereotypes that assume form under the guise of liberation and "new woman" rhetoric, but being conformist nonetheless. Thus what we witness is a brand of assimilationism that often displays the verbiage and outward life-style of liberation. Assimilationists frequently view their emancipation as a freedom from the world of traditional women, as well as from the world of feminist women. Very often, they exaggerate declarations that they are not feminists, or they take pains to proclaim that they have moved beyond feminism. In the latter case, many women have used the term *postfeminist* to describe their stance. The irony of such disidentifications with feminism is that often assimilationist women engage in quite extraordinary activities that are feminist in the sense that these endeavors require unconventional capabilities, courage, determination, and persistence. One also thinks of women scientists, truck drivers, welders, and presidents of colleges who are not only excellent at what they do, but very often are more astute and humane than men in the same fields. However, many of these women, when asked, would deny any kind of woman-identification in a strong sense of the word.

Assimilationist women want no social roots in any community of women. Liberation, as understood by them, means *freedom for men* and *freedom from* the *women* and woman-identified behavior they perceive as holding them back from the male-defined world. Their emancipation is their assimilation. Hence assimilation, like dissociation, leads to a worldlessness that constricts rather than constructs female friendship.

VICTIMISM

Victimism is a third response that women have assumed toward the world. I use the word to describe women whose primary female or feminist identity seems to be grounded in women's shared state of having been victimized by men. In relationships with each other, such women emphasize their heritage of shared pain, although the ways in which various women have been victimized differs by age, class, race, or other factors.

I am not trying to minimize the pain of women's victimization by men in a patriarchal culture. It is extremely important that women understand and act on the full picture of female oppression. However, one-dimensional emphasis on the "state of atrocity" can have the unintended effect of stressing that what women have in common is only, or mostly, our shared pain. Such an emphasis, as reflected in women's relationships, in women's sharing of experiences, and in feminist literature and activism, can also create the impression that because women have been historically bound to and by men, that woman is *for man*, no matter how she might have to be forced to do his bidding.

Victimism drives women further away from strong female friendships by de-emphasizing the primordial reality that women can be *for women* in other than sisterly suffering ways. Among many feminists, the emphasis on victimism bolsters the conviction that female friendship can only arise negatively—i.e., because men are so bad, and/or in reaction to the atrocities promoted by a woman-hating culture. Here female friendship seems spawned by the results of the oppression of women. Thus in a better world, presumably one in which men were good to women, female friendship would not be necessary.

171

It is obvious that any feminist analysis and action has to be well acquainted with the varieties of male terrorism perpetrated against women and must name this for what it is. But it should be as obvious that an emphasis on female friendship and a vision of Gyn/affection is a vital counterpart to the emphasis on women as abused, battered, and killed. Behind many apparently colonized women, there have been women of strength and fortitude who en-courage them Selves and each other.

Sustained and one-dimensional emphasis on victimism reduces the history of women to an eternal state of atrocity over which women have never had any control. While it is necessary for women to recognize the prevalence and the longevity of anti-feminism across historical ages and cultural lines, the necessity for such recognition should not lead women to the conclusion that the force of anti-feminism is almost natural and eternal—so overwhelming that any will to feminist action is lost.

Women have indeed been broken by men. Yet men would make it the case that it is they who have been damaged by women. For example, they blame mothers who gave them too much or too little attention, or wives who dominate or are too dependent. Men have always claimed the wounded role. The overcoming of brokenness by women, as well as the rejection of men as broken creatures in need of women's restorative power, is necessary to the process of female friendship.

Ultimately, what victimism does is to negate Self-definition and Self-responsibility in the world. When women do not define themselves beyond the role of sufferer, then women will settle for the world as men have made it. Victimism means being overwhelmed by the world. It makes women world-sufferers rather than world-makers. It views the world largely from the perspective of the persecuted and establishes itself in the world negatively. Women's commonality is reduced to our shared oppression. There is the unstated, and perhaps unintended, premise that feminists might lose their feminist identity if anti-feminism disappeared from the world.

Women, as a people, cannot be held together nor move in the world linked primarily by a common enemy or by a negative identity of oppression. Only within the framework of female friend-ship can a woman live as a woman, working for a reconstituted world, without exhausting herself in the struggle against woman-hating, and without despairing at the enormity of the task.

It is my contention that friendship provides the ethical basis for a feminist worldliness and by providing this restores a moral nature to the politics of feminist worldliness. Friendship achieves this reunification of ethics and politics because it gives feminist political activity a moral passion and depth.

There has been a certain hostility to ethical analysis in feminist circles. This hostility stems from a modern division between the ethical and the political and a tendency to categorize issues of power and control as political, relegating the ethical to the individual or interpersonal spheres. One woman expressed her objections in the following way to the ethical focus of a conference whose expressed goal was to do a feminist ethical analysis of reproductive technologies. To a certain extent, her opinion is representative of a wider feminist disapprobation of ethical analysis: "It seems to me that the stress on ethics confuses the analysis in terms of power and control. ... To turn questions of 'who has power over whom' into ethical issues is to depoliticize them, whereas I think we need to politicize these issues even more."[14] I would argue, in contrast, that an adequate feminist politics needs the depth and value of a moral passion and purpose. The emphasis, in some feminist theory and circles, on a one-dimensional view of politics has, in my opinion, de-ethicized issues of power. When power is de-ethicized, decisions often get made from, for example, a cost-benefit or purely consequentialist analysis. And when politics is disjoined from ethics, politics frequently gets reduced to policy.

Feminist ethics can restore a *teleology* to feminist politics. Where politics and political activity can be distorted by the emphasis on the *means*, ethics revives the emphasis on ends. Without Gyn/affection, feminist politics and political activity can more easily become short-circuited and tend toward the monodimensional and superficial. Female friendship gives depth and spirit to a political vision of

14 Ruth Hubbard as quoted in the DES Discussion in *The Custom-Made Child*, ed. Holmes, Hoskins, and Gross (Clifton, NJ: The Humana Press Inc., 1981), 57.

feminism and is itself a profoundly political act. Feminists must be defined by the reality of female friendship, not only in our personal lives, but in our political lives. Female friendship reminds feminists that our political activity consists in more than just conflict and struggle with men and male supremacy. Its end is to bring women together with our Selves and with each other.

12

Parenting, Mutual Love, and Sacrifice

Christine E. Gudorf

"I am a student of theology; I am also a woman." So began an article in the *Journal of Religion* over twenty years ago.[1] That article by Valerie Saiving (Goldstein), "The Human Situation: A Feminine View," became the starting point for this article and for many feminist forays into theology in the last decade. "The Human Situation" is the starting point for this work in that it both demonstrated the importance of doing theology out of particular experience, and first raised for me the question of the appropriateness of the concept of Christian agape.

Within the discipline of ethics there is a commonly recognized division between individual and social ethics, between, in the terminology of Christian realism, love and justice. Ever since Reinhold Niebuhr made his distinction between love and justice based on the different behavior of human beings as individuals and in groups,[2] it has been a risky undertaking in ethics to make analogies between individuals and groups. It seems to me that this separation has gone too long unchallenged. As a feminist ethicist, I begin with my experience. My peculiar experience as a parent has suggested serious questions concerning this separation of individuals and groups based

---

1 *Journal of Religion* (April 1960).
2 Reinhold Niebuhr, *Moral Man and Immoral Society* (New York: Charles Scribner's Sons, 1960), 257.

on expectations concerning their moral behavior. As a feminist, I have been brought to see that there is agreement between the picture of individual human nature originating in my experience and the picture of human nature culled from the study of history and sociology. This is especially true in considering my experience as a mother.

I arrived at the following understanding after years of grappling with a severe personal uncomfortableness and periodic anger toward the way my decision to parent was universally perceived—as heroic, self-sacrificing, Christian love. I believe this interpretation is very faulty, and results from a radical misunderstanding of parenting, personal relationships in general, and the ethic of Jesus.

PARENTING MY CHILDREN

Besides a natural child my husband and I have two medically handicapped children who were adopted at the ages of five and two, after severely deprived early years spent solely in institutions.[3] Both children at placement were developmentally backward, especially the younger. The five-year-old could barely walk, would not be left in a room alone even with a parent in sight, and could not dress, wash, or undress himself. The two-year-old could not walk, talk, or eat. He had to be force-fed liquid; he refused all food, and did not know how to chew, despite a full mouth of teeth. He did not respond to speech, and could not, apparently, distinguish sounds, even his own name. Both children went through a very difficult period of six months to two years after adoption. This is not uncommon in the adoption of older children (meaning older than babies). Both refused to cooperate; the younger, who had never formed any

3 There is a very real issue here regarding my right to recount in public an experience which is not only mine, but the children's as well. Feminist theologians and others need to grapple with this issue, for we say that we need to do theology from our experience. And yet rarely is any experience of ours not also the experience of another person. What of the privacy of the other? This is complicated within the family, where it is impossible to protect the identity of the other. In addition, when we write as parents, we violate the privacy of minors to whom we stand guardian. Moreover, one could ask whether the attempt to theologize from the experience of parenting alters the parenting itself, introducing new factors detrimental to the child.

relationship before, totally refused. Often we suspected after the first few months that he understood more than he acknowledged and was forcing himself to vomit back food.

My experience with these children has been basic for my understanding of human nature. I anticipate some outrage at the comparison of individual, "maladjusted" children to the groups with which social ethics deals. I, too, am leery of condescension and paternalism in doing ethics. But I also think that my experience has radical implications for the conventional view of parent-child relationships. My husband and I were never in control of the relationship with either of these children, and are not now. Even when force-feeding Mike, the younger child, we found that he kept down only as much as he wanted—never enough to gain weight, barely enough to stay alive. The children were in control, not only of themselves, but of us, as least as much as we were. They dictated where we went and didn't, what we ate, all home activities, whom we saw, even how much sleep we got. Moreover, they made it clear that they knew they controlled our public image; everyone took their side—not only strangers on the street when we forced the elder child to walk short distances, refusing to carry him, but even our relatives, who felt it cruel of us to force Mike to eat when he "wasn't hungry."

They kept us thoroughly unbalanced, never sure of where we were in the process. I was more than once reminded of a historian's comments on the lack of freedom of slave owners, who, although having legal and physical control of the slaves, lived in psychological slavery to the fear of reprisal and rebellion. This fear dictated much of their lifestyle.[4]

But more than being in charge of the process, the children gave to us. We are radically different people now. They have given us, after long trial, love, trust, a new view of people in general, and hope that the world can be made significantly better. I can say this last at the same time knowing that the ongoing uncertainty as to whether they will survive childhood has forced us, agonizingly, to deal with the

4 This is also reminiscent of George Jackson's description of the insecurity of prison guards and its effects upon them, in "From Dachau, Soledad Prison, California," in Robert Lefcourt's *Law Against the People* (New York: Random House, 1971), 219.

existence of death and evil against which one can only hope in the resurrection. The children have given us not only themselves, but ourselves, and in more than one way. Through the process of making these children ours, we came to identify with new groups of people whose causes became ours. Not only did we come to feel connected with the plight of Hispanic refugees because of the origins of our eldest son, but we developed an interest in Latin America that has led to travel, learning Spanish, and membership in Latin American interest groups. Similarly, our relation to refugees through this son, Victor, led to our sponsorship of a Vietnamese refugee family of eight.

In the course of parenting Michael, who was born to a white mother and a black father, we purposely cultivated close associations with blacks in a well integrated neighborhood, church, and school. This has led to many different kinds of involvement in the issue of race, not least of all to a new circle of friends who share the richness of their traditions and experiences with us. Such involvement has made us see our world in radically different terms; it has made us choose sides, realizing that in a racist society there is no neutral territory, no neutral attitude.

Last but certainly not least, we have come to have common cause with the multitudes of people who haunt the hospitals, doctors' offices, and clinics of our nation due to severe illness and medical handicaps. We share common cause with the hundreds of thousands who ache because there is no cure for the chronic illness which threatens life or health, and/or because of a lack of respect for the dignity and suffering of the chronically ill and their families. We have a perspective on the American health care system radically different from that of healthy families. And that radically different perspective extends beyond the field of medicine to other areas of our society, especially education and social work. Because of both minimal brain damage (due to cardiac arrest as an infant) and neglect during his first two years in the hospital, Mike does not fit into any established educational programs. He is neither simply delayed so that he could be expected to catch up over time with normal children, nor is he retarded in such a way that special classes for the trainable or educably retarded could include him. My children repeatedly fall through the cracks in our society, thus illustrating for us the existence of both these cracks and the many other children who are abandoned, unloved, and/or excluded from normal social patterns. Our children have given us new communities, new loyalties, new insight—new identities.

These two aspects of our situation, the control and beneficence of the children, are, I think, true of all children, only more dramatic in our situation. They are certainly true of our biological son as well as our adopted ones. Much revision needs to be done in how we as a society view our children and child-rearing.

EGOISM AMONG INDIVIDUALS AND GROUPS

Niebuhr differentiated individual and group behavior primarily on the ground that the checks which serve to limit natural selfishness in immediate situations do not exist, or at least not as strongly, in social situations, and that altruism is overstrained when stretched to cover large social situations.[5] While he acknowledged that egoism also rears its head in individual relations such as in the family, he felt that there is a qualitative difference in favor of such individual relationships. While many attack Niebuhr's assessment of social relations as the problem with his comparison,[6] I would suggest that, in addition, he idealized individual relations. In the years since Niebuhr composed the bulk of his writing, we have learned a great deal more about the workings of family. Millions of children in this country alone have suffered from parental abuse. Thousands have died from it. Wife- and even husband-beating are common occurrences. Millions of people are raised in families which leave them emotionally and psychologically crippled due to neglect, incompetence, and intentional cruelty. We no longer know what the

5 It is interesting to read Niebuhr within the current sociobiology debate. Wilson's assessment of altruism as intended by nature only within basic units for their preservation, not to be extended beyond clan boundaries, is not far from Niebuhr's observation that, though only the fostering of social altruism can limit conflict and promote justice, altruism is exceedingly difficult to find in social relations. Edward O. Wilson, *On Human Nature* (New York: Bantam, 1978), 155–75.

6 Gene Outka, *Agape: An Ethical Social Analysis* (New Haven and Yale: Yale University Press, 1972), 42–43.

"normal" family is, and experience real doubts about the healthiness of the "average" family.

But the existence of this degree of sinfulness in individual relationships is not recognized in Niebuhr's work. The statement in his 1932 *Moral Man and Immoral Society* that women had won a "complete victory" over the "vestigal remnants of male autocracy" in modern society itself reveals his less than critical stance on the family and other relationships between the sexes.[7]

It is because of the common tendency, illustrated by Niebuhr, to idealize individual relations that pessimism tinges our view of social relations. And yet more and more we are coming to learn through history, sociology, and psychology that the family and other individual relations cannot be understood separately from social relations. Research into family and individual relations reveal that it is largely social relations which determine structure and roles in individual relations.[8] Most children were workers, not students, until the worker movement recognized them as a threat to adult employment. In the establishment of childhood as a haven of innocence and education where children were to be protected from contact with harsh reality, women's role, no longer that of producer since the Industrial Revolution moved production out of the home into the factories, came to be understood in terms of custodial care and nurturance of innocent, carefree youth. As is well known, where family size decreased around the world, it did so not in response to

7 Niebuhr, *Moral Man and Immoral Society*, 46.

8 Dorothy Dinnerstein's *The Mermaid and the Minotaur* (New York: Harper and Row, 1976) traces social decisions (such as the sex of childrearers) to resulting social misogyny. Philippe Aries' *Centuries of Childhood*, trans. Robert Baldick (New York: Vintage, 1962) outlines the changes in attitudes toward and structures of childhood which resulted from other social forces since the Middle Ages. Eli Zaretsky's *Capitalism, the Family and Personal Life* (New York: Harper and Row, 1976) and Jacques Donzelot's *The Policing of Families* (New York: Random House, 1979) both connect the structuring of the modern familial experience with social institutions and decisions. Hilda Scott's *Does Socialism Liberate Women? Experiences from Eastern Europe* (Boston: Beacon, 1974) examines this in contemporary Eastern Europe; Francis Fox Piven's and Richard Cloward's *Regulating the Poor: the Functions of Public Welfare* (New York: Random House, 1971) considers the effect of welfare on the behavior and self-understanding of poor families. In fact, the list of such studies connecting social and private relations is large and growing.

the availability of contraception, but in response to the rising mass prosperity associated with industrialization. All these changes in *individual* relations resulted from social groups working to protect their self-interest—their jobs, their social value, their prosperity.

Not only in terms of long-ranging historical trends are the two areas connected, but in current trends as well. Two causes of divorce in this country for years have been money problems and job dissatisfaction. Rising rates of unemployment translate into rising rates of spouse and child abuse. Not only is it sometimes the case, as Niebuhr noted, that anger, insecurity, alienation and frustration are vented in social and political action while love protects our individual associations from our wrath. It is also true that we vent our frustrations at alienating jobs, inefficient bureaucracies, and the general absence of avenues for self-creative activity not on or through the impersonal systems which create them, but on our spouses, our children, the person in the car ahead of us. *They* are reachable, they are usually "safe" to take it out on, and they give us the satisfaction of a response.

AGAPE: DISINTERESTED AND SACRIFICIAL

Much treatment of individual relations assumes that this is the realm of disinterested sacrificial love, of agape. Now this is strange, since the strongest individual relation would seem to be the marriage tie, which is by modern definition one of eros, or mutual love. Moreover, it is this tie which structures the social unit in and from which other relationships take place: the family. It has always seemed to me that only if one dealt solely with individual acts, refusing to link them in relationships, could one understand the family as the center of disinterested love. For the family is really the center of give and take, as the historical specialized division of labor within it makes clear.

With our own children we realized very clearly that though much of the early giving seemed to be solely ours, this was not disinterested, because the children were considered extensions of us, such that our efforts for them rebounded to our credit. Failure to provide for them would have discredited us. And we had expectations that the giving would become more mutual.

181

This led to the most revealing lesson the children taught us: that complete agape as either intention or result is impossible. Love can never be disinterested. It can be patient, but never disinterested. Christian preachers consistently point out, especially during Lent, that all actions are tainted with self-interest to some degree, if only by pride in one's own goodness. But a common understanding is that agape, disinterested, self-sacrificing love, is the ideal which always stands over against our actions as the standard impossible of achievement.[9] It is the standard because it exemplifies the love of God as expressed in Jesus Christ.

I have come to criticize this understanding. This conception of agape does not prove adequate in its application, which must be the final test of adequacy. Nor does it correspond to the historical event from which it is supposedly deduced, i.e., Jesus Christ. Christian love should not be construed as disinterested or set apart from other love as essentially self-sacrificing. All love both involves sacrifice and aims at mutuality. We need to rework the understanding of Christian love. What Christianity does for "natural" love, as for

9 Many major Christian figures have not been explicit on this point. The real question is whether Christlike love consists primarily in the sacrifice of self, or in devotion to the other, as well as whether any degree of self-interest invalidates Christian love. Luther clearly thought it did; Nygren reports that Luther called self-love "vicious," and held that love of one's neighbor has the task of completely dispossessing and annihilating self-love (*Agape and Eros,* trans. Philip S. Watson [New York: Harper and Row, 1969], 712–13). Kierkegaard agreed (*Works of Love,* trans. Howard and Edna Hong [New York: Harper and Row, 1964], 68, 133–34). The Christian tradition before Luther did not exclude the self so rigorously—major figures of the patristic period described Christian love in terms of eros, or mutual love, as Nygren reports. Thomas argued that the proper objects of love are both those having a more excellent good, and those to which we are more closely united (*Summa Theologica,* 2a2ae26, 9–12). Neither way of speaking about love excludes the self; rather the reverse. In this he follows Aristotle, who understands love and friendship in terms of mutuality: "And in loving a friend men love what is best for themselves; for the good man in becoming a friend becomes a good to his friend. Each, then, both loves what is good for himself, and makes an equal return in goodwill and in pleasantness, for friendship is said to be equality, and both of these are found most in the friendship of the good" (*Nicomachean Ethics,* Bk VIII, 1157b). However clear this split may be in the theological traditions, I do not think that it is reflected in popular piety. The Lutheran Protestant view is almost universal in the churches. I suspect that the strong influence yet today of medieval passion-mysticism is responsible for the present state of affairs in Catholicism.

human nature in general, is to articulate forcefully its end and meaning.

Of agape as essentially self-sacrificial, others have also been critical. Gene Outka writes out of an extended discussion of Christian writers on this theme:

> Generally, therefore, I am inclined to think that instead of appraising self-sacrifice as the purest and most perfect manifestation of agape, the difficulties I have considered are avoided if one allows it only *instrumental* warrant. Self-sacrifice must always be purposive in promoting the welfare of others and never simply expressive of something resident in the agent.[10]

To understand self-sacrificing love in any other way is to condone and even encourage the worst abuses of human dignity. As for agape as disinterested love, not only is this incapable of achievement, but its idealization as *the* Christian love destroys human relationships and distorts the God/human relationship. While we should realize that we constantly fail to achieve the best of which we are capable, it is wrong to identify this failure with a lack of total disinterestedness. To make this identification is to refuse to see how interdependent we are, to insist instead on our radical separation, to encourage masochism and domination, as well as to fail to understand the kingdom of God which Jesus preached.

The problems we faced with these children revolved around making the children able to participate in normal society. There was no way to do that without also gratifying our own self-interest, in that when they learned to walk, talk, eat, use the toilet, attend school, and form other relationships not only would their horizons expand, but ours also. As with all children, every achievement of the child is both a source of pride and a freeing of the parent from responsibility for the child. This sounds very simple. But in the case of our children, the medical, psychological, physical therapy, and other specialists counseled against thwarting the children's wishes,

10 Outka, *Agape*, 278. Also Margaret Farley, "New Patterns of Relationship: Beginnings of a Moral Revolution," in *Woman: New Dimensions*, ed. Walter Burkhardt (New York: Paulist, 1975), 51–70. And, since this article was written: Barbara Hilkert Andolsen, "Agape in Feminist Ethics," *Journal of Religious Ethics* 9 (Spring, 1981), 69–83 and Beverly Harrison, "The Power of Anger in the Work of Love: Christian Ethics for Woman and Other Strangers," *Union Seminary Quarterly Review* 36 (1981), 41–57.

against letting them cry, against pushing them to achieve with other children their age. In the case of the elder child, we were accused of selfishness for not accepting the medical judgment that the child was terminal within two years; we should "let the poor child die in peace in a family" rather than put him through more doctors and hospitals. Yet our efforts in finding experimental surgery have paid off in eleven normal years of school, camp, swimming, and bikes thus far. In the case of our youngest son, a diagnosis of brain damage from temporary heart failure led many "experts" to counsel us to expect nothing of Mike, though he continues to progress. One's self-interest is often, but not always, also the interest of the other. When we assume that to do the hard, self-sacrificing thing is to do the loving thing, we have, in fact, defined the interest of the other in terms of ourselves, and not in terms of the person and conditions of the other.

Even more, in the original decision to adopt these children, we found that apparently selfless love is not so. There is, as C. S. Lewis observed, not only Gift-love, but also Need-love.[11] We adopted a hard-to-place child, we said, because such children needed homes, and because we felt they had a right to parents. But in living with the decision, we saw that two people from large families living eight hundred miles from our homes in a large, strange city were lonely, and wanted a child to make them a family. But not a baby, for that would interfere with plans for graduate school for both of us. The wait was shortest for hard-to-place children.

In the second adoption, we wanted a girl, because we had two boys. We asked for a healthy, two-year-old, biracial girl. We were offered Mike, a two-year-old biracial boy with the same medical condition as our elder son. We cringed—if the elder son died could we go on, waiting for Mike to be stricken? But the agency used real moral pressure: since there were no other adoptive or foster homes open and the hospital would no longer keep him, Mike would be placed in a nursing home for the elderly. Our sons settled the question, the elder asking "Are you sorry you took me?" No matter how it seemed, our adoption of Mike was not a case of simple self-sacrificing love of another. I do not know how we would have

11 C. S. Lewis, *The Four Loves* (New York: Harcourt, Brace, Jovanovich, 1960), 11.

responded if no one else had known of the offer made us, if our moral pride were not on the line.

When we overemphasize the Gift-love in our loving and deemphasize the Need-love, we end up disguising our needs by calling them gifts for others. This can seriously damage the other, distorting his/her real needs and desires. A well-meaning woman (a social worker!) once told our eldest son that he should be grateful every day of his life that we had adopted him. Only because we had come to see the two-sidedness of both our intention and the result of that adoption was I able to respond furiously that *no* child should have to be grateful for parents, *especially* one who had been through so much and waited so long for them.

Much love is mutual; all is directed at mutuality. It could not be any other way, for we find love rewarding. If we love the other, we want him/her to experience that reward to the utmost, and that includes loving us. In a more impersonal sense, we may do a deed for another we do not know well—but in the action is the hope that the deed opens the other to love, if not specifically to us as individuals, then at least to the humanity which includes us. This is why Aquinas says, " ... hope precedes love at first; though afterwards hope is increased by love. Because from the fact that a man thinks that he can obtain a good from someone, he begins to love him; and from the fact that he loves him, he then hopes all the more in him."[12]

This is true of the divine love for us. It is true in the life of Jesus. Jesus did not come to earth to give himself disinterestedly to save us. Jesus was motivated by a mutual love with "Abba." Love expands; Jesus felt impelled not only to love others, but to bring others into the relationship he shared with "Abba," to share himself and "Abba" with others and to show these others to share themselves with each other, with himself, and with "Abba." This sharing was the kingdom he announced; in the kingdom all relationships, individual and social, would be restructured to reflect this mutual love.

This mutuality is true of God's love also. If God is love, then he/she needs an object for his/her love; he/she needs us. The

12 *Summa Theologica*, 2a2ae64, 4 reply obj. 3.

community within the Trinity was not alone sufficient, for one person of the Trinity, the Son, presupposes in his historical function our existence, and the third member of the Trinity, the Spirit, presupposes in her historical function both the Son and us. Moreover, the history of our interaction with God has been one of God's making known to us his/her desire for a relationship of mutual love. The moments of self-sacrifice, such as we find in the crucifixion of Jesus, are just that—moments in a process designed to end in mutual love.

ADVANTAGES OF LOVE AS MUTUALITY
IN SOCIAL RELATIONS

Understanding Christian love as essentially self-sacrifice has contributed to the common view that Christian love is inappropriate in social decision making. To move to an understanding of Christian love as intending mutuality could alter this view. Social decisions are not made by the whole, but by representatives pledged to act in the best interests of the group. Since self-sacrifice is not considered in the best interest of the group, the present, essentially sacrificial understanding of Christian love prevents representatives from heeding the demands of love, or at least limits them to those loving acts which have clear mandates and/or minimum impact.

With love understood as intending mutuality, instead of rejecting actions which call for some degree of sacrifice from the group in question, leaders might be led to consider the long-term situation and the possibilities for mutual benefit. In social relations, as in individual relations, all units are related. It is never the case that a group's action stands alone. It affects other groups which react to it. The group which dominates other groups must constantly stay vigilant to prevent their combination and rebellion, and must maintain the muscle necessary to subdue others. This does not leave the dominant group free to do other things—it has exacted a cost. No situation is without cost, though we tend to be blinded to the cost of dominance. One of the most common errors in policy making is to reject plans which do not maintain the advantages the group presently enjoys (which sacrifice its dominance). But we need to ask: does the plan eliminate the present cost? Does it benefit the group in the long run? Can the present advantage be maintained indefinitely without additional cost?

The failure to take into consideration the long term is common not only in decisions to reject alternatives to the present, but also in decisions deemed of mutual benefit. The U.S. Food for Peace Program has been a good example of this. Without even considering the mechanisms of the bill which made the immediate benefit to hungry nations less than optimal, critics could ask whether it benefits hungry nations to indefinitely depend on another country for their food. Does it detract from the independence of that country's decisions and leave them open to manipulation? Does it encourage self-sufficiency? How does it affect their economy? (The program has, in fact, been amended to attempt to deal with many of the problems.) In being very critical concerning the formulation of the interests of both sides, we must be careful to cast these formulations in terms of the long run.

When we consider the long run, what appears to be sacrifice now can be in our best interest, as the Marshall Plan to rebuild Europe after World War II intended and demonstrated. Many decisions involving sacrifice now—foreign aid plans, affirmative action plans, job training programs, ecology plans—can also be considered just smart, self-interested long-term planning.

JESUS ON SACRIFICE AND REWARD

This seems strange and repugnant to many of us who have interpreted Jesus to demand disinterested, sacrificial love for neighbor. But I believe that the message of Jesus is more ambiguous than that. He did not only say, "But love your enemies, and do good, and lend, expecting no return." He also gave us the second great commandment, "Love your neighbor as yourself." Not *more* than yourself, but as yourself. This should give us pause, for the golden rule is the basis of natural law ethics; it assumes that mutual peace and cooperation—the end—is obtained through treating the neighbor as oneself.

Yet Jesus did constantly urge action usually regarded as sacrificial—giving possessions to the needy, leaving relatives and friends, undergoing persecution. These actions were not, however, disinter-

187

ested, for he continually added that the reward or punishment for the response to this demand would be great in the kingdom now on the horizon. In these circumstances he often stressed that to follow him was not only righteous, it was shrewd, a looking to one's own best interest. The parable of the dishonest steward is a good example of this, as are the verses of Luke 12 ending: "Instead, seek the Kingdom and these things will be yours as well."[13] Throughout the Gospels Jesus told those who follow him, "Ask and it shall be given to you; seek, and you shall find; knock, and it shall be opened to you."[14]

Jesus connected his demand for sacrifice with the promise of reward, making sacrificial actions not one-sided, but mutually beneficial. I am not claiming that Scripture inspired the conception of Christian love as mutual. Only because I see this in my own experience did I look for it in Scripture. The scriptural issue is not whether Jesus promised reward for loving—that much is clear. The issue is whether the reward is the natural result of the love, or whether it is an addition, a gift from God extrinsic to the love of neighbor. Was Jesus telling us to open ourselves to a dynamic process of love in which we experience God's promise of fulfillment, or was he urging us to deny ourselves in the present so as to receive promised fulfillment in the future? When is the kingdom? I believe the kingdom has begun, that Jesus opened us to an ongoing process of kingdom, and I hope that the fulness of this kingdom is to come.[15] We experience the kingdom in partial ways, within the struggle against injustice and indignity.

It is better to derive one's strength and hope from the partial experience of kingdom than solely from the belief in ultimate reward in the culmination of kingdom. Kingdom is not a bifurcated entity in which our efforts toward kingdom in the present incur only

13 The New Testament: Luke 16:1–9, 12:31. Also, John 16:23–24, 5:24; Matt 25:34–36, 6:1–33, 24:45–51, 5:11–12, 21:22, 19:21, 7:7–8; Mark 9:41, 10:21, 29–31, 43–44; and Luke 13:22–30, 14:7–14, 18:29–30.

14 Luke 11:9.

15 In this position I am not alone. See, for example, Robert W. Funk, "Apocalyptic As a Historic and Theological Problem in Current New Testament Scholarship," in *Apocalypticism, Journal for Theology and Church* 6, ed. Robert W. Funk (New York: Herder and Herder, 1969), 182 and Ernst Käsemann, "On the Topic of Primitive Christian Apocalyptic," p. 104 in the same volume.

misery and occur in pitch darkness, with the joyful realization postponed to an indefinite future. We have partial realizations of kingdom, and not to be fed on these, not to rely on the energy and hope they generate, but to keep our eyes fixed only on the far-off future, is to refuse God's gift, to risk burnout in one's work of resisting evil and suffering. What is it that keeps people going through years of working to alleviate starvation, persecution, or epidemic disease amidst overwhelming odds? It is the small moments of victory, the moments where people really touched each other, where the barriers of evil and suffering were broken in a brief moment of resurrection. If not for such moments, how could we positively envision the meaning of kingdom?

These partial realizations are, I think, what Jesus referred to in the parables of the kingdom. The unexpected surprise, the wondrous discovered amongst the ordinary—these partial realizations of kingdom are experiences of love returned. Love is not always returned as we had hoped, or when we would have wished; it often engulfs us far more radically than we had envisaged and stretches us beyond what we had understood as our limits. Love is not happy, so much as it is joyful, in the way that resurrection is not a moment of carefree happiness, but a moment of deep joy. The impetus to love is the experience of kingdom. Love is an act of hope, and experiences of kingdom feed that hope, allowing us to sacrifice in love. Our experiences of mutual love, of love returned, love victorious, are the concretization of Jesus' promise of reward.

MUTUALITY NOT IMMEDIATE

One way in which the preaching of love as disinterested and self-sacrificial has been useful is in depressing expectations of the immediate return of love. This is good in that mutual love seldom begins mutually. Certainly God's love is prior; he/she initiates the relationship with us beginning with our creation. Often persons who have been deprived of love require much love and reassurance before they become confident enough to make themselves vulnerable to love. To expect immediate return of love from these is naive. Love is a process. Sometimes one's gifts are greater and one's needs lesser in the beginning of relationships, but the balance often shifts. Sometimes time runs out before the balance shifts. But the intention is always that it shall.

Nevertheless, the preaching of self-less love has had some disastrous consequences in the history of Christianity. It has sometimes distorted the understanding of Jesus, presenting him as a masochist, searching for a way to suffer and die. It has also distorted some people's understanding of God, suggesting a depiction of God as a vengeful Lord demanding the slaughter of his/her Son. The insistence on Christian love as self-less has created tremendous guilt in people who constantly find that they cannot forget themselves completely in their loving as they feel they should. The experience of having their love rewarded, returning fourfold, frustrates many, who come to assume that Christian love must be only for the saints, not for ordinary people. Even worse, the understanding of Christian love as self-sacrificing has pushed some to mistake destructive acts of self-sacrifice as Christian love precisely *because* there is no return of their love. Counselors who deal with battered women hear often that women recovering from beatings intend to return to abusive spouses, expecting further abuse, because that is what Jesus did: "he took what they did to him, and turned the other cheek." This notion of love as self-less, says John Cobb, "has promoted a 'love' that is devoid of genuine sensitivity to the deepest needs of the loved ones."[16]

This is not to argue against the need for sacrifice. Sacrifice is essential in the furthering of the kingdom. But we need to be very clear that self-sacrificing love is always aimed at the establishment of mutual love. An act is only a loving act if it has the potential to provoke loving response, however far in the future. Acts of no matter how much self-sacrifice, which support or encourage unloving actions or attitudes, are not acts of love. Agape is valuable in the service of eros and does not exist otherwise.[17]

16 John B. Cobb, Jr. and David Ray Griffin, *Process Theology: An Introductory Exposition* (Philadelphia: Westminster, 1976), 46.

17 This is, I think, the corrective to the situation pointed out by Saiving in the article discussed above. Saiving pointed out that in the Christian tradition sin has been defined in terms of the self-sacrifice missing in male conditioning. Agape, the corrective to sin is, however, *not* a corrective to the sinful tendency in the socialization of women, which is passivity and diffusion. Rather, agape confirms women's sinful tendency. I would say that the function of agape-istic teaching for men has been to increase their capacity and tendency for mutuality; for females

In conclusion, I propose that we have been led to emphasize dissimilarities between individuals and groups by idealizations of individual relations and mistaken notions about Christian love. Love in both individual and social relations involves the intention of mutuality and the probability of self-sacrifice to establish the interdependence of all which dictates that our ultimate self-interest demands sacrifice in the interest of the disadvantaged other.

it has served to reduce possibilities for mutuality. Women are already over-socialized to give (see Margaret Adams' "The Compassion Trap," *Women in a Sexist Society*, ed. Vivian Gornick and Barbara Moran [New York: Basic Books, 1971]), but have often not learned to recognize their own needs. Agape teaching prevents them from recognizing their own needs and directs them to serve others' needs. In this process, ironically, women become less able to give towards the real needs of others. That is, women are encouraged to ignore self needs and to fulfill those of others, although recognizing the needs of others is best done by those who recognize their own. At the same time, women's self needs go unmet because unrecognized, resulting in a frustration which manifests itself either in feelings of self-pitying worthlessness, or in demands for gratitude for their services, and often in both. Women can both give too much (they surrender the possibility of real personhood) and too little (for often they do not give what others really need).

13

Ethics and Justice in Goddess Religion

Starhawk

The religions of the Great Goddess, which are presently undergoing a rebirth and a re-creation, especially among women, are sometimes accused by those unfamiliar with their philosophy and practices of lacking a conception of justice or a system of ethics. This paper is written to explore and clarify the ethics and morality inherent in a worldview centered on immanent divinity found within nature, human beings, and the world.

Most writers on contemporary Goddess religions, womanspirit, or Witchcraft cite the past to offer a historical basis for the present traditions. I am not going to do that here. Historical points are always arguable, and while the past may serve us with models and myths, we need not look to it to justify the reemergence of the feminine principle. Whether or not there was a religion of the Great Goddess in prehistoric times, there is one today. Whether or not women ever ruled in matriarchies, women are taking power today. Whether or not contemporary Witchcraft has its roots in the Stone Age, its branches reach into the future.

And it is with the future that any system of ethics and justice must be concerned, because the ethics of the unarguable, historical, well-documented, and patriarchal religions and cultures have brought us to a point at which our chances of destroying ourselves and poisoning the biosphere seem much greater than our chances of preserving life into the future. Never before have we as a species had the potential for causing such widespread social, biological, and irreversible destruction, yet never before have we had such potential for the alleviation of poverty, hunger, disease, and social injustice, and for the fostering of individual freedom, growth, and creativity. The choices we must make, although they are rarely posed in these terms, are essentially ethical choices.

The conceptions of justice in the western, patriarchal religions are based on a worldview which locates deity outside the world. Of course, within each tradition there are exceptions, but in the broad view of Christianity, Judaism, and Islam, God is transcendent, and his laws are absolutes, which can be considered in a context removed both from the reality of human needs and desires and the reality of their actual effects. They are the laws of heaven—and must be followed whatever their consequences on Earth. So, as I write this paper, the newspaper greets me with headlines stating that the pope has reiterated the ban on birth control. I doubt if any Catholic, in good conscience, would hold that God wants to doom the poor to inescapable hunger and poverty. Yet such is the effect of this absolute morality. Because when we believe that what is sacred—and, therefore, most highly valued—is *not* what we see and sense and experience, we maintain an inherent split in consciousness that allows us to quite comfortably cause pain and suffering in pursuit of an unmanifest good.

The major difference between patriarchal religions and the evolving Goddess religions—perhaps even more central than the image of the divine as female—is the worldview that includes regarding divinity as immanent: in the world, not outside the world, as manifest in nature and in human beings, human needs and desires.

In such a system, justice is not based on an external Absolute who imposes a set of laws upon chaotic nature, but on recognition of the ordering principles inherent in nature. The law is the natural law. We break it at our peril, not because we fear hellfire or damnation or a Day of Judgment after the end of the world, but because its consequences are also inherent in the structure of the world. So, if I "break" the law of gravity by jumping out of a third-story window, I may break my neck in consequence, not because the Goddess is punishing me for my effrontery, but because that is the way the law of gravity works. So, if we continue to spray our forests with mutagenic chemicals that leach into local water supplies, we will continue to see increases in miscarriages and birth defects. If we continue unsafe storage of nuclear wastes, rates of cancer will continue to rise. That is the way it works.

The Goddess is manifest not just in human life, but in the interwoven chain of relationships that link all forms of life. We are not given dominion over the birds of the air and the fish of the sea; rather, human life is recognized as part of the animal world. We are conscious, but consciousness itself is *of* nature, not separate from nature. And we do not have the right to damage or destroy other species in order to further purely human aims. Witches, of course, are not Jains, nor are most of us vegetarians. The Goddess in her aspect as the Crone or Reaper and the God in his aspect of the Hunter embody the principle that all of life feeds on other life. Death sustains life. But the hunt, the harvest, the reaping of herbs— or of profits—must be practiced with respect for the balance of life and its continuation in the greatest possible richness and diversity of forms. The herds are culled, not obliterated. When herbs are cut, only a few are taken from each separate clump, so that they may grow back in future years. Human communities limit their numbers to what the land can support without straining its resources or displacing other species. We do not, for example, have the ethical right to destroy a species—even the lowly snail darter—in order to build a dam, regardless of how much money has already been invested in the project. When we consider ourselves as a true part of the fabric of life, then each time we irrevocably destroy an aspect of life we have destroyed an aspect of ourselves.

Diversity is highly valued—as it is in nature—in a polytheistic worldview which allows for many powers, many images of divinity. In ecological systems, the greater the diversity of a community, the greater is its power of resilience, of adaptation in the face of change, and the greater the chances for survival of its elements.

Diversity is also valued in human endeavors and creations. Ethics are concerned with fostering diversity rather than sameness, and they are not concerned with enforcing a dogma or a party line. Individual conscience—itself a manifestation of the Goddess—is the final court of appeals, above codified laws or hierarchical proclamations.

Such a statement makes many people uneasy. If ethics are based on the individual's sense of right and wrong, then don't we open ourselves to the horrors of a Hitler, to crime, anarchy, and blind selfishness? Yes, if the individual self is seen out of context. But in Goddess religion, the individual self is never seen as a separate, isolated *object:* it is a nexus of interwoven relationships, an integral and inseparable part of the human and biological community. The Goddess is manifest in the self—but also in every other human self, and the biological world. We cannot honor and serve the Goddess in ourselves unless we honor and serve her in others.

In Witchcraft, the coven structure fosters the dynamic balance between the individual self and the interrelated community that is necessary for true personal responsibility to develop. A coven, the congregation of the Craft, is a small group, not more than thirteen in membership. Coveners participate in rituals together and develop an intimate bond of trust and support. Because the group is small, each individual personality stands out and affects its direction. Yet within the group there is community; it becomes a laboratory in which we experience the divine in others, in diverse and usually strong-willed individuals rather than as an abstract glow of appreciation for humanity in the mass.

Each individual self, then, is linked by ties of blood and affection to a family, and by the bonds of love and trust to the coven, which in turn is a part of the larger human community, the culture and society in which it is found, and that culture is part of the biological/geological community of planet Earth and the cosmos beyond, the dance of being which we call Goddess.

Inherent in Goddess religion, then, is an ethical imperative to work toward relationships and communities that serve the Goddess manifest: the interplay of diversity and richness of life in its fullest expression. No one can live out the fullness of self when she is hungry or condemned to a life of poverty and discrimination, when as woman her roles are circumscribed and she is not free to be strong, creative, to control her own body and her own sexuality, to be a leader, and to be in touch with her internal power; when the color of her skin limits her freedom and opportunities; when her life is overshadowed by the fear of war or the threat of ecological disaster. Whenever the Goddess is diminished, self is diminished;

and given the conditions of our society, a commitment to the Goddess carries with it an inherent demand to work for social change. Regardless of how fortunate and privileged we as individuals are, regardless of how many growth seminars we attend, how often we meditate, how many miles we jog each day, or how often we meet with our coven and perform the rituals of the changing seasons, we cannot fulfill ourselves in a world of starvation, pollution, and hopelessness. As Witches, the rituals we perform reinforce that identification of self with Larger-Myriad-Self, so that it becomes not an intellectual affirmation but a deep, constant psychological state. They do not offer an escape from the world of suffering, but a source of healing and energy we can use to heal the wounds of the world. And their mood—in spite of the suffering we recognize—remains one of joy and wonder, of celebration of life.

Because divinity is manifest in human beings, our needs and desires are not seen as evil or negative, but as sacred evidences of the life-force. Witchcraft is not a religion of self-abnegation. We celebrate our hunger, our creativity, our successes in the world, and our sexuality.

Sexuality is sacred not just because it is the means of procreation, but because it is a power which infuses life with vitality and pleasure, because it is the numinous means of deep connection with another human being, and with the Goddess. Witches value diversity in sexual expressions and orientations, recognizing that different people have very different needs and capacities. Sexual ethics are based on honest recognition of one's own impulses and desires and honoring one's true feelings rather than either repressing them or feigning a level of desire which does not exist.

Force or coercion of any sort, however, is extremely unethical. Sexuality is sacred because through it we make a connection with another self—but it is misused and perverted when it becomes a means of treating another as an object, or treating oneself as an object, or attaining power *over* another. Sex is not an obsession, it is the moving energy of the Goddess wherever it is honored and recognized with honesty—in simple erotic passion, in the unfathomable mystery of falling in love, in the committed relationship of marriage, in periods of abstinence and chastity, or in its infinite other appearances which we will leave to the reader's imagination.

197

Coercion, however, is often more subtle than physical rape or overt economic pressure. It includes psychological pressures which influence people to ignore their needs or repress their impulses, political pressures to focus one's sexual drives in "acceptable" orientations, and social pressures. By these standards, the attitudes promulgated by most of the "major" religions are extremely coercive and immoral. When the individual self and will are considered sacred, no one has the right to interfere with another's exercise of free choice or control of energy, mind, or body.

The issue that comes to mind here is abortion. While the so-called "right-to-life" movement tries to pose this question as one involving the rights of fetuses, Goddess religion recognizes that to value life as an untempered absolute is ridiculous—it is to maintain the right of every cancer cell to reproduce blindly, of every sperm and every egg to unite a new embryo, of every flea and cockroach to populate the world endlessly. Life is interwoven in a dance of death, the limiting factor that sustains the possibility of new life. The predator is as necessary to an ecological balance as the prey—because it is the richness and diversity of the interplay between species that manifests the Goddess.

Human life is valuable and sacred when it is the freely given gift of the Mother—through the human mother. To bear new life is a grave responsibility, requiring a deep commitment—one which no one can force on another. To coerce a woman by force or fear or guilt or law or economic pressure to bear an unwanted child is the height of immorality. It denies her right to exercise her own sacred will and conscience, robs her of her humanity, and dishonors the Goddess manifest in her being. The concern of the anti-abortion forces is not truly with the preservation of life, it is with punishment for sexuality. If they were genuinely concerned with life, they would be protesting the spraying of our forests and fields with pesticides known to cause birth defects. They would be working to shut down nuclear power plants and dismantle nuclear weapons, to avert the threat of widespread genetic damage which may plague *wanted* children for generations to come—if there are generations to come.

"All acts of love and pleasure are my rituals" is a saying from the Goddess, and in her religions sharing love and pleasure with each other are considered among the best things human beings can do with our time here. An ethical society would encourage all that allows that expression to be most honest, all that makes us free to listen to our own deep desires.

Justice, then, in Goddess religion operates in the world as it is inherent in the world and the ecological balance of the biosphere. Consequences may not be distributed fairly on an individual level: it is not the owner of the chemical company who will give birth to a defective child, nor are we confronted by the belief that he will burn eternally in an afterlife. Consequences are suffered collectively, because it is our collective responsibility as a society to change those practices that destroy the lives of individuals and the interplay of life-forms around us. No external God, Goddess, angel, or convoy of visitors from another planet will do this for us: *we* must create justice and ecological and social balance; this is the prime concern, the bottom line, the nitty gritty of ethics in a worldview that sees deity as immanent in human life and the world we live in.

Life, being sacred, demands our full participation. The ethical person engages in life and does not withdraw from it. Our ideal is not monastic seclusion or asceticism, but the fully human life lived in the world, involved in community. To be human is, by definition, to be imperfect, and Goddess religion holds out no superhuman standard to perfection which we are expected to emulate and at which attempt we inevitably fail. One acts ethically not out of a sense of guilt or self-hate brought on by constant failure, but out of pride: honor of the divine within.

Life demands honesty, the ability to face, admit, and express oneself. It demands integrity—being integrated, having brought together and recognized our conflicting internal forces, and being integrated into a larger community of selves and life-forms. Life demands courage and vulnerability, because without them there can be no openness and no connection; and it requires responsibility and discipline, to make choices and face the consequences, to carry out what we undertake. And, finally, life demands love, because it is through love, of self and of others, erotic love, transforming love, affectionate love, delighted love for the myriad forms of life evolving and changing, for the redwood and mayfly, for the blue whale and the snail darter, for wind and sun and the waxing and waning moon, caring love for the Cambodian child and the restless ghetto teenager, love of all the eternally self-creating world, love of the light and the mysterious darkness, and raging love against all that would diminish the unspeakable beauty of the world, that we connect with the Goddess within and without.

Yet Witches, like everyone today, face life in a society that makes ethical actions difficult and a purely ethical life impossible. We all, by participation in the life of our culture, participate in exploitation, destruction, and pollution. It is a conflict with no easy resolution. Some Witches have removed themselves from the city, not to withdraw from the world but to explore the possibilities of creating new communities. Most of us, however, continue to drive our cars, run our electric typewriters, buy coffee, and eat bananas, while recycling our garbage sporadically, if at all.

If I have a personal guiding principle, it derives from my friend Mary, who used to go with her small son out to open land north of Los Angeles where they could walk under live oaks and play in the stream that ran down from the coastal foothills. A rough, beer-drinking crowd frequented the area and left the stream littered with cans and trash. Mary always brought some large bags with her, and when they were leaving she and her little boy would fill them with beer cans. It was a discouraging task, as the supply was so vast that their efforts barely seemed to make a difference. I asked her once why she bothered to try. "I know I can't clean it all up," she said, "but I believe in picking up the garbage that you find in your path."

Each of us must determine for ourselves what path is ours and where it takes us; the garbage is not hard to recognize. And that is what I would like to offer as an ethical guide for a modern age.

14

Where Is the Love?

June Jordan

The 1978 National Black Writers Conference at Howard University culminated with an extremely intense public seminar entitled *Feminism and the Black Woman Writer.* This was an historic, unprecedented event tantamount to conceding that, under such a heading, there might be something to discuss! Acklyn Lynch, Sonia Sanchez, Barbara Smith, and myself were the panelists chosen to present papers to the standing-room-only audience. I had been asked, also, to moderate the proceedings and therefore gave the opening statement, *Where Is the Love?*, which was later published in *Essence* magazine.

From phone calls and other kinds of gossip, I knew that the very scheduling of this seminar had managed to divide people into camps prepared for war. Folks were so jumpy, in fact, that when I walked into the theater I ran into several Black feminists and then several Black men who, I suppose, just to be safe, had decided not to speak to anyone outside the immediate circle of supportive friends they had brought with them.

The session was going to be hot. Evidently, feminism was being translated into lesbianism, into something interchangeable with lesbianism, and the taboo on feminism, within the Black intellectual community, had long been exceeded in its orthodox severity only by the taboo on the subject of the lesbian. I say within the intellectual Black community, because, minus such terms as *feminist* and *lesbian*, the phenomena of self-directed Black women or the phenomena of Black women loving other women have hardly been uncommon, let alone unbelievable, events to Black people not privy to theoretical strife about correct and incorrect Black experience.

This blurring of issues seemed to me incendiary and obnoxious. Once again, the Black woman writer would be lost to view as issues of her sex life claimed public attention at the expense of intellectual and aesthetic focus upon her work. Compared to the intellectual and literary criticism accorded to James Baldwin and Richard Wright, for example, there is damned little attention paid to their bedroom activities. In any case, I do not believe that feminism is a matter, first or last, of sexuality.

The seminar was going to be a fight. It was not easy to prepare for this one. From my childhood in Brooklyn I knew that your peers would respect you if you could hurt somebody. Much less obvious was how to elicit respect as somebody who felt and who meant love.

I wanted to see if it was possible to say things that people believe they don't want to hear, without having to kick ass and without looking the fool for holding out your hand. Was there some way to say, to insist on, each, perhaps disagreeable, individual orientation and nonetheless leave the union of Black men and Black women, as a people, intact? I felt that there had to be: if the individual cannot exist then who will be the people?

I expected that we, Black panelists and audience, together, would work out a way to deal, even if we didn't want to deal. And that's what happened, at Howard. We did. Nobody walked out. Nobody stopped talking. The session ended because we ran out of time.

As I think about anyone or anything—whether history or literature or my father or political organizations or a poem or a film—as I seek to evaluate the potentiality, the life-supportive commitment/ possibilities of anyone or any thing, the decisive questions is, always, *where is the love?* The energies that flow from hatred, from negative and hateful habits and attitudes and dogma do not promise something good, something I would choose to cherish, to honor with my own life. It is always the love, whether we look to the spirit of Fannie Lou Hamer, or to the spirit of Agostinho Neto, it is always the love that will carry action into positive new places, that will carry your own nights and days beyond demoralization and away from suicide.

I am a feminist, and what that means to me is much the same as the meaning of the fact that I am Black: it means that I must undertake to love myself and to respect myself as though my very life depends upon self-love and self-respect. It means that I must everlastingly seek to cleanse myself of the hatred and the contempt that surrounds and permeates my identity, as a woman, and as a Black human being, in this particular world of ours. It means that the achievement of self-love and self-respect will require inordinate, hourly vigilance, and that I am entering my soul into a struggle that will most certainly transform the experience of all the peoples of the earth, as no other movement can, in fact, hope to claim: because the movement into self-love, self-respect, and self-determination is the movement now galvanizing the true, the unarguable majority of human beings everywhere. This movement explicitly demands the testing of the viability of a moral idea: that the health, the legitimacy of any status quo, any government force, must be measured according to the experiences of those who are, comparatively, powerless. Virtue is not to be discovered in the conduct of the strong *vis-à-vis* the powerful, but rather it is to be found in our behavior and policies affecting those who are different, those who are weaker, or smaller than we. How do the strong, the powerful, treat children? How do we treat so-called minority members of the body politic? How do the powerful regard women? How do they treat us?

Easily you can see that, according to this criterion, the overwhelming reality of power and government and tradition is evil, is diseased, is illegitimate, and deserves nothing from us—no loyalty, no accommodation, no patience, no understanding—except a clear-minded resolve to utterly change this total situation and, thereby, to change our own destiny.

As a Black woman, as a Black feminist, I exist, simultaneously, as part of the powerless and as part of the majority peoples of the world in two ways: I am powerless as compared to any man because women, *per se*, are kept powerless by men/by the powerful; I am powerless as compared to anyone white because Black and Third World peoples are kept powerless by whites/by the powerful. I am the majority because women constitute the majority gender. I am the majority because Black and Third World peoples constitute the majority of life on this planet.

June Jordan

And it is here, in this extreme, inviolable coincidence of my status as a Black feminist, my status as someone twice stigmatized, my status as a Black woman who is twice kin to the despised majority of all the human life that there is, it is here, in that extremity, that I stand in a struggle against suicide. And it is here, in this extremity, that I ask, of myself, and of any one who would call me *sister, where is the love?*

The love devolving from my quest for self-love and self-respect and self-determination must be, as I see it, something you can verify in the ways that I present myself to others, and in the ways that I approach people different from myself. How do I reach out to the people I would like to call my sisters and my brothers and my children and my lovers and my friends? If I am a Black feminist serious in the undertaking of self-love, then it seems to me that the legitimate, the morally defensible character of that self-love should be such that I gain and gain and gain in the socio-psychic strength needed so that I may, without fear, be able and willing to love and respect women, for example, who are not like me: women who are not feminists, women who are not professionals, women who are not as old or as young as I am, women who have neither job nor income, women who are not Black.

And it seems to me that the socio-psychic strength that should follow from a morally defensible Black feminism will mean that I become able and willing, without fear, to love and respect men who are willing and able, without fear, to respect me. In short, if the acquirement of my self-determination is part of a worldwide, an inevitable, and a righteous movement, then I should become willing and able to embrace more and more of the whole world, without fear, and also without self-sacrifice.

This means that, as a Black feminist, I cannot be expected to respect what somebody else calls self-love if that concept of self-love requires my suicide to any degree. And this will hold true whether that somebody else is male, female, Black, or white. My Black feminism means that you cannot expect me to respect what somebody else identifies as the Good of the People, if that so-called Good (often translated into *manhood* or *family* or *nationalism*) requires the deferral or the diminution of my self-fulfillment. We *are* the people. And, as Black women, we are most of the people, any people, you care to talk about. And, therefore, nothing that is Good for the People is good unless it is good for me, as I determine myself.

When I speak of Black feminism, then, I am speaking from an exacerbated consciousness of the truth that we, Black women, huddle together, miserably, on the very lowest levels of the economic pyramid. We, Black women, subsist among the most tenuous and least likely economic conditions for survival.

When I speak of Black feminism, then, I am not speaking of sexuality. I am not speaking of heterosexuality or lesbianism or homosexuality or bisexuality; whatever sexuality anyone elects for his or her pursuit is not my business, nor the business of the state. And, furthermore, I cannot be persuaded that one kind of sexuality, as against another, will necessarily provide for the greater happiness of the two people involved. I am not talking about sexuality. I am talking about love, about a steady-state deep caring and respect for every other human being, a love that can only derive from a secure and positive self-love.

As a Black woman/feminist, I must look about me, with trembling, and with shocked anger, at the endless waste, the endless suffocation of my sisters: the bitter sufferings of hundreds of thousands of women who are the sole parents, the mothers of hundreds of thousands of children, the desolation and the futility of women trapped by demeaning, lowest-paying occupations, the unemployed, the bullied, the beaten, the battered, the ridiculed, the slandered, the trivialized, the raped, and the sterilized, the lost millions and multimillions of beautiful, creative, and momentous lives turned to ashes on the pyre of gender identity. I must look about me and, as a Black feminist, I must ask myself: *where is the love?* How is my own lifework serving to end these tyrannies, these corrosions of sacred possibility?

As a Black feminist poet and writer I must look behind me with trembling, and with shocked anger, at the fate of Black women writers until now. From the terrible graves of a traditional conspiracy against my sisters in art, I must exhume the works of women writers and poets such as Georgia Douglas Johnson (who?).

In the early flush of the Harlem Renaissance, Georgia Johnson accomplished an astonishing, illustrious life experience. Married to Henry Lincoln Johnson, U.S. Recorder of Deeds in Washington,

D.C., the poet, in her own right, became no less than Commissioner
of Conciliation for the U.S. Department of Labor *(who was that
again? Who?)*. And she, this poet, furthermore enjoyed the intense,
promotional attention of Dean Kelley Miller, here at Howard, and
W. E. B. DuBois, and William Stanley Braithwaite, and Alain
Locke. And she published three volumes of her own poetry and I
found her work in Countee Cullen's anthology, *Caroling Dusk*,
where, Countee Cullen reports, she, Georgia Douglas Johnson,
thrived as a kind of Gwendolyn Brooks, holding regular Saturday
night get-togethers with the young Black writers of the day.

And what did this poet of such acclaim, achievement, connection,
and generosity, what did this poet have to say in her poetry, and
who among us has ever heard of Georgia Douglas Johnson? And is
there anybody in this room who can tell me the name of two or three
other women poets from the Harlem Renaissance? And why did she
die, and why does the work of all women die with no river carrying
forward the record of such grace? How is it the case that whether we
have written novels or poetry or whether we have raised our
children or cleaned and cooked and washed and ironed, it is all
dismissed as "women's work"; it is all, finally, despised as nothing
important, and there is no trace, no echo of our days upon the earth?

Why is it not surprising that a Black woman as remarkably
capable and gifted and proven as Georgia Douglas Johnson should
be the poet of these pathetic, beggarly lines:

> I'm folding up my little dreams
> within my heart tonight
> and praying I may soon forget
> the torture of their sight
> —"My Little Dreams"

How long, how long will we let the dreams of women serve merely
to torture and not to ignite, to enflame, and to ennoble the promise
of the years of every lifetime? And here is Georgia Douglas
Johnson's poem "The Heart of a Woman":

> The heart of a woman goes forth with the dawn,
> As a lovebird, softwinging, so restlessly on,
> Afar o'er life's turrets and vales does it roam
> In the wake of those echoes the heart calls home.

Where is the Love?

The heart of a woman falls back with the night
And enters some alien cage in its plight,
And tries to forget it has dreamed of the stars,
While it breaks, breaks, breaks on the sheltering bars.

And it is against such sorrow, and it is against such suicide, and it is against such deliberated strangulation of the possible lives of women, of my sisters, and of powerless peoples—men and children—everywhere, that I work and live, now, as a feminist trusting that I will learn to love myself well enough to love you (whoever you are), well enough so that you will love me well enough so that we will know exactly where is the love: that it is here, between us, and growing stronger and growing stronger.

Staking Our Claims

SITUATING FEMINIST ETHICAL CLAIMS
IN THE ETHICS ENTERPRISE

Part Three

15

A Framework
for Feminist Ethics

Carol S. Robb

INTRODUCTION

The diversity among feminist perspectives is reflected in the diversity of feminist ethical theories. A major indicator of this diversity is the way feminists answer the question, who is accountable to feminist ethics? The seat of accountability rests in some of the following areas: to women solely, according to radical feminists; to families and schools, for sex-role theorists; to the working class, according to Marxist-Leninist feminists; to all women and the working class, for socialist-feminists. Considering these responses, this paper takes the position that feminists are making claims on social structures and aggregates of people—government, childcare systems, families, schools, churches, and the corporate sphere. In this light, feminist ethics are social ethics, and can guide our reflection with the tools and questions which pertain to the discipline of social ethics.

On the other side, social ethics is a discipline still in the forge, in process, with some of its outlines yet to be shaped. Developments in feminist ethical theory provide the basis for a contribution to the formation of social ethics: a vision of the breadth of scope that the discipline must encompass. Without a scope broad enough to include, among other things, the task of analyzing the roots of women's oppression, our ethical reflection is subject to a major difficulty, to fail to account for the systematic quality of the ground for women's complaints and claims. Secondarily, without recognizing the importance of that analysis to feminist ethics, we will miss understanding a major reason why feminists take such diverse and even conflicting normative stances, ranging from separatism to institutional reformism to commitment to socialist revolution.

Yet the analysis of women's oppression is only one aspect of feminist ethics, as the analysis of the root of any situation is only one aspect of social ethics in general. Several factors constitute ethical theories, and ethicists, including feminist ethicists, may differ along any or all of these factors, thus expressing different normative stances. In this paper I propose a schema which can make explicit how ethical theories differ from each other and share points of commonality. This schema can be shared by feminist ethics and social ethics.

This schema contains many factors which appear in contemporary and traditional ethical theory, though this particular configuration is one which I propose to encourage viewing the ethical enterprise in a broad way. Ethicists in general, including feminist ethicists, tend to focus their attention on one or a few of these factors, as the notes will indicate, making contributions to the total enterprise in the context of others' contributions in different ways.

ELEMENTS OF ETHICAL THEORIES

Proposing this schema necessitates attentiveness to a dialogue between the traditions of the discipline of ethics and new voices which are both appropriating and challenging the traditions. One of the outcomes of this dialogue is an awareness of the impact on ethical reflection of the analysis of the roots of oppression. We have seen attention to analysis before in the ethics of Latin American liberation theology. My concern is to make this aspect of ethical reflection explicit, since to do so confronts us with the importance of making explicit the social theories at the base of our various social ethics.

Specifically in relation to feminist ethics, analyses among feminists differ, as I shall take some care to show. Thus, while all feminist ethics begins with or assumes a criticism of the historical, including contemporary, roles of women in society, or a complaint about those roles, the attempt to understand the grounds for the criticism and the requirements for liberation requires analysis. Because the analyses of the roots of women's oppression yield such divergent normative stances, I will make the case that this particular factor is heavily weighted in relation to all the other factors.

Starting point for ethical reflection   The starting point is the first of nine analytically distinct aspects of ethical reflection. In the tradition of ethics we have learned the significance of how people define problems appropriate for ethical reflection, or pose issues, and in this sense *start* the ethical enterprise.

On the one hand, one can proceed by reflecting on very concrete historical experiences, and attempt to arrive at more general understandings of the ethical situation by that "reflection on praxis," to borrow liberation theology teminology. On the other hand, one can begin with a definition of the good life, the virtuous person, the "nature" of anything in an idealist sense, and deduce the definition of an ethical situation from that basis.[1]

To date there has been a nearly consistent tendency for feminist ethicists to take as their starting points reflection upon very concrete situations. This procedure is one way, and a main way, in which dominant ideology is unmasked. In this procedure, there is commonality or at least a basis for commonality with those who articulate ethical reflections from other oppressed groups. For until the dominant ideology of a social structure can be exposed as manufactured instead of natural, the terms of an ethical problem will tend to reflect assumptions which support a dominant ideology. For this reason, the act of defining a problem is a political act; it is an exercise of power to have accepted one's terms of a "problem."[2]

1 For an illustration of this particular distinction in terms of the abortion question, see Jane English, "Abortion and the Concept of a Person," in *Feminism and Philosophy*, ed. Mary Vetterling-Bragin, Frederick A. Elliston, and Jane English (Totowa, NJ: Littlefield, Adams and Company, 1977), 417–28. Also see Howard Cohen, "Abortion and the Quality of Life," pp. 429–40 in the same volume.

2 Carol Gilligan claims that the proclivity of women to reconstruct hypothetical dilemmas in terms of the real, to request or supply the information missing about the nature of people and the places where they live, shifts their

Carol S. Robb

Data about the historical situation   Ethical decisions must take into account all of the relevant data. Social ethicists are accountable for basing their definition of the ethical situation on inclusive data. Those formulating feminist ethical theory are inclined to challenge social ethicists in two ways, as to the *sufficiency* of the data to be considered, whether it adequately reflects what is happening to women and what it is that women are doing, and as to the *weight given* to the data which reflects or impacts women's lives.[3]

Analysis of the roots of oppression   Dependent upon, but not collapsible to, the data about the historical situation, the location of the roots of oppression informs all aspects of ethical reflection. The purpose of this factor is to locate causal dynamics.[4]

Feminist ethical theory reflects at least four different analyses of

---

judgment away from the hierarchical ordering of principles and the formal procedures of decision-making that are critical for scoring at Kohlberg's highest level ("In a Different Voice: Women's Conceptions of Self and Morality," *Harvard Educational Review* 47 [November 1977], 481–517).

3 Claudia Card claims we cannot presuppose a requisite publicity of the data for our inquiries, thus the need for autobiographies ("Feminist Ethical Theory: A Lesbian Perspective," unpublished manuscript 1978). Karen Lebacqz says that if only logical analysis of "facts" is considered appropriate data, one takes the decision away from those most intimately involved, and obfuscates the value-laden nature of data ("Bioethics: Some Challenges from a Liberation Perspective," World Council of Churches Conference on Faith, Science and the Future, 12–24 July 1979, Cambridge, MA). Mary Pellauer used to teach a course, "Violence and Violation," at Union Theological Seminary which organized often-ignored data about various forms of violence against women.

4 For an illustration of the significance of analysis on a common data fund, compare Barbara Ehrenreich and John Ehrenreich, "The Professional-Managerial Class," *Radical America* 11 (1977), 7–31, with Mary Daly, *Gyn/Ecology: The Metaethics of Radical Feminism* (Boston: Beacon Press, 1978) on the treatment of the development of gynecology in the medical profession. The Ehrenreichs argue that the development was part of the de-skilling of the working class. Midwifery, which played an important role in the culture of European immigrant groups and rural black and white Americans, was outlawed or discredited in the early 1900s and replaced by professionally dominated care. De-skilling the working class was involved in the rise of the professional managerial class, whose function is to reproduce capitalist class relations. Daly views that rise of the professional field of gynecology as a reactionary response of men to the first wave of feminism. "For of course the purpose and intent of gynecology was/is not healing in a deep sense but violent enforcement of the sexual caste system" (see p. 227).

the roots of oppression which I will examine later. They share one perspective, however: that the causative factors in women's situation, whether prehistorical, historical, or currently operative, are not collapsible to, even if they are related to, causes of other social inequalities. Women's oppression cannot be "liquidated" by abolishing the class structure alone, racism alone, or the need for democratic reforms alone.

Loyalties   On whose behalf ought we to make ethical judgments? Some ethicists have treated this factor as a pre-ethical factor, one about which persons have made some judgment when they enter into ethical reflection. However, the approach I suggest is that one may intentionally and after reflection take a position of partiality, or loyalty to a particular group, and consequently it is appropriate to treat "loyalties" as an ethical factor.

Feminist ethical theory confronts all proponents of justice in the social-ethical tradition as to whether loyalty to women *as women* is operative. It is not sufficient to espouse justice for women solely or even primarily as a means to achieve justice for the underdeveloped, a racial or ethnic group, or a nationality. On the other hand, there is among feminist ethicists a continuing search for the relationship between loyalty to women and loyalty to other oppressed groups. With some exceptions, feminist ethicists are loyal to women in a way which is consistent to a loyalty to all of humanity.

Theory of value   Value theories contain rank orders of value according to priority. Rank orderings are based on an assumption that many if not all ethical decisions are made in situations in which some values must be chosen at the expense of others. Thus theories of value may posit how to choose between life and freedom, unity and justice, affiliation and autonomy, to name some examples of choices often posed. Theories of value are often implied in anthropologies, theologies, and visions of future social orders as they are expressed in utopic science fiction, for example.

An ongoing discussion among those developing theories of feminist values concerns whether feminists have claim to any values independent of either a theory that biology is determinative, or a commitment to social justice shared with others with commitments

215

Carol S. Robb

to racial or economic justice. The substance of feminist value theory remains an open discussion.[5]

Mode of making ethical decisions   The discipline of social ethics generally recognizes three primary models for decision-making, and there is some discussion about whether there are in fact only two. That is, in reflecting upon the teleological, deontological, and situation-response modes, one can detect within the third mode aspects which are essentially teleological or deontological, depending on the ethicist in question.

Feminist ethics is in large part done in the teleological mode when the understanding of teleology allows for inclusion of the relational mode. Feminist ethics is oriented toward the liberation of women and weighs the value of acts or policy in those terms, but it is important to distinguish teleology from utilitarianism.[6] For while

---

5 Haney has articulated a notion of feminist ethics as a vision for a values revolution, and proposes the paradigm nourishment-friendship as the central values. It is the task of feminists, she claims, to redefine moral excellence, virtue, and the good person, and to hold suspect definitions from the past of justice, love, and mercy (Eleanor Haney, "What Is Feminist Ethics? A Proposal for Continuing Discussion," *Journal of Religious Ethics* 8 [Spring 1980], 115–24).

6 Just as H. Richard Niebuhr is credited by Gustafson as having claimed that ethics is reflection upon ethos, when that means that his task is to analyze "ethos," to lay bare the roots and fundamental character of a community's moral life (James Gustafson, "Introduction" to H. Richard Niebuhr, *The Responsible Self* [San Francisco: Harper and Row, 1978], 13), so too might the metaethics of Daly be understood:

I would say that radical feminist metaethics is of a *deeper intuitive* type than "ethics." The latter, generally written from one of several (but basically the same) patriarchal perspectives, works out of hidden agendas concealed in the texture of language, buried in mythic reversals which control "logic" most powerfully because unacknowledged. Thus for theologians and philosophers, Eastern and Western, and particularly for ethicists, woman-identified women do not exist. The metaethics of radical feminism seeks to uncover the background. . . . It is able to do this because our primary concern is *not* male ethics and/or ethicists, but our own Journeying. (*Gyn/Ecology,* 12)

Further considering the mode of decision-making, Gilligan characterizes women's patterns of moral reasoning in terms of an ethic of responsibility: "Sensitivity to the needs of others and the assumption of responsibility for taking care, lead women to attend to voices other than their own and to include in their judgment other points of view. Women's moral weakness, manifest in an apparent diffusion

216

utilitarian theories are teleological, not all teleological theories are subject to the difficulties of utilitarianism. That is, when utilitarianism calculates the greater good, it can be done in such a way as to make minority groups, including women, pay the cost for social policy. There are trends of feminist ethics which view the liberation of women as inclusive of or consistent with the liberation of other oppressed groups, and also of white men.[7]

Source of justification of ethical claims   Some typical sources of ethical claims have traditionally included reference to the revelation of God, tradition, rational reflection, history, or lived experience. When lived experience is the source of ethical claims, further questions must be asked to clarify *whose* experience and under what interpretation. A further issue involves how persons are able to claim objectivity for their ethical sources when cultural, personal, and political perspectives on those claims are significant.

In relation to the various modes of making ethical decisions, it appears unlikely that those using a teleological mode would claim revelation as the source or justification of ethical claims, whereas those using a deontological or relational mode might do so. There is no rigid relation between the various sources and modes. For instance, one might claim natural law as the source for ethical claims and use either a teleological or a deontological mode of making ethical decisions, or justifying them.

Those developing feminist ethical theory are overwhelmingly inclined to refer to lived experience as the source for ethical claims, granting the complexities of this method.[8]

and confusion of judgment, is thus inseparable from women's moral strength, an overriding concern with relationships and responsibilities. The reluctance to judge itself can be indicative of the same care and concern for others that infuses the psychology of women's development ..." (Carol Gilligan, "Woman's Place in Man's Life Cycle," *Harvard Educational Review* 49 [November 1979], 431–46).

7 I am indebted to a March, 1980 discussion within the Consultation on Social Ethics in Feminist Perspective, at Andover-Newton Theological School, Newton Centre, Massachusetts, in which Lisa Cahill made the point that the inclusiveness of ends may distinguish teleological ethics from utilitarian ethics.

8 Lived-world experience, feminist consciousness, "our bodies/ourselves," women's efforts to achieve full recognition as persons—all serve as sources for norms in the work of Beverly Harrison ("The New Consciousness of Women: A Socio-Political Resource," *Cross Currents* [Winter 1975], 445–61, and "Toward a

Presupposition of ethical action, autonomy   The theory with regard to autonomy must necessarily be complex if it is to take seriously both the meaning of ethical propositions as well as behavioral research uncovering the very powerful forces which limit autonomy. While a measure of autonomy is necessary before moral choice can be exercised—and in this sense is an important goal—the notion of the moral agent as dispassionate and disengaged is distinct from the former notion of autonomy, and has come under criticism for its failure to recognize the social foundation of self.

Feminist ethical theory, in general terms, presupposes a criticism of the forces which limit women's autonomy in the ethical realm. In this sense, the economic dependency of women in the family, the inequality of pay and promotion in the labor force tied to women's role as child-bearer and child-rearer, the possibility of sexual harassment or physical abuse from a stranger or an intimate, and further, in psychological terms, the tendency toward lack of ego differentiation in women's personality formation, are all factors impinging upon women's sense of self which can be autonomous confronting or defining ethical situations.[9]

Motivation   How do we view the way ethical action begins and what keeps it going, recognizing that knowledge of what is the right thing to do does not necessarily result in the will to do the right? This is a classical question in the ethical tradition. Developing feminist perspectives bring to light the energy unleashed when women become engaged in collective efforts of self-definition, an energy which overcomes or at least mitigates against the alienation between the will and the right.[10]

To include all these factors in the ethical reasoning process is

Just Social Order," *Journal of Current Social Issues* 15 [Spring 1978], 63–70).

9 In response to this and related issues, Ruth Smith has developed a notion of the social self as moral agent, infra, and Katie G. Cannon is judging the applicability of the autonomous self to survival ethics of black women.

10 Barbara Ehrenreich says that Marxism and feminism are both outlooks which "lead to conclusions which are jarring and disturbing at the same time that they are liberating. There is no way to have a Marxist or feminist outlook and remain a spectator. To understand the reality laid bare by these analyses is to move into action to change it" ("What Is Socialist Feminism?" *New American Working Papers on Socialism and Feminism* [Chicago: National Office, 1978], 3).

significant in itself, as there is not general agreement that the scope of social ethics should be so broadly conceived. While ethicists have proposed schemas including some of these factors, or more factors than these, it has been only recently, in relation to Latin American theologians of liberation, that the analysis of the roots of oppression has been suggested as necessary.[11] In the field of social ethics we have had no trouble viewing "data" as a significant factor in ethical theory. However, *analysis* is the process of organizing data according to a theory which attempts to locate the historical causes of the situation. Some of the most important work impacting ethical reflection on women's experience is explicitly in this area, as I will presently outline.

In addition, there is another reason to broaden the scope of ethics to include this factor alongside the others. It provides a framework in which we can see the way the divergent agendas relate to each other. For instance, the work of Daly, Haney, and Pellauer, emphasizing heretofore ignored data and reversing value systems in which women have no honor, can be seen *in relation to* work which emphasizes sources and justification in ethics, as in Lebacqz and Harrison, or the analysis of the roots of oppression, as in Lenin, Gordon, Ehrenreich, or Vogel, or the method of deciding what is to be done, as in Gilligan.[12]

In sum, to do feminist ethics we need a view of ethics in this broad scope. And in particular, we need to recognize analysis of the roots of oppression as an ethical factor.

DIVERGENT FEMINIST SOCIAL-POLITICAL THEORIES

This discussion should illustrate the value of this scope of the discipline of social ethics. One basis from which all feminists begin

11 Carol S. Robb, "Ethical Procedures of Gutierrez and Alves," in The American Society of Christian Ethics, *Selected Papers*, 1979.

12 See notes 3, 4, 5, and 8. Also Vladimir Lenin, *The Emancipation of Women* (New York: International Publishers, 1978); Linda Gordon and Allen Hunter, "Sex, Family and the New Right: Anti-feminism as a Political Force," *Radical America* 11, 12 (November–February 1978), 9–25; Ehrenreich, "What Is Socialist Feminism?"; Lise Vogel, "Questions On The Woman Question," *Monthly Review* 31 (June 1979), 39–59; and Gilligan, "In a Different Voice: Women's Conceptions of Self and Morality" and "Woman's Place in Man's Life Cycle."

doing social-political theory is by reflecting upon what is happening to women and what it is that women are doing. Our starting point is in our own experience, as that is revealed in women of different races, classes, religions, and nationalities. Socialist feminists in particular have contributed a wonderful way of talking about this in terms of reuniting the personal and the political. To reunite the personal and the political means two things. First, it means that the areas of women's lives heretofore thought to be "private" and "personal"—for instance, her relations to individual men or women—were part of a systematic division of labor between men and women (male supremacy). This division of labor is reinforced by a set of attitudes and ideas (male chauvinism), that serve to justify and maintain this division. The home, for instance, is considered the personal and private domain of a family, and women often exercise what control they have only in the context of the home. Men, on the other hand, have had more control in the public sphere or the market place. "Women's work" is then systematically undervalued. To recognize that the personal is political is a challenge to that equation of women and personal, men and public or political.

Second, if the personal is political, the attempt by women to understand our personal lives within small groups is political. It is a political action for a woman to say what she believes or is coming to believe about her life instead of what she has always been told to say.[13]

In a fundamental way, feminist ethical theory criticizes the alienation of the personal from the political, and seeks both to integrate these aspects of personality and to institutionalize this integration. In order to institutionalize the integration of the personal and the political, however, we need more than the integration of women into the paid labor force, or the proliferation of women's support groups. While these measures heighten women's awareness of the weaknesses in the ideology of male chauvinism, they do not constitute a far-reaching strategy to liberate or emancipate women in the broadest sense. Arriving at such a strategy requires careful attention to the history of women in different societies, an assess-

13 John Judis, "The Personal and Political," *Socialist Revolution* 2 (January–February 1971), 9–29.

ment of the current situation, an analysis of the causal or key factors in the oppression of women, and a program to guide our action together.

What follows are four contemporary social-political analyses of the oppression of women, chosen to illustrate the importance of such analysis for ethics. The major limitation to the following outline of these analyses is that they appear to be mutually exclusive. In fact, women often identify with parts of several of these four descriptions. Nevertheless, they are representative of major feminist political formations which are significant within the women's movement in the U.S. and internationally.

Radical Feminism   One very important perspective is radical feminism.[14] According to the analysis of radical feminism, the roots of women's oppression are very simply *men*. Men have in their makeup some tendencies, say brutishness or weak egos, for instance, which result in goals for social organization which are different from women's. At some historical moments, perhaps different moments in different parts of the populated globe, men overthrew egalitarian social orders and through physical strength consolidated political and economic control. They continue to use that strength to maintain their control.

According to radical feminists, women have their own culture which has not been recognized by the dominant culture since the patriarchal revolt. Women have different aesthetics, priorities, and perceptions. Men have feared, and in their fear reviled, women's culture and therefore have kept women isolated and ignorant of their sisterhood. Daly writes concerning this fear:

> All of the so-called religions legitimating patriarchy are mere sects subsumed under its vast umbrella/canopy. They are essentially similar, despite variations. All—from buddhism and hinduism to islam, judaism, christianity, to secular derivatives such as freudianism, jungianism, marxism, and maoism—are infrastructures of the edifice of patriarchy. All are erected as parts of the male's shelter against anomie.[15]

14 The term "radical feminism" is used here because it is a nomenclature of persons with this perspective. Where there is disagreement with radical feminists about the roots of women's oppression, and hence strategy, there will be reluctance to grant such usage of this term.

15 Daly, *Gyn/Ecology*, 39.

Eventually, according to radical feminist arguments, women will have to take power away from men in order to establish a truly egalitarian society, because egalitarianism is only possible under matriarchy. But for now, women must create our own enclaves to nurture and support each other. By living out in the present the freedom of the future, the revolution will grow *by example* to other women. And if we decide that it will never be worthwhile to reestablish the egalitarian society, at least we have a parallel nation, regardless of the patriarchal order.

According to this analysis, racism, capitalism, and imperialism are results of male supremacy and can only be eliminated by eliminating male supremacy:

> We identify the agents of our oppression as men. Male supremacy is the oldest, most basic form of domination. All other forms of exploitation and oppression (racism, capitalism, imperialism, etc.) are extensions of male supremacy: men dominate women, a few men dominate the rest. . . . Attempts have been made to shift the burden of responsibility from men to institutions or to women themselves. We condemn these arguments as evasions. Institutions alone do not oppress; they are merely tools of the oppressor.[16]

The weakness in this argument is that it does not in itself offer the prospect of dismantling the society that is being criticized. Political program in this view is masculinist. Therefore, the only real option for women who adopt this line is to withdraw from the struggle for liberation for themselves and for other women who can't take the option of withdrawal.

On the other hand, a major insight of this analysis must be taken seriously: the institution and ideology of heterosexuality in its historical development is a cornerstone of male supremacy. As long as the majority of adult women allow themselves to be linked in intimate and emotionally sustaining relationships primarily with men, it will be difficult for us to engage in a long-term struggle to destroy male supremacy.

Though the notion that heterosexuality is a cornerstone of male supremacy is an important notion to be considered and tested,

16 "The Redstocking Manifesto," in *Voices From Women's Liberation*, ed. Leslie B. Tanner (New York: Signet, 1970), 109–10.

another approach may offer the basis for broader political unity: it is not heterosexuality *per se* that must be conquered. Rather, we must target the ideology which limits appropriate sexual expression and relationships to heterosexual ones. In addition, we must dismantle the various material support systems of male supremacy which tie women's economic support to husbands and make child-rearing women's work.

Sex-rolism   A second perspective on women's oppression focuses on the importance of sex roles. A broad base of the population first engages feminist thought through the investigation of the notions of "masculine" and "feminine" as socially-defined role expectations, discovering the extent to which such notions are social constructions, and then identifying feminism with a critical perspective on sex roles.

In its simplest version, this line absolves men from any but psychological responsibility for the oppression of women, and blames it all on "sex-roles" or society. According to this version, the program for change is primarily education, with complementary incremental reforms in schooling practices and workplace/home relationships. Women should learn how to fix automobiles and other machines, and men should learn how to maintain the home. Women should take courses in college that are oriented toward specific careers, and men should take equal responsibility for parenting. Women should practice acting assertively and self-consciously check behaviors reflecting internalized oppression, and men should try to exercise some restraint over their typically domineering and hierarchical interaction patterns.

Clearly, education and incremental reforms do fit into a strategy of changing society and behavior, including sexist behavior. And the attempts at destroying stereotypical sex roles are important for obvious reasons. But this analysis has several weaknesses if it stands by itself. The qualities that sex-rolists say are ascribed to all women are really only ascribed to middle and upper class women. Sarah Small, a campus minister at the University of Massachusetts-Boston, has often said that America creates two kinds of women: those who can't take care of themselves and those who have to. The existence of the second group indicates that sex roles are not the basis of women's oppression, but rather the result of other factors. Sex roles are symptoms of male supremacy, not the cause or the cure.[17]

A second and closely related weakness is that adherents to this perspective never articulate a political program to ensure that all races and classes will benefit from the educational and incremental reforms. They fail to do so because they *assume* that their goals can be achieved by working within constitutional means, given the current political process and the current general view of the rights and responsibilities of individuals. Those who work within these assumptions do not feel the necessity of articulating a political program, because they accept the existing one. While, on the other hand, those who work within the other perspectives have the double burden of articulating their analyses of the roots of oppression and the vision of the new society, sex-role feminists do not perceive the need to envision radically new social-political arrangements.[18]

There is a second and deeper version of this analysis of the roots of the gender system which, while calling for similar programmatic commitments, describes the psychological dynamics of sex-role divisions of labor in the home and public spheres. For example, in attempting to account for demonstrated tendencies for boys to be oriented toward achievement and self-reliance and girls toward nurturance and responsibility, Chodorow and Dinnerstein cite in a somewhat different way the identification process between mother and daughter and the lack of such identification between mother and son as the factor which results in daughters differentiating less, while sons are encouraged to separate and individuate.[19] Therefore, cultural definitions of personality and behavior are not simply taught. The structural situation of child-rearing, wherein women are universally the primary child-rearers, produces these differences.

17 Brooke L. Williams, "What's Wrong With Sex-Rolism," *Feminist Revolution* (Red Stocking, P.O. Box 413, New Paltz, NY 12561).

18 Barbara Hilkert Andolsen contributed this perspective on the political program of sex-rolism at the abovementioned consultation.

19 Nancy Chodorow, "Family Structure and Feminine Personality," in *Woman, Culture and Society*, ed. Michelle Zimbalist Rosaldo and Louise Lamphere (Stanford: Stanford University Press, 1974), 43–56, and Dorothy Dinnerstein, *The Mermaid and the Minotaur* (New York: Harper and Row, 1977).

Women lactate, and for convenience, not biological necessity, mothers, and females in general, have tended to take care of all babies. Social and self-help reforms will not succeed, ultimately, unless there is a shift in the quality of the very early social environment of child-rearing. It is Chodorow's perspective that,

> Daughters and sons must be able to develop a personal identification with more than one adult, and preferably one embedded in a role relationship that gives it a social context of expression and provides some limitation upon it. Most important, boys need to grow up around men who take a major role in child care, and girls around women who, in addition to their child-care responsibilities, have a valued role and recognized spheres of legitimate control. These arrangements could help to ensure that children of both sexes develop a sufficiently individuated and strong sense of self, a well as a positively valued and secure gender identity, that does not bog down either in ego-boundary confusion, low self-esteem, and overwhelming relatedness to others, or in compulsive denial of any connection to others or dependence upon them.[20]

This second version of sex-rolism is explicit in the work of Gilligan, who draws on Chodorow's contributions and concludes that women not only define themselves in a context of human relationship but also judge themselves on their ability to care, while men devalue that care and define moral excellence in terms of male development up to the period of adolescence.[21]

20 Chodorow, "Family Structure and Feminine Personality," 66.

21 To summarize and paraphrase her description of moral patterns in men and women, Gilligan claims that the morality of rights, characteristic of men's moral reasoning, differs from the morality of responsibility, characteristic of women's, in its emphasis on separation rather than attachment, in its consideration of the individual rather than the relationship as primary. When the categories of women's thinking are examined, the moral problem is seen to arise from conflicting responsibilities rather than competing rights and to require for its resolution a mode of thinking which is contextual and inductive rather than formal and abstract. This reconstruction of moral understanding is based not on the primacy of and universality of individual rights, but rather on a very strong sense of being responsible to the world. This orientation focuses on the limitations of any particular resolution and describes the conflicts that remain, whereas the rights conception of morality that informs Kohlberg's principled stages is geared toward arriving at an objectively fair or just resolution to the moral dilemma to which all rational men could agree (Gilligan, "Woman's Place in Man's Life Cycle").

To recapitulate an earlier point, the weakness of both versions of this analysis is that they never ask about the broad social-political conditions, costs, and consequences of restructuring child-rearing practices to allow for the recommended role redefinitions. The contribution of this analysis, however, is to hold up as essentially irrational the basis for the sexual division of labor and for gender-defined behavioral expectations in the current day.

Marxist-Leninist Feminism   The social-political theory of Marxist-Leninist feminism stands within the tradition of Marx, Engels, Lenin, Luxembourg, Zetkin, and Kollontai, all of whom were committed to leading the working class and its allies to overthrow the dictatorship of the bourgeoisie, to establish socialism under the dictatorship of the proletariat, and eventually to achieve communism. This tradition sees private property as the basis of all alienation in the social sphere and thus holds that the struggle for women's rights must be linked with the *principal aim:* the conquest of power and the establishment of the dictatorship of the proletariat. "At present, this is, and will continue to be, our alpha and omega."[22]

Engel's and Marx's writings acknowledge that sexual domination preceded capitalist economic formation. Their documents have historically served as part of the basis for commitment to the liberation of women within the socialist agenda. But it is to Lenin that we look for the manner in which such a commitment took shape in the midst of political struggles for socialism. In his speeches, articles, and conversations, aspects of the woman question, as it is put in this tradition, include the struggle for equal rights under the law, both in bourgeois and socialist countries; freeing women from slavery to the home and small farm (in Russia) because housework is drudgery and degrading, and because when she is isolated under the rule of the father or husband she cannot broaden herself or her view of the world; the politicization of women whose lives have been so dominated, so that, "We say that the emancipation of the workers must be effected by the workers themselves, and in exactly the same way the emancipation of working women is a matter for the working

---

22 Lenin, *The Emancipation of Women,* 113.

women themselves."[23] Other aspects involve drawing women into various social spheres, such as social production, the administration of socialized enterprises, and of the state, as well as the reconstruction of the economy and of sexist ideology[24]:

> We demonstrate thereby that we are aware of these needs and of the oppression of women, that we are conscious of the privileged position of the men, and that we hate—yes, hate—and want to remove whatever oppresses and harasses the working women, the wife of the worker, the peasant woman, the wife of the little man, and even in many respects the woman of the propertied classes.[25]

The implementation of these measures requires a mass movement of women before, during, and after seizing state power, and Lenin encouraged systematic political work among women. He inveighed against separate organizations of communist women, but declared that within the Party there must be organs—working groups, commissions, and committees with the special purpose of rousing the broad masses of women and integrating them into political work under the influence of the Party.

But the relationship between revolutionary struggle and feminist organizing is not simple. An exchange between Lenin and Zetkin gives some indication of the historical importance of the woman question in revolutionary Europe. When Zetkin organized evening study groups for women in Germany, Lenin called her to account why she was focusing on sex and marriage problems as main objects of interest in her political and educational work. She defended her work, saying that knowledge of the historical modifications of the forms of marriage and family and their dependence on economics was important in politicizing women. Such knowledge served to rid women's minds of the notion that bourgeois society structured marriage and family along natural and eternal lines. Lenin's concern was that Zetkin was treating sex and marriage problems as the *main* social problem, rather than as *part* of the main social problem. One of the ongoing issues for Marxist-Leninist feminists is how to acknowledge that "sex and marriage problems" are part of

23 Lenin, *The Emancipation of Women,* 70.
24 Lenin, *The Emancipation of Women,* 112.
25 Lenin, *The Emancipation of Women,* 110.

the main social problem—the dominance of industrial monopoly capital—without implying that they are *secondary* issues.

Lenin perceived the broad-ranging character of the woman question, though the politics of sexuality were not developed either in his own thinking or in western thought in general in the early part of the twentieth century.[26] Lenin was aware of sexuality as a political issue. He characterized bourgeois marriage and legislation on the family as perverse, because they treated women as property and thus gave license to forms of violence against women. Communism would not, should not breed asceticism, but rather "joy and strength, stemming among other things from a consummate love life."[27] He was distressed that some of the communist youth subscribed to the theory that satisfying sexual needs was as simple as taking a drink of water. But he recognized that new sexual values in keeping with the proletarian revolution were being formed, and that the process was a part of the liberation of women.

The distinctiveness of feminism within the context of Leninism is that it poses the need for a Marxist-Leninist party organized according to the principles of democratic centralism, and engaged in building a mass political base to seize state power, as the prerequisite for the liberation of women. The major weakness of this analysis is that it has not sufficiently grasped and criticized the way that democratic centralism became *bureaucratic* centralism in the history of major Marxist-Leninist parties, the Communist Party of the U.S.A. and the Communist Party of the Soviet Union. The past practices of the socialist movements with regard to women's leadership and commitment to women's issues do not warrant our trust in the context of bureaucratic leadership—a leadership that has historically been shown to be insensitive to the concerns and the wisdom of the base.

The strength of this analysis is that it is the most clear of all those presented herein about the implications of the demands of feminism for social reorganization.

---

26 Sheila Rowbotham, *Women, Resistance and Revolution* (New York: Vintage, 1974), 107.

27 Lenin, *The Emancipation of Women*, 107.

Socialist Feminism   Socialist feminism stands in the tradition of socialist struggles, but criticizes this tradition for not being able to account for the reality of patriarchy, the near universal domination of men over women, existing in all societies regardless of economic organization. The criticism is aimed at two aspects of socialism: the practice of socialists which often reflects the sexism of the surrounding society; and the theory of Marxism, which is unable to account for relations within the mode of reproduction (sexuality, home, family) or the deep significance of sexuality in the formation of human social relations.[28]

Socialist feminists build on the radical feminist empirical data regarding male supremacy. But they criticize radical feminists for having a nonhistorical understanding of what patriarchy is, equating the effects of male supremacy across cultures and across historical eras, and not making qualitative distinctions between female infanticide and under-representation on the central committee.[29]

In general terms, socialist feminism is not a uniform theory with consistency in its formulations. Theorists ally themselves with that trend within Marxist theory which emphasizes the connections between culture, politics, and the economic base, with attendant organizing implications, and oppose that trend which emphasizes the primacy of workplace organizing on economic issues. This is a strength in their perspective. A weakness, however, is that when socialist feminists criticize leftist theory and practice, mechanical Marxism, or economism, their criticisms are rarely linked closely to texts or events. Thus, it is difficult to assess their criticisms.

The distinction between socialist feminism and mechanical Marxism is described by advocates of the former in terms of their intent to transform the sphere of reproduction as well as the sphere of production. Rather than collapse the issues involved in reproduction—family, child-rearing, socialization, cooking, housework—into a category of relations which will *automatically* change after the control of the productive forces has passed to the proletariat, socialist feminists contend that they should be bases for organizing in the

28 Holly Graff, "The Oppression of Women," *New American Working Papers on Socialism and Feminism*, 32.
29 Ehrenreich, "What Is Socialist Feminism?" 5.

Carol S. Robb

working class now. Since the rise of monopoly industrial capitalism, these issues together with sexuality have become the last domain of control of workers, who have lost control over the productive or public sphere. Zaretsky, who has developed this aspect of the "personal is political" slogan, theoretically dates this split as a process that took most of the nineteenth century and culminated around 1900.

> With the rise of corporate capitalism the family became the major institution in society given over to the personal needs of its members. Within it new needs began to take shape: for intimacy, self-understanding and emotional connection. ... A special concern for personal life has been called a "petit bourgeois" or "middle-class" preoccupation, but in fact it is only with the full scale development of a proletariat that we can truly speak of personal life in the modern sense.[30]

The implication of Zaretsky's analysis is that "the personal is political" should not be seen as an addition to a Marxism *manqué*. Rather it should be seen as a reflection of historical developments within industrial capitalism, which we are compelled to understand and compute into our political theory and organizing, *using* the theory and method of historical materialism.

What this means for organizational structure, however, is unclear; for socialist feminists, while claiming that a socialist revolution is a necessary though not sufficient condition for the liberation of women (with which Marxist-Leninist feminists would agree), do not advocate party-building in Leninist perspective. Political formations tend to be described as autonomous groups, characterized by democracy, consensus decision-making, but not democratic centralism. Just how autonomous groups of women, blacks, gays, lesbians, poor people, and the elderly will relate to each other in mass-based political struggle to make a revolution is not made explicit in socialist feminist documents, and this unclarity is another weakness.

Mitchell and Rowbotham are theorists of some import for the development of early socialist feminist theory.[31] Mitchell put for-

---

30 Eli Zaretsky, "Socialist Politics and the Family," *New American Working Papers on Socialism and Feminism*, 17.
31 Juliet Mitchell, *Woman's Estate* (New York: Vintage Books, 1971) and Rowbotham, *Women, Resistance and Revolution.*

230

ward the view that women are oppressed in terms of their roles in production, reproduction, socialization, and sexuality, and that any program which does not address all these aspects will not fully liberate women. Because such views do not clearly identify the primary contradiction with women's liberation, their adherents lend only qualified support to socialist programs and organizations.

Rowbotham is credited with having reviewed much of the history of women's struggles within socialist struggles in Britain and Europe. Her work underlines the necessity of maintaining a strong women's movement within socialist organizing efforts as well as in socialist countries after revolutions. She is critical of feminist movements which do not have a social commitment.

CONCLUSION

In the preceding discussion, my purpose was to indicate why the term "feminist ethics" does not by itself indicate the content of feminist ethical theory. Indeed, there are at least four different social-political theories and programs which could provide a foundation for feminist ethics. However, the analysis of the roots of oppression is a key factor in feminist ethics. It has a direct bearing on the way we pose problems, gather data, commit our loyalties, rank values, engage in moral reasoning, justify claims, structure autonomy, and heighten motivation. Some examples might point to the validity of the exercise.

I made the point earlier that feminist ethicists generally agree that the appropriate starting point for ethical reflection is to attend to the very concrete situations, the fabric of women's lives. But just as few ethicists use the inductive mode at the expense of the deductive mode, feminists take into their reflection some assumptions which affect how they define the problem. Consequently, one can compare a radical feminist way of posing the problem, "In what ways are problematic situations the results of patriarchal control?" to a sex-rolist approach, "Is this a problem for both women and men, or do the conditions which resolve it apply equally for women and men?" A socialist feminist approach might look for concrete ways in which race and sexual dynamics benefit the owners of capital in the situation, and Marxist-Leninist feminists would probably share this starting point. Thus, at a fundamental level, the analysis of women's oppression affects the way the problem is posed.

Again, earlier I made the point that feminist ethicists have a loyalty to women *as women*, but that there is not across-the-board agreement as to how this loyalty relates to loyalties to other oppressed groups. Hence, the loyalties of radical feminists are to women, and perhaps even to radical feminist women, whereas the loyalties of sex-rolists are to all people, in the vision of situation-specific behaviors rather than sex-defined behaviors. Marxist-Leninist feminists have loyalties to women and men in the working class, and to all groups exploited by capital, as well as to those women and men who swing in their class allegiance toward the working class, thereby committing class suicide. Socialist feminists, because of a class analysis which views many professionals and white-collar workers as working class, would view their loyalties in similar but broader terms than Marxist-Leninist feminists.

Values take on new meaning when they are defined in terms of the different political theories. "Control over our own bodies" can evoke images of the petit bourgeoisie, a class of individualists, in light of a Marxist-Leninist feminist position on reproductive rights. On the other hand, reproductive rights as democratic rights needed by working class women to participate in the revolutionary struggle can sound like a mask of male hegemony in the context of a socialist feminist or a radical feminist perspective.

Yet there is no necessary disagreement among feminists about a value theory. Self-determination for women, autonomy, and an inviolable sense of embodiedness figure prominently in all feminists' visions of a new social order. There might be disagreement, however, on the understanding about why to articulate a feminist value theory, which would determine the weight it is given. Ethicists who have integrated an historical materialist worldview are likely to articulate a feminist value theory as one task to be accomplished in addition to other, more social-structural tasks. It could be that ethicists who do not operate with an historical materialist worldview project the reordering of values as primary among the tasks involved in creating new structures for social relations. This thesis explains in some measure the emphasis given to value theory among radical feminists and sex-role theorists. However, some sex-role theorists actually place more emphasis on restructuring the institutions of family and school than socialist or Marxist-Leninist feminists. Since the sex-role theorists do not face the task of restructuring the economic and political relations, they can attend to and focus on a limited range of institutions.

In the radical feminist perspective, motivation to ethical activity is a function of coming to awareness of being female in a woman-hating culture. In sex-rolism, motivation is the result of having insight as to all the levels of experience which have been defined as socially inappropriate by virtue of an irrational factor, gender. Socialist feminism and Marxist-Leninist feminism acknowledge a motivation of commitment to justice for all victims of private property, even if one has race, class, or sex privilege.

And so on. These paragraphs should be suggestive of further possibilities in connecting the analysis of the roots of oppression to other factors in ethical theory. The emphasis on the role of this factor in feminist ethics reflects two things: first, that social-political theory contains a broad range of ethical factors, and, second, that ethicists, in the narrow sense of this term, do have social-political analyses, often unacknowledged.

By implication, ethicists are accountable to make clear their analyses of the roots of oppression, so that they can be held accountable for adequacy to the full range of data. In so doing we are broadening the range of accountability for attending to such analyses in two directions: to all ethicists, insofar as their work is in any way related to the social sphere; and to claims for adequacy to women regardless of race and class. In the context of such claims we can sense that the discipline of social ethics is full of possibilities for people seeking to take control of their lives in the midst of community formation.

16

Feminism and the Moral Subject

Ruth L. Smith

INTRODUCTION

In this essay I will present some of the challenges which the feminist movement and feminist theory pose to traditional moral theory. The focus of my discussion will be the moral subject. While it does not always receive direct attention by theorists, the moral subject is one of the fundamental assumptions in moral history. This concept is particularly significant because it carries with it assumptions about human nature or ontology, that is, about how human beings are constituted and what in this constitution is relevant for the moral life.

The question of ontology or individuality has been central in contemporary feminist thought. However, at this point there is no general feminist theory of individuality just as there is no general feminist theory of society. Nor is it clear precisely what form such theories might take given the transdisciplinary character of feminist theory and given the variance and, at points, conflict among the several feminist perspectives.[1] This conflict includes the definitions of the problem and the social, economic, and political goals seen to be necessary for its solution. It includes the concerns among women across different races and classes.

---

1 For a discussion outlining the different feminist perspectives see Carol S. Robb, "A Framework for Feminist Ethics," supra.

Nevertheless, one can see some common directions and perspectives in feminist thinking about the individual. Generally, feminist perspectives involve the claim that the individual is social or relational. To say that the individual is social or relational means that the relations and groups of which we are part are in some sense constitutive of individuality itself. Such relations are not just an environment external to the individual. This notion of individuality is in contrast to the notion of individuality which has been dominant in the historical period of liberalism and in the moral theory of that period. From this perspective the individual is defined as a separable discrete entity whose fundamental constitution exists apart from all social-historical relations. In moral theory the hallmark of this form of individuality is characterized by the term "autonomy."

The focus on autonomy means that the qualities relevant and necessary for the moral life and the process of moral choice are qualities that 1) inhere in the individual as a discrete self-contained entity and that 2) can only be exercised in their full power when the individual removes her- or himself from all relations of social-historical life. These relations include our institutional and structural relations in society, our direct relations with other people, and our self-relation with regard to aspects like race, gender, and economic class.

In the following pages I will explore the notion of autonomous individuality in moral theory. I will then summarize certain feminist views of individuality and discuss the implications of these views for moral theory. In this essay I will not present a fully developed feminist concept of individuality or of the moral subject.

AUTONOMY AND MORAL AGENCY

The notion of autonomy as a concept of individuality and moral agency takes its modern form from both the historical development of western society and the influence of Enlightenment philosophy. As an historical phenomenon it involves the development of bourgeois society out of feudal society and the concomitant shift in notions of individuality. Feudal society was structured hierarchically. One's position was fixed by birth and this position set the terms by which one participated in social life. Individuals had clusters of rights by virtue of their membership in a particular class. The individual was classified as a type according to that particular set of social relations of which he or she was a part.[2]

In bourgeois society the individual is, in principle, no longer defined by those relations which place one in the social hierarchy as in feudal society. Participation in the affairs of the world is not fixed, permanently prescribed by birth. Such particularities of relationship are seen as accidental and external. Real individuality is defined apart from such relations, which are from this perspective seen as fetters.

The accounting of bourgeois social relations in bourgeois thought is in terms of contract theory. The contract theorists of the seventeenth and eighteenth centuries struggled in different ways with the problem of cohesion in a society of individual peers. The development of contractual relations and contract theory itself provided, in theory, a form of relationship among equals. However, this society of equals and the theoretical account of it limit the notions of any form of collective life to external relations which are contingent and have no primary, intrinsic value. Individuality is defined apart from group life. Social-historical relations appear as a context or an environment for the individual but not as defining or prescribing. This environment may even enhance individuality but it is not seen as a part of the constitution of individuality itself.

The notion of autonomy has its most definitive philosophical statement in the thought of Immanuel Kant. Kant defines the individual as a knowing subject who, by constitution, stands apart from the world of empirical contingency. This subject is formal and universal. In this way the freedom of the subject in relation to self-determination and responsibility is upheld in contrast to the determinism of nature. We can be held morally responsible only for choices made, acts committed, under conditions of freedom. Freedom in this sense is a transcendental inner state of the human being and must be distinguished from the various factors of our particularity. These factors of historical circumstance and of social condi-

2 For a discussion of this point see Ernst Troeltsch, *The Social Teaching of the Christian Churches* 2, trans. Olive Wyon (New York: Harper and Brothers, 1960), 540.

tions are contingent and have the status of natural phenomena. That is, their movement and effect is considered to be mechanistically deterministic. The subject of moral activity is identified with and by moral freedom and the will and reason to enact it. The subject in Kant has no other essential identifying features. In the *Critique of Pure Reason*[3] the subject is defined as the transcendental ego, and in the *Critique of Practical Reason*[4] this notion is represented by the self as legislative will.

The influence of this view of the individual and the moral subject has been continuous since the Enlightenment. The assumptions about the individual as a formal entity autonomous of social and historical relations are evident in philosophical ethics, for example, in the ideal observer theory of Roderick Firth in which the moral individual assumes a posture of omniscience.[5] The Kantian assumptions are also evident in John Rawl's theory of the original position. In the original position the moral individuals do not know what characteristics apply to them and thus what the consequences would be for them should a particular decision be made one way or the other.[6] From either Firth's or Rawl's view, the moral actor must separate her- or himself from all social and historical relations in order to achieve the rationality and objectivity necessary for a moral decision. Such relations are seen not only as an impediment to moral judgment but as separable from and an encroachment on the "real individual," and it is this "real individual" who is the moral subject.

In Christian ethics the questions of human anthropology and moral agency are taken up by H. Richard Niebuhr and Reinhold Niebuhr. While each of these thinkers develops the issues differently, each remains influenced by neo-Kantianism. H. Richard Niebuhr attempts to develop a view of the self as social and historical. In *The Meaning of Revelation* he explores the significance of this perspective for the claims of religious faith and

3 Immanuel Kant, *Critique of Pure Reason,* trans. Norman Kemp Smith (New York: St. Martin's Press, 1965).

4 Immanuel Kant, *Critique of Practical Reason,* trans. Lewis White Beck (Indianapolis: Bobbs-Merrill, 1956).

5 Roderick Firth, "Ethical Absolutism and the Ideal Observer," *Philosophy and Phenomenological Research* XII (1952), 317–45.

6 John Rawls, *A Theory of Justice* (Cambridge: Harvard University Press, 1971).

theology.[7] In *The Responsible Self* he explores the significance of the socialness of the individual for a phenomenology of the moral life.[8] Niebuhr defines the self as follows:

> To say the self is social is not to say that it finds itself in need of fellow men in order to achieve its purposes, but that it is born in the womb of society as a sentient, thinking, needful being with certain definitions of its need and with the possibility of experience of a common world. It is born in society as a mind and as moral being, but above all it is born in society as self.[9]

Thus, Niebuhr emphasizes the fundamentally social nature of the self in a way that has yet to be integrated into ethics.

However, apart from the fact that he was not able to complete his work, several problems remain. Theologically, the concept of the relational or social self is not reconciled with the Calvinist view of the majesty and remoteness of God. Further, in his distinction between inner and outer history H. R. Niebuhr preserves the Kantian conceptuality of a world posited apart (outer history) from the factors of subjectivity and historical particularity: "Events may be regarded from the outside by a non-participating observer; then they belong to the history of *things*"[10] (my emphasis). He does not recognize that both objective and subjective factors are present in both the "inner" and "outer" worlds. Further, the meaning of the term "social" is not sufficiently considered in its historical and political content. The reality to which this term refers remains undefined. The problems of historically particular social selves amidst particular social arrangements are not considered, a problem also in George Herbert Mead on whom Niebuhr draws.[11]

Reinhold Niebuhr argues for a biblically based anthropology which takes seriously both the human capacity for reason and self-transcendence and the limitations of human sinfulness.[12] He argues

7 H. Richard Niebuhr, *The Meaning of Revelation* (London: The MacMillan Company, 1941).

8 H. Richard Niebuhr, *The Responsible Self* (New York: Harper and Row, 1963).

9 Niebuhr, *The Responsible Self*, 73.

10 Niebuhr, *Meaning of Revelation*, 47.

11 For a discussion of these issues in Mead, see Ray Holland, *Self and Social Context* (New York: St. Martin's Press, 1977), 26–30.

12 Reinhold Niebuhr, *The Nature and Destiny of Man* 1 (New York: Charles

this position against modern views of the self which are optimistic in their assessment of human reason (idealists and liberals) and against those views which are reductionistic in their assessment (naturalists). Niebuhr puts forth a "unified view" of the individual which embraces the aspects of both nature and spirit. While these aspects cannot, in Niebuhr's terms, be neatly separated, nature refers to our embeddedness in time, the particularities of historical existence such as language, race, gender, and to our social or collective (group) relations. Spirit refers to our capacity for reason and self-transcendence and for what Niebuhr calls "our transcendence to a world beyond time."[13]

The consequences of Reinhold Niebuhr's view for moral agency is the bifurcation of individual and collective morality. Individuals are creatures of self-interest and the will-to-power, but are also distinguished by their capacity for reason and transcendence. Further, in the intimate relations of the private sphere, individuals may achieve a level of morality higher than that possible for collectives. Niebuhr puts it this way: "In every human group there is less reason to guide and to check impulse, less capacity for self-transcendence, less ability to comprehend the needs of others and therefore more unrestrained egoism than the individuals, who compose the group, reveal in their personal relationships."[14]

Niebuhr's analysis of human nature and moral agency is extended to an analysis of political life. In this sense he gives serious attention to social-historical relations. However, this attention remains limited to political relations as defined by interest, power, and the balance of power. Other forms of social relations are not addressed. Niebuhr also recognizes the Christian value of community. However, the notion of community remains residual. It is not analytically developed and integrated into his theory.

Not only is Reinhold Niebuhr's analysis of social relations limited, but his analysis of the individual involves the basic assumptions of the autonomous perspective. The division of nature and spirit rep-

Scribner's Sons, 1940), 27.

13 Reinhold Niebuhr, *The Self and the Dramas of History* (New York: Charles Scribner's Sons, 1955), 239.

14 Reinhold Niebuhr, *Moral Man and Immoral Society* (New York: Charles Scribner's Sons, 1932), xi, xii.

licates the Kantian distinction between the empirical contingency of relations in time and the transcendental ego which exists beyond them. This separation is evident in his argument that higher morality is associated with individuals who are free and transcendent of social relations. Social relations are part of the individual as a social being but this is only an outer layer which remains outside the "real individual." Niebuhr's analysis, however powerful at points, illustrates the fact that the consideration of social issues does not necessarily provide a theory of the socio-historical nature of the individual and the moral agent.[15]

I do not attribute a stark individualism bereft of concern for others and for society at large to the constructions of agency outlined here. At issue instead is the particular orientation of their social thought and their assumptions about human nature as they relate to individuality and the moral subject.

AUTONOMY, SOCIALITY, AND FEMINISM

Before discussing sociality and feminism I will comment on the notion of autonomy and feminism. Certain aspects of the idea of autonomy have been an important part of the claims of the feminist movement. These claims have included particular rights, for example, equal opportunities in the work place, equal pay for equal work, health care, and legalized abortion. The notion of autonomy has also included related but more general claims about the power of selfhood and its social expression in self-determination, self-realization and becoming the subject of one's own history. The particular form these claims take depends on the particular feminist perspective and analysis, as noted earlier.

Within liberal feminism the expressions of autonomy are tied to the social and political goals of equality of opportunity, individual freedom, and increased individual rights for the exercise of choice and self-realization. Within cultural or radical feminism the notion of autonomy refers to the feminist movement itself. That is, feminist self-social transformation is to be achieved through the development

15 For a more extensive discussion of these aspects of Niebuhr see Ruth Smith, *The Individual and Society in Reinhold Niebuhr and Karl Marx* (Ann Arbor: University Microfilms, 1982), dissertation, Boston University.

of a separate (autonomous) feminist culture. It is to be autonomous of all patriarchal vestiges for only in this way can the evils of patriarchy be overcome.

The perspectives of feminist groups politically identified on the left are distinctive as between socialist feminists and Marxist-Leninists. Feminists of the left criticize autonomy as a part of the ideology of bourgeois culture, the class structure, and the liberal individualism of social programs based solely on personal liberty and individual choice. However, these feminists are also interested in a type of autonomy which refers to the significance of women as subjects of their own identity and decision making, not that derived from men. As a consequence, women's issues and analysis must be given space in the political analysis of the left.

At this point it appears that the stress on autonomy in feminism renders invalid my earlier claim that the idea of sociality is central. Certainly its various meanings and the use of the term itself need further theoretical attention within and across the various perspectives. That is not the task of this paper. However, even in liberal feminism in which the notion of autonomy is most closely tied to its classical assumptions, the notion of individuality and social relations pushes beyond the liberal view, a point to which I will return. Here I will simply note that at no point is the autonomous individual in its classical form fully intact within feminism.

Having raised the issue of sociality in the feminist movement, it is appropriate to look more closely at the meaning and significance of this issue. I will identify several aspects of particular significance for ethical theory: the meaning of the group, explorations of gender and socio-psychological development, and relations and ontology.

Perhaps the most concrete and immediate referent of sociality is the value and meaning of the group. The significance of the group in feminism is not just a theoretical proposition but is more primarily a statement of the experience of the movement as a movement. In this context the group is the unit of consciousness raising, of hearing and speaking a new self-relation and relation to others into being. For many women this group is not just an association but is a community of people with shared problems, goals, and language as well as an experience of collective work and collective power relations.

Certainly there were and are serious limitations to this experience of the movement, most notably in its predominantly white middle- and upper-class membership and definition of problems and needs. Further, a seamless view of community can develop which may attempt to absorb rather than face conflicts within it. Nonetheless, this experience of the movement in which social goals are deeply intertwined with self redefinition provides an impetus for social criticism and for envisioning alternative social relations.

It is also through the experience of the movement that many women come to understand that relations among women are not just casual and private. Women constitute a group that is public and political. It is at this point that liberal feminism itself pushes beyond the liberal tradition. Within the liberal tradition we exist and have political significance only as individuals, as citizens, not as classes of people based on any "accidental" characteristics. Thus liberalism can only account for exclusion on an individual, not a class basis. Yet liberal feminists recognize that women are not excluded as individuals but as a class. In tracing the history of liberal feminism, Zillah Eisenstein makes this point: "Liberal feminism is not feminism merely added onto liberalism. . . . Early feminists argued for the individual rights of woman on the basis that she was excluded from citizens' rights as a member of a sexual class."[16] Thus sociality in this context refers to the awareness of women as a sexual class as well as to the value of the group as a source of consciousness, language, and community.

A second aspect of sociality can be seen in research which examines the construction of selfhood in psychological terms. Here perhaps the more accurate term is "relational." The term "relational" expresses the idea that women not only place primary value on relationships but that the egos and personalities of women are themselves constructed in terms of relations. This mode is distinct from the ego structure of men which is constructed in terms of objects.

The development of personality in men and women is discussed by Nancy Chodorow in the language of ego boundaries. Male

---

16 Zillah Eisenstein, *The Radical Future of Liberal Feminism* (New York: Longman, 1981), 6.

identity develops in relation to the father and is "positional." Female identity develops primarily in relation to the mother and is "diffuse."[17] This distinction involves socialization but within the framework of the experience of motherhood, childcare, and the consequent experiences of male and female children with each parent. The formation of gender personality results in a different mode of being in the world for males and females. The female mode is marked by a communal or participatory sense of self within the relations of the world while the male mode is marked by agency or action upon the world as an object to be mastered and controlled by the lone, isolated self.[18]

The distinction between male and female modes is explored by Carol Gilligan in an analysis of the stages of the moral development of women.[19] She ties the male sense of self as discrete with the moral concept of right. The female relational self is tied to the moral concept of responsibility. Gilligan analyzes women's accounts of their decision-making processes in terms of the connection between the growth of self identity and the perception of what responsibility entails. In this way she seeks to broaden and critique Kohlberg's work in the stage theory of moral development.

In this paper I will not give full consideration to an analysis of these views, but only concentrate on two issues. The first pertains to Gilligan and involves the issue of the character of morality, both as knowing and acting. While she attempts to expand Kohlberg, here it takes the form of being Kohlberg plus. Gilligan does not address fundamental issues in the whole project of stage theory. She does not address the assumption in Kohlberg that morality can be equated with rational facility of a certain sort, that morality is to be equated with an abstract rational calculus which stands above as a measure of moral action.[20] Nor does she examine the historical character of the

17 Nancy Chodorow, "Family Structure and Feminine Personality," *Woman, Culture, and Society,* ed. Michele Zimbalist Rosaldo and Louise Lamphere (Stanford University Press, 1974), 49.

18 Chodorow, "Family Structure and Feminine Personality," 56.

19 Carol Gilligan, *In a Different Voice* (Cambridge, MA: Harvard University Press, 1982).

20 For a discussion of this point see Debra Nails, "Social Scientific Sexism: Gilligan and the Mismeasure of Man," *Social Research* 50 (1983), 643–64.

view of individuality implied, either of the autonomous individual of Kohlberg or of her own notion. This point brings me to the second issue which relates more generally to the relational perspective.

While the authors mentioned above all note the force of socialization, the consideration of its force is not primarily historical. The term "relational" refers to the internal structure of the female self. While this structure develops in response to learned behavior (socialization), the learning too easily assumes the status of biology, that is, it is in the structure of things with no particular historical identity. The interaction of the relations in which the ego is constructed with other aspects of social relations such as race and economic class is not examined.

Further, the experience of motherhood or childhood becomes not only primary but isolated as an experience. The political structure of these experiences in our society is not examined nor are other experiences in the history of the individual seen to interact or compete with them to any significant extent. The value of this research on the important and complex problems of ego construction, gender, and socialization can only be enriched when better integrated with their historical, political, and economic contexts.

The third cluster of issues regarding sociality directly involves the character of ontology or human nature. This idea is perhaps best exemplified in the work of Mary Daly. Daly, one of the articulators of the radical or cultural feminist perspective, places the phenomenon of being at the center of feminism. The centrality of being is grounded in the foundations of language and of life itself: "*Be-ing* is the verb that says the dimensions of depth in all verbs, such as intuiting, reasoning, loving, imagining, making, acting, as well as the couraging, hoping, and playing that are always there when one is really living."[21]

Feminism itself is "a new mode of being."[22] This mode is not to be understood in static terms but as a process. Be-ing is becoming. The becoming of women is at the center of the liberation process. The notion of selfhood as a process, or "I" as a verb, stands in critical

21 Mary Daly, *The Church and the Second Sex* (New York: Harper and Row, 1975), 49.
22 Mary Daly, *Beyond God the Father* (Boston: Beacon Press, 1973), 113.

distinction to the autonomous self, which as a completed formal entity does not essentially change through time. Daly does not appear to extend this possibility to men, however. Thus, it appears that patriarchy is an inherent evil not separable from "the patriarchs" themselves and that the ontology of men and women differs.

A second aspect of Daly's ontological construct is that it is communal. The transformation of the "I" takes place within the liberating relations of sisterhood even as these relations are themselves created.[23] The group is not simply an instrument for the realization of individuality but is significant for the formation and re-formation of individuality itself. Again, this point is distinct from the autonomous perspective in which social relations are not part of one's essential individuality. In this context it is recognized concretely that we not only come to know ourselves in relation to others but that we come *to be* in relation to others.

Daly develops the feminist notion of the subject as a process and as communal as against the view of the subject as static and individualistic. However, her mythic, cultural approach neglects a third aspect of ontology which is more continuous with the socialist and Marxist perspectives, that of the historical aspect of human nature. In the latter perspectives it is recognized that we are changing and that we are intrinsically social, but that change and sociality take place in relation to the historical processes of a particular time and place. Daly's ontology lacks a historical dimension which would analyze the subject within concrete historical experiences.

SOCIALITY AND MORAL AGENCY

At the beginning of this essay I noted that for Kant autonomy signifies two aspects which become foundational for subsequent moral theory. First, the moral subject is autonomous of all social and historical relations. This autonomy is a necessary condition for the second aspect, the autonomy of the will in the application of rational principles to moral dilemmas. This view has three consequences for the understanding of human nature. 1) Essential human nature is separable and defined apart from social-historical relations. 2) While

23 Daly, *Beyond God the Father*, 155.

246

moral reasoning is distinguished by the primacy of the will, rationality remains the attribute of human nature most relevant for morality. 3) The moral subject is formal and as such is abstract and appears to be without limits within the sphere of moral deliberation. Philosopher Robert Paul Wolfe speaks to this issue in a discussion of his struggle with the classical liberal model. He describes the perspective of Bentham (prudential agency) and Kant (moral agency) and responds from his own biography.

> In both accounts of rational agency—the prudential and the moral—man is portrayed as not essentially located in a time, a place, a culture, or a history. The limitations of his will and the constraints of his body are seen as accidental to his nature as a moral and a political being.[24]

> (However) I am not a person who just happens accidentally and irrelevantly, to be a man, forty years old, the husband of a professor of English literature, the son of two aging and sick parents, the father of two small boys six and four, a comfortably well-off member of the upper middle class, American-Jewish, born and raised in New York. I am *essentially* such a man.[25]

Thus Wolfe expresses the important point that moral deliberation necessarily occurs in individuals who are a confluence of socio-historical elements. I will now consider the aspects of social relations, rationality, and formalness in relation to feminism.

To view essential moral human nature as separable from social relations is *a priori* to relegate social relations to a lesser moral status and is to view society as only a collection of autonomous agents. The relations which would in fact constitute a community remain external to the individual and to the society itself. In this way, community, often the expressed goal of moral theories, is contradicted in the social theory and assumptions which many ethicists employ. This problem can be seen in Reinhold Niebuhr's claim that the morality of individuals is inherently higher than that of groups.

In the first instance, such a view ignores the significance of culture

24 Robert Paul Wolfe, "There's Nobody Here but Us Persons," in *Women and Philosophy*, ed. Carol C. Gould and Marx Wartofsky (New York: G. P. Putnam's Sons, 1976), 130.
25 Wolfe, "There's Nobody Here but Us Persons," 136–37.

and social relations in the process of becoming human. But such an assumption also renders moral theory unable to account for the alternative experience in which groups themselves improve the morality of the individual. For many women the feminist movement provides an example of this alternative experience in which the group is a context for the development of a critical social analysis, of accountability of women to other women, and of moral agency itself. Moral theorists need to account for the moral efficacy of group behavior.

The aspect of human nature which is morally significant in the autonomous individual is rationality. Rationality refers to the application of principles in choosing means toward ends. Social relations are an impediment to this process because they are a source of self-interest and of particularity. Thus, this form of rationality entails the objectivity of nonparticularity. The moral vantage point is theoretically one of nonlimitation, of omniscience. While I will not provide a lengthy critique of this position, it is important to note that this view works with a very limited conception of human nature. Further, it assumes that 1) in moral deliberation we become creatures without limits; 2) human rationality and objectivity are not themselves social and historical; 3) we are detached spectators of life rather than embodied participants in life.

In feminist literature we see the development of a view of human nature different from the one used in traditional moral theory. In turn, the feminist view of human nature implies a different moral theory. The moral perspective is not one of detachment because we are not detached. We are attached in nature and in history. We are not social in general but in specific historical ways, ways which make our rationality and our moral freedom not *a priori* givens but problems to be struggled with within the social structure of relations and within the relations of our identity as subjects.

From the feminist perspective moral knowing and acting are part of and informed by the entirety of our experience. Morality involves not just particular choices but the whole context of choice, including the question of whether some choices should even have to be made at all or of whether new possibilities of choice should not be created. The decision about how to feed a family on an inadequate welfare income is a moral decision about survival but it is a decision which should not have to be made at all. Agency involves responding to the needs, responsibilities, and choices within the constraints of our experiences and situations. Agency also involves the changing historical conditions of our particular nexus of relations and the critical self-consciousness and activity through which we become aware of our relations and seek to change them. Morality then involves not only the application of principles in conscience but also, and more broadly, consciousness.

At least since Kant it has been assumed that ethical theory needs a concept of the generic self to function as theory at all. The generic self is formal and universal, having no particular attributes of its own. Like the citizens of the political sphere, all moral agents are alike as agents. On one level, if agency is understood only in formal terms, we are all agents. But in fact, on that basis, only some can be agents. Like the formal equality of the citizen, the formal equality of agency masks real and significant differences. The inner capacity for choice as a property of the human being is too easily equated with actual historical freedom.

Nonetheless, the universalistic dimension of agency in Kant cannot be easily dismissed. If our ontology has no universal aspect then we have lost a fundamental source of moral appeal and we have ignored our nature as a human species and our global interdependence. The full contours of what the concept of universality would involve in an historical ontology are not developed in this paper, but it would not be the universality of the omniscient rational spectator who stands behind all particular experiences and actions. It would not be formal but concrete, which means it would have to recognize conflict as well as harmony in social relations. Nor would all agents look alike. The particularity of agency does not mean we can have no common goals, that we are left with an autonomy and egoism of ends, but that our relation to these goals differs. In the United States we all live in a racist society but black people and white people have different freedoms and responsibilities with regard to racism. Likewise, the task of men and women in relation to sexism is not the same.

Finally, feminists recognize that our moral activity includes not only actions, decisions, and loyalties to persons, ideals, and projects. Moral activity includes ourselves. To become a moral subject is itself a moral task, if not the central moral task.[26] The moral subject is not a completed, closed entity but is unfinished and open. The terms and implications of this process are particularly relevant to women and others currently involved in their own liberation struggles. Becoming the subject of one's own actions is a social and historical process key to liberation politically, socially, and psychologically so that we no longer collude in our own oppression and so that we can attempt to change conditions of life negation and alienation into conditions of affirmation and fulfillment.

The notion of becoming a subject demands that we recognize the historical incompleteness of all of us and the ways in which we make and remake ourselves, our relations, and our society in our moral activity. Becoming a moral subject means recognizing that morality is a structure of socio-historical relations, not a detached calculus performed by autonomous individuals.

26 Katie G. Cannon discusses this point with regard to black women in "The Black Woman as Moral Agent: A Paradigm for Liberation Ethics," paper delivered at the American Academy of Religion, 21 December 1983.

17

Feminism and the Ethic of Inseparability

Catherine Keller

She say, my first step from the old white man was trees. Then air. Then birds. Then other people. But one day when I was sitting quiet and feeling like a motherless child, which I was, it come to me: that feeling of being part of everything, not separate at all. I knew that if I cut a tree, my arm would bleed.

—the character Shug, in *The Color Purple* by A. Walker

I. GITTING MAN OFF YOUR EYEBALL

When Shug experiences this epiphany of interconnection, she is female, black, and poor, living in a small town in the deep South between the wars. In other words, she dwells in the margins of the triply disestablished. No wonder her revelation comes as an ultimate answer to the "old white man," the establishment God—or, conversely, the establishment as God. She does not flee from her marginality into traditional spirituality, but rather discovers, through a kind of *via negativa* by which she steps free of the ultimate image of oppression, a radical vision. "Being part of everything" evokes an anti-establishment metaphysic, divinely charged and ripe with ethical implications.

And yet this epiphany must give a feminist pause. No matter how well-credentialed by oppression, no matter how beautifully conjured by the black feminism moving Alice Walker's pen—a doubt arises. How can a feeling of being "not separate at all" do a woman any favors? Doesn't freedom demand separation and independence? Such inseparability blurs the boundaries between self and world, subject and object, spinning the universe into a web of relations. Does it not then threaten the self of woman so tenuously getting loose of the grip of defining and confining relations—above all to the traditional patrilineal family? Has not woman through great travail only begun to achieve a sense of distinct, focused, and intentional subjectivity? In other words, don't we as women need to move toward separateness (which need not entail separatism) rather than toward this mystical state of pan-participation? Aren't women already all *too* empathetic—why should we now bleed with the *trees?*

Well, Shug might reply, it's not that we *should:* we already do; we are part of everything whether we realize it or not. So it might provide more power and indeed more self to feel *with* and *into* this reality of interconnection, rather than to flap about in the illusion of separateness, feeling "motherless." Separateness, her vision implies, characterizes the transcendent modality of the "old white man." Thus freedom requires iconoclasm, negation: "You have to git man off your eyeball, before you can see anything a'tall."[1] It is a matter of seeing things as they are: and the interdependence of all things summarizes the content, form, and force of the vision.

Let us then in response turn to the work of a pioneering feminist who pumped her lifeblood into the empowerment of an *independent* self for women. The Simone de Beauvoir of *The Second Sex,* which inaugurated the second wave of the woman's movement, would want nothing to do with such inseparability. We will examine certain fundamental presuppositions supporting her argument for woman's authenticity as a subject *over against* the object, the other, the world. This will focus our doubt (though this doubt may have intrinsically to do with the peculiarity of woman's oppression within a white bourgeois context). But if de Beauvoir's approach—taken as prototypical—itself arouses doubts, we will suggest in conclusion a

1 Alice Walker, *The Color Purple* (New York: Harcourt, Brace, Jovanovich, 1982), 168.

strategy for considering Shug's epiphany in terms explicitly related to woman's experience. We will draw upon an example of contemporary theory that may corroborate the intuition of interconnection for precisely feminist purposes.

II. HOSTILE SUBJECTS, INESSENTIAL OBJECTS

Posing her famous question "What is woman?" de Beauvoir formulated what has remained perhaps the most incisive statement of the relationship between man and woman within patriarchal culture: "She is defined and differentiated with reference to man and not he with reference to her; she is the incidental, the inessential as opposed to the essential. He is the Subject, he is the Absolute—she is the Other."[2] Woman as the Other—de Beauvoir's brilliant deployment of Sartrian-Hegelian terms echoes throughout the work of women in religion.[3] It is the classic anti-Freudian declaration that anatomy is not only *not* destiny; gender difference is merely biological to whatever extent it is not culturally created. And the culture expresses the aims of the dominant male Absolute. She calls her perspective that of "existential ethics."

Because of the exclusive claim of the male upon normative subjectivity, he "represents both the positive and the neutral, as is indicated by the common use of man to designate human beings in general; whereas woman represents only the negative, defined by limiting criteria, without reciprocity."[4]

Religion has been crucial in the maintenance of male absoluteness: "the males could not enjoy this privilege fully unless they believed it to be founded on the absolute and the eternal."[5] De Beauvoir traces the derivative status of woman as Other through its bountiful history in myth, psychoanalysis, economics, and literature,

2 Simone de Beauvoir, *The Second Sex*, trans. H. M. Parshley (New York: Vintage Books/Random House, 1974; original, 1949), xix.

3 For example, Mary Daly's first book, *The Church and the Second Sex* (New York: Harper and Row, 1975), is a straightforward application of de Beauvoir's notion of woman as "Other" to Roman Catholic treatment of women; Rosemary Ruether's influential work, *New Woman, New Earth* (New York: Seabury, 1975), also uses de Beauvoir's thesis as its starting point.

4 De Beauvoir, *The Second Sex*, xviii.

5 De Beauvoir, *The Second Sex*, xxv.

seeking to understand how it is that half the human race could seem to acquiesce in its own alterity—its identity as Other: "Why is it that women do not dispute male sovereignty? No subject will readily volunteer to become the Object, the inessential; it is not the Other, who in defining himself as the Other, establishes the One. The Other is posed as such by the One in defining himself as the One."[6] She will answer the question of woman's acceptance of her own otherness in terms both of man's coercion and woman's complicity. This arrangement suited not only men's economic aims but their "ontological and moral pretensions as well";[7] and at the same time a good many women could enjoy the derivative privileges of their class while being spared the existential burdens of "transcendence," of becoming an authentic, self-responsible subject. De Beauvoir's account of this elusive interplay of coercion and complicity relies upon two arguments: 1) women have always been subordinated to men and so lack, unlike other objectified groups, even the memory of a subjective existence, for they lack a historical religion or culture of their own; 2) every human consciousness is constantly tempted to retreat into its own subjectivity—i.e., into "immanence." De Beauvoir means by immanence the Sartrian sense of a fundamental stagnation, "the brutish life of subjection to given conditions," all that resists the "transcendence" of freely-chosen projects expanding "into an indefinitely open future."[8] But a problem with her fundamental approach disturbs both arguments, I believe.

She claims that "Otherness is a fundamental category of human thought."[9] Perhaps one cannot dispute this axiom without forfeiting any self, surrendering to a spiritual or a material monism in which there is no individuality at all. Rather than question that a relation of self to other "is as primordial as consciousness itself," I would draw attention to the particular sort of relation of Self and Other and hence the kind of consciousness her analysis presumes. For she draws the relation on the model of oppositions like right-left, good-evil, day-night. At least one culture-critic suggests that whenever "oppositionalism" appears we must be on the lookout for a particular kind

---

6 De Beauvoir, *The Second Sex*, xxi.
7 De Beauvoir, *The Second Sex*, 157.
8 De Beauvoir, *The Second Sex*, xxxiii.
9 De Beauvoir, *The Second Sex*, xix.

of subject: the heroic ego, "who divides so he can conquer."[10] And the mythos of the hero as free-wandering warrior has provided the most pervasive or the most patriarchal of our culture-patterns. The heroic ego is not accidentally imaged as "he."

In fact we find the warrior-hero's metaphysically outfitted (and outmoded) descendant, the Hegelian absolute Ego, at work in de Beauvoir's own argument. The telling problem does not lie so much with de Beauvoir's own thinking as with what it presupposes. Recall that by catching such presuppositions at work we rehearse our ability to recognize their persistence in our own perspectives.

Duality is here the privileged form of plurality, for only the confrontation of the Hegelian subject with an object which it negates brings the subject into being at all; she explicitly follows Hegel (via Lévi-Strauss) in this analysis of all culture as a dialectic of symmetrical opposition: "We find in consciousness itself a fundamental hostility toward every other consciousness; as the subject can be posed only in being opposed—he sets himself up as the essential as opposed to the other, the inessential, the object."[11]

Ironically *The Second Sex*, which could be described as a single protest against the Freudian essentialism (that "anatomy is destiny"), lets echo in its very foundations another Freudian axiom: that of the "primary mutual hostility of human beings."[12]

Of course Freud did not invent the idea of an essential enmity, primal aggression, at the root of human relations. But even granted that such "a fundamental hostility" characterizes the psychological metaphysic of male sovereignty, does it disclose the essence of any human subject whatsoever? Or does de Beauvoir here succumb to an unnecessary generalization? In our dialogue with de Beauvoir, we must now ask: what price are we to pay as women if we "authentically assume" *this* subjective attitude? To what extent is culture's "inside man" authoring this authenticity? What are the consequences for the relation of self to other, for relatedness, including its most theological and cosmological limits?

10 James Hillman, *The Dream and the Underworld* (New York: Harper Colophon, 1979), 82.

11 De Beauvoir, *The Second Sex*, xx.

12 Sigmund Freud, *Civilization and its Discontents*, trans. James Strachey (New York: W. W. Norton, 1961), 59.

III. COMPLICITY AND IMMANENCE

Above all, this subjective style would require us to forfeit any identity based on immanence, in favor of "transcendence," of the creative liberty whereby we become more than the natural, the given, the mechanical. As an act of the subject positing itself as One over against the Other, transcendence moves outward, forward, upward and can scarcely find itself in the circumscribed feminine spaces of house, garden, embrace.

The ideal relation between subjects is what de Beauvoir terms "reciprocity," in which selves are not vying to dominate one another but rather recognize one another as transcendences, face to face. However, in the field of consciousness generated by the supposedly inevitable hostility, can reciprocity finally mean more than an anxious peace treaty based on common projects? To be sure, such reciprocity would offer an immeasurable improvement over the continuing attempt to abort transcendence in self and other, to dominate or to submit. De Beauvoir demonstrates patriarchy's own refusal of freedom, and does not display its culture as facilitating even for males the expression of the transcendence she advocates; *au contraire:* "He would be liberated himself in their liberation. But this is precisely what he dreads. And so he obstinately persists in the mystifications intended to keep woman in her chains."[13]

As patriarchy learns at least in such statements to abort male transcendence as well, it is never for her a matter of simply achieving for women what men already have; of dressing women in masculine egos and three-piece suits (a contemporary Athena's armor). But at a deeper level do we discern after all a certain philosophical complicity—not to be reduced to a relationship to Sartre!—at work in her categories, a complicity between de Beauvoir and an ethic grounded in the culture of male dominance?

The presupposition of the unmitigated self-assertion of the transcendent subject shows its true colors in her historical account of the origins of culture. The critical balance of male coercion and female complicity has persisted in history so effectively, according to her analysis, because she believes male supremacy to have no beginning:

13 De Beauvoir, *The Second Sex*, 800.

"Slave or idol, it was never she who chose her lot."[14] It is true that little trustworthy work, anthropological or archaeological, had been accomplished suggesting any pre-patriarchal stages of culture: Lévi-Strauss's analysis of the universality of patriarchy was understandably more persuasive to her than Bachofen's speculations. I would here argue not so much with her choice of historical theory as with the assumptions that come to light in her evaluative descriptions of that history. The following account is telling. She discusses woman's role in the early agricultural communities to which patriarchal-patrilineal structures can only be attributed by inference:

> In no domain whatever did she create: she maintained the life of the tribe by giving it children and bread, nothing more. She remained doomed to immanence, incarnating only the static aspect of society, closed in upon itself. Whereas man went on monopolizing the functions which threw open that society toward nature and toward the rest of humanity. The only employments worthy of him were war, hunting, and fishing; he made conquest of foreign booty and bestowed it on the tribe; war, hunting and fishing represented an expansion of existence, its projection toward the world. The male remained alone the incarnation of transcendence.[15]

According to this chain of thought, the labors that produce and nurture life, agriculture and child-rearing, count as "immanence"; whereas those privileged vocations of slaughter, either of humans or animals, count as "transcendence." Contrary to the previous passage, a patriarchal pastoral stimulates transcendence in men. Does "world-openness" mean warfare? The spear rises in this analysis as the symbol of transcendence, and makes manifest the phallic-aggressive energy of the outward bound, projectile subject in its "fundamental hostility." Especially disturbing is its ability to determine the thought of a most radical and pioneering feminist!

We may acknowledge the strain of picturing any culture in which "woman's work," especially mothering, does not circle aimlessly within the confines of life-maintenance. But the question of the very relation of self to other, to nature and to its world is at stake here. De Beauvoir effectively exposes the use of the institution of motherhood as the privileged means for at once subjugating and valuing the

14 De Beauvoir, *The Second Sex*, 89.
15 De Beauvoir, *The Second Sex*, 83.

privileged object through which he subdues Nature. The dream of a rejuvenating, virgin, delightful nature joins the extremes of cultural artifice, out of which "the feminine" is wrought. Thus the patriarch must dissociate the "dreaded essence of the mother" from the woman he possesses. For the mother holds for him the terror of an uncontrollable Mother Nature along with its promises of security and refreshment: "Man is on the defensive against woman in so far as she represents the vague source of the world and obscure organic development."[16]

What is de Beauvoir's own attitude toward this "nature" men find so threatening and yet so seductive, to be controlled through the subjugation of women? In her discussion of "Early Tillers of the Soil," she speculates that history might have taken a different turn at the vital juncture between the worship of the Great Mother (whom de Beauvoir considers an idol, yet one that granted women at least the dignity of idols) and the law-encoded patriarchy:

> Perhaps, if productive work had remained within her strength, woman would have accomplished with man the conquest of nature; the human species would have made its stand against the gods through both males and females; but woman was unable to avail herself of the promised benefits of the tool.[17]

By "tool" de Beauvoir means a technology based on "weapon," for she attributes the invention of agricultural tools, which did not "conquer" nature, to women. De Beauvoir simply does not question the absolute right of the Absolute Ego to conquer and subdue the earth—she disputes only the bad faith of its projection, its injustices, its denials of finitude. "Nature" remains for her a means to human ends, "immanence" resisting "transcendence," cosmos devoid of the authenticity of anthropos.

In this context her atheological commitment collaborates with the existentialist alienation from the natural universe. She laments the failure of woman to divest herself of an identity invested in nature and religion. The divine and the natural are both together to be vanquished, drained of the projections of human subjectivity which keep humans in bondage. The divine in her thought must stand over

16 De Beauvoir, *The Second Sex*, 170.
17 De Beauvoir, *The Second Sex*, 87.

against the human, as must the natural: both are inhuman objects *par excellence,* awesomely Other than human, rendered alien in the course of human exploits of transcendence. As the embodiment of the zone between nature and spirit, subject and object, woman ever after "enables her group, separated from the cosmos and the gods, to remain in communication with them."

There can be no doubt that woman has been trapped, trivialized, and exploited in these margins of heaven and earth. Woman projected as Madonna mediates between the divine and the human; as Whore she seduces the human toward the animal. Woman has been rendered multilaterally marginal. In a certain sense, Shug's experience as socially marginal person confirms de Beauvoir's thesis. Shug blurs the boundaries between the natural, the divine, and the human in her normative epiphany. Yet where de Beauvoir might spy the effects of oppression, Shug locates the source of liberation.

Could it be, we must now ask, that the transcendent subject, in as much as it constitutes itself by a "fundamental hostility" toward the other, whether human, cosmic, or divine, is none other than the perennial "male ego," a cultural construct dependent on the nurture, flattery, and suspension of disbelief offered by its feminine counterpart? If so, the attempt to achieve the ethos of such a subject— requiring as it does the maintenance of the female Other—is doomed to failure from the outset. For its mode of consciousness might represent not human reciprocity but only the project of an essentially patriarchal self disguised as the normatively human. Yet de Beauvoir's analysis of the metaphysical conditions of subjectivity *within* the cultural status quo, which in its broadest self-definition means simply patriarchy, remains unsurpassed. Is there some way to receive back into a newly empowered sense of self certain of those values she discards as "immanent," without diluting the strength of freedom, individuality, and transcendence she has inspired within the feminist trajectory?

IV.

Let us turn to the experience which inaugurated this discussion: to Shug's "feeling of being part of everything, not separate at all." As there is a profound problem with the sort of feminist position which stands against such inseparability, we may pursue Shug's sense of things with less anxiety. To support the intuition with a more systematic rationality, we could choose a method somewhat parallel to de Beauvoir's. That is, in the way that she uses existentialism as the basis for her ethic of transcendence, we could evoke that philosophical system which best elaborates the intuition of interconnection: the process, or process-relational metaphysic classically developed by Whitehead. In this organicist vision, the interrelatedness of every being to every other emerges—yet in conjunction with a doctrine of *mutual transcendence*. All beings take account of each other, take part in each other, literally internalizing one another, however unconsciously, as each others' very stuff. They then fashion their individuality out of this immanence of inflowing matter (the other, the world) in a momentary act of self-creation not unlike the existentialist transcendence. The ethic which emerges from this nondualistic account of subject-object relations approximates the sentiment which Shug summarizes as "if I cut a tree, my arm would bleed."[18]

Does any other method suggest itself, however, than such an immediate turn for legitimation to the male philosopher? Can we tread a path better coordinated with the feminist insistence upon woman's experience of herself as the basis for reflection and action? Indeed we need only look to the work of certain women in psychological theory to find both corroboration of Shug's intuition and an important explanation for the association of patriarchy with the separate self. Gilligan's *In a Different Voice*[19] proves especially valuable for the task of considering a specifically female structure of self as the basis for an alternative ethic.[20]

Gilligan found that women and men in fact understand and make moral decisions differently. The three studies which provided the data for her claim enable her to challenge normative theories of

18 Walker, *The Color Purple*, 167.

19 Carol Gilligan, *In a Different Voice: Psychological Theory and Women's Development* (Cambridge: Harvard University Press, 1982).

20 Nancy Chodorow, who especially in *The Reproduction of Mothering* (Berkeley: University of California Press, 1978) reaches similar conclusions by way of a more rigorous sociological and psychoanalytic argument, provides Gilligan her starting point. Dorothy Dinnerstein, Jean Baker Miller and Ann Wilson Schaef are psychologists who propound related theses.

development and ethical maturation, especially Erikson's and Kohlberg's, and in the background, Freud's. In these maturity is identified with separation, independence, and autonomy; and women invariably seem to count as derivative or underdeveloped—if they are counted at all. While for women, she claims, "the moral problem arises from conflicting responsibilities" within an inclusive "network of relations," it is for men more a matter of "competing rights" requiring a hierarchical ordering of claims for its resolution.[21] Gilligan derives the difference between the two moralities from a radical difference in personality development between genders. Thus "the morality of rights differs from the morality of responsibility in its emphasis on *separation* rather than *connection*, in its consideration of the *individual* rather than the *relationship* as primary."[22]

The typically male sense of morality as Gilligan describes it presupposes a universe of aggressive others who must be kept in line, ordered, controlled. Through her critique of Freud, she illumines a crucial bond between the psychology of separateness and the primacy of aggression: the "primary separation" of infant-ego from object, "arising from disappointment and fueled by rage, creates a self whose relations with others or 'objects' must then be protected by rules, a morality that contains this explosive potential and adjusts 'the mutual relationships of human beings in the family, the state and the society.'"[23] De Beauvoir—naturally enough—presupposed precisely this sort of self, concocted of aggression and separation: the "fundamental hostility" of the subject as the very energy of transcendence. But Gilligan offers evidence that such a description at most fits the personality profile of typical males by demonstrating that women consistently describe *themselves* differently.

Thus in all of the women's descriptions, identity is defined in a context of relationship and judged by a standard of responsibility and care. Similarly, morality is seen by these women as arising from the experience of connection and conceived as a problem of inclusion rather than one of balancing claims.[24]

21 Gilligan, *In a Different Voice*, 19, 33.
22 Gilligan, *In a Different Voice*, 19. My emphasis.
23 Gilligan, *In a Different Voice*, 46.
24 Gilligan, *In a Different Voice*, 160.

If de Beauvoir's acceptance of male preconceptions concerning the normative autonomy of a mature self have become more transparent, it is not surprising to find a sentiment echoing Shug's imagery voiced by one of the women interviewed in Gilligan's study:

> You have to love someone else, because while you may not like them, you are inseparable from them. ... *They are part of you;* that other person is part of that giant collection of people that you are connected to.[25]

v.

This loving, derived from the intuition of interconnection, is vulnerable to criticisms of solipsism, narcissism, and stagnation if it collapses into sheer immanence. De Beauvoir's voice must not fade. Yet such loving need not eliminate transcendence and individuality. Taking part in each other presupposes and creates differentiated selves in which to take part! Then the ethic implied by the ecological—and almost animistic—sense that I harm myself by harming another, even nonhuman, creature embodies the ethic of loving-others-as-I-love-myself. But it corrects Christian anthropocentrism, while eliminating also the antinatural and antitheistic animus of de Beauvoir's ethic.

Gilligan's theory contributes to a growing commitment in feminism to tap the special strength of women's history trapped and hidden beneath the facades of femininity, rather than to flee to prevailing androcentric norms of subjectivity and ethics—norms which men themselves may begin to abandon. Of course any affirmation of gender "difference" raises the spectre of biologism, essentialism, and the stereotype. Yet the dangers of succumbing to apparently "human" and actually patriarchical values and ontologies is every bit as dire. As Gilligan says elsewhere, criticizing whatever tendency we may have today to consider gender a difference that makes no difference in any but the most limited biological sense, "femininity may contain values and ways of seeing whose release

---

25 Gilligan, *In a Different Voice,* 160. Her emphasis.

would benefit all." "Connection," as a value arising from a recent and rich variety of feminist perspectives offers a critical, perhaps the most important, key to such a release.[26] It may just happen to be a spacious, wildly diverse, and differentiated world of interwoven entities which comes into focus—when you "git man off your eyeball."

26 For instance, Nancy Chodorow analyzes the gender-difference in a way that frees it of any biological or archetypal determinism, while Stephanie Demetrakopoulos, in *Listening to Our Bodies: The Rebirth of Feminine Wisdom* (Boston: Beacon Press, 1983), partially in response to Chodorow, would want to affirm some sort of innate, body-linked tendency. And the proliferating metaphor of web, of weaving, arising in the poetics of woman's vision (notably in Mary Daly and Adrienne Rich) depicts the dynamism of a collective female insight into a universe of interknit subjectivities.

18

On Doing Religious Ethics

June O'Connor

Although the word feminist never appears in the following essay, the article presents a view of ethics that shares with feminist thought several features. *One* is a concern for wholeness which requires us to see the various processes involved in ethical inquiry and reflection in terms of the larger pattern and total process of which they are a part. Central to this wholistic view is the recognition that ethical reflection is rooted in experience and requires studied attention to experience. Feminist analysis highlights the fact that attention to women's experience is mandatory, given the androcentric bias that has prevailed cross-culturally and for centuries. A *second* feature is an integrated appreciation of the roles of reason and emotion as important voices in the search for ethical insight and wisdom. Discernment of the true, the good, the valuable occurs affectively and cognitively. Both. Feminist thought supports this perspective also. *Third*, the essay urges a sensitivity to ways in which our inherited and assumed visions of reality inform our feelings and reasoning processes. Feminist critiques of society detail ways in which attitudes about women shape personal behaviors and social policies. *Fourth*, the essay points out the importance of examining the sources of our viewpoints or visions of reality which often operate pre-reflectively; these are frequently held as self-evident truths unless explicitly and critically examined. To examine them means we are willing to ask the questions, how do we know what we know? and where are we standing as we see and speak? Feminist thought centers in on questions such as these with decided interest:

June O'Connor

how do we know what we know (about women and about men)? What are the sources of our views (regarding gender identity and ability and power)? The feminist challenge, like this view of ethics, is ultimately epistemological in nature, challenging us to notice anew the angle of our vision, thereby examining *how* and *why* we see as we do, as well as examining *what* we see.

Recent discussions addressing methodological issues in religious ethics indicates that there is a wide variety of views on the nature of the religious ethical task.[1] Some ethicists employ philosophical analysis, others focus on social and economic analysis, still others are fascinated with psychological dimensions of ethical inquiry and behavior or pursue historical-descriptive studies. In principle, all of these approaches have legitimacy, as individual ethicists narrow their perspective in the effort to do "one thing well" and focus their attention on particular topics of special concern (such as war, abortion, or international relations). I sense a need, however, to look

1 See *The Journal of Religious Ethics* since its first appearance in Fall 1973: Max Stackhouse, "The Location of the Holy: An Essay on Justification in Ethics," *Journal of Religious Ethics* 4 (Spring 1976), 63–104; Glenn C. Graber, "A Critical Bibliography of Recent Discussions of Religious Ethics by Philosophers," *Journal of Religious Ethics* 2 (Fall 1974), 53–80; Frederick S. Carney, "On Frankena and Religious Ethics," *Journal of Religious Ethics* 3 (Spring 1975), 7–25; John P. Reeder, Jr., "Religious Ethics as a Field and Discipline," *Journal of Religious Ethics* 6 (Spring 1978), 32–53; and James Wm. McClendon, Jr., "Three Strands of Christian Ethics," *Journal of Religious Ethics* 6 (Spring 1978), 54–80. See also articles listed in note 3, and the Spring 1977 issue of *Journal of Religious Ethics* which is devoted to the question of method in religious social ethics and presupposes familiarity both with Ralph Potter's "The Logic of Moral Argument," in *Toward a Discipline of Social Ethics*, ed. Paul Deats (Boston: Boston University Press, 1972), 93–114 and with Douglas Sturm's written but unpublished response, "Ethical Reflection and the Art of Life" (1974). Additional pertinent writings on the nature of the religious ethical task include Arthur J. Dyck, "Questions of Ethics," *Harvard Theological Review* 65 (October 1972), 453–81; James Gustafson, "Context Versus Principles: A Misplaced Debate in Christian Ethics," and "Theology and Ethics," *Christian Ethics and the Community* (Philadelphia: Pilgrim Press, 1971), 83–126; James F. Smurl, *Religious Ethics: A Systems Approach* (Englewood Cliffs, NJ: Prentice-Hall, 1972); and Gibson Winter, "Introduction: Religion, Ethics and Society," in *Social Ethics: Issues in Ethics and Society*, ed. Gibson Winter (New York: Harper and Row, 1968) and, from the point of view of moral philosophy, Henry Aiken, "Levels of Moral Discourse," *Reason and Conduct* (New York: Knopf, 1962), 65–87.

at the task of religious ethics as a whole; in what follows, I shall attempt to sketch my view of what we do when we do religious ethics, what questions we ask, the order in which we tend to ask them, and how they relate one to the other.

To describe the nature of the ethical task is to describe a process in which one attempts to bring sensitivity, method, and discernment to discovering moral value. This process is religious ethics when the ethicist approaches her work attuned to a religious worldview, which is to say, attuned to a perspective that acknowledges an experience of ultimacy. The religious ethicist may personally affirm and speak from within an experience of ultimacy (normative religious ethics), or, although she may not share a given perspective on ultimacy, she remains attuned to its presence in the ethics of those she studies (descriptive religious ethics).

The experience of ultimacy may be identified as an experience of the "transcendent" or of an "ultimate concern" in an effort to differentiate it from our routinized experience of daily life. It may be identified further as the presence of God in Jesus, of enlightenment through the Buddha, of union between the individual self (atman) and the Universal Self (Brahman). Additional designations abound, and students of religion strive to identify a common element in these diverse formulations, all of which seem to point to an encounter either with a whole new dimension of life or with an awareness of the meaning of daily life that is more full, more rich, and more valuable than our routinized experience of the here-and-now often suggests. Religious ethical inquiry and reflection flow naturally from religious perspectives on life as people ask themselves questions about how to live in harmony with their convictions of what is.[2]

Ethical inquiry and reflection revolve around a variety of questions about decision-making that represent two distinct but related directions of thought. On the one hand, ethics is concerned with duties, obligations, and rights, asking such questions as: what must I do? What rights must I honor in others? What rights are mine?

2 On the relationship between theology and ethics, see John P. Crossley, Jr., "Theological Ethics and the Naturalistic Fallacy," *Journal of Religious Ethics* 6 (Spring 1978), 121–34.

What can I demand from others regarding justice or freedom or dignity or privacy? These questions continue to be asked, with low levels of deliberation and with high, with self-interest dominating some questioners, with compassion for the neighbor motivating others. They reflect an imperative approach to ethical inquiry, offering an ethic of demand and command in the name of humane behavior.

On the other hand, ethics is also concerned with values and virtues, with unrealized possibilities as well as with *oughts;* it addresses questions such as: what can I do? How might I respond? What kind of person do I want to become? What kind of society do we want to become? How can we use our power in creative and constructive ways? And so on. These questions reflect a broader approach to ethical inquiry, offer a more open-ended view of creativity and possibility, and express an indicative ethic of invitation rather than command.[3] In a word, ethics is concerned with possibilities as well as with imperatives, with *mights* as well as with *oughts*, with *coulds* as well as with *shoulds*.

The two approaches designated and the questions articulated take shape in varying form within specific ethical traditions. I trust that all traditions grapple with the same fundamental human dilemmas such as the ethics of war, care of the sick, treatment of the neighbor and stranger alike. But their formulations of these questions as well as their resolutions to them might well be different due to their differing standpoints. The question of duties and rights in the context of the Hindu caste system, for example, will be perceived differently from the way this question is heard in a Christian

---

3 For more extended discussions regarding the relationship these two sets of interests and questions bear to one another, see the debate among Carney, Dyck, Frankena, Hauerwas, Robbins, and Schenk: Carney, "The Virtue-Obligation Controversy"; Arthur Dyck, "A Unified Theory of Virtue and Obligation," *Journal of Religious Ethics* 1 (Fall 1973), 37–52; William K. Frankena, "Conversations with Carney and Hauerwas," *Journal of Religious Ethics* 3 (Spring 1975), 45–62; Stanley Hauerwas, "Obligation and Virtue Once More," *Journal of Religious Ethics* 3 (Spring 1975), 27–42; J. Wesley Robbins, "Frankena on the Difference Between an Ethic of Virtue and an Ethic of Duty," *Journal of Religious Ethics* 4 (Spring 1976), 57–62; David Schenk, Jr., "Recasting the 'Ethics of Virtue/Ethics of Duty' Debate," *Journal of Religious Ethics* 4 (Fall 1976), 269–86. On ethics and creativity, see Daniel Maguire, *The Moral Choice* (Garden City, NY: Doubleday, 1978), 189–217.

community because the caste system, the samsaric cycle, and the laws of karma provide an interpretive framework not found in Christianity. Likewise, Christian convictions about the uniqueness of each individual creature, prophetic themes regarding the importance of social justice, and God's will that all be one in Christ provide a framework for understanding that is notably different from the Hindu view.

The identification of goals and values, likewise, will be one thing for a Buddhist who seeks ultimate emptiness through enlightenment and quite another thing for a Christian who seeks personal communion with God through Christ, and it will be something else again for the secular humanist whose sense of meaning has no transhistorical reference.

These interpretive frameworks need to be recognized, acknowledged, and examined in the effort to do good ethics just as much as decision procedures and rationales for action need to be assessed. To study and to do religious ethics is to be engaged in a three-tiered task which I think of as not unlike climbing a three-step ladder. The climber is free to move both up and down depending on the need at hand, depending upon what it is that is to be reached for. Let me elaborate.

The *first level* is the most obvious and the most visible level of reflection; it rests upon and presupposes the ground level of daily experiences where we confront nagging problems, specific dilemmas, particular issues—concrete questions that emerge from life experience and that demand resolution. Issues such as revolution and war, violence and nonviolence, euthanasia, suicide, and involvement in the internal affairs of foreign countries exemplify concerns addressed. To do ethics at level one is to step out of the mire of confusion and crisis into the act of reflection. It is to address conflicting value claims and to engage in decision-making processes. Ethical reflections at this level involve a number of activities.

1. Collecting the empirical facts is a fundamental first step and can be accomplished by asking a variety of questions: what is going on? Who is involved? Why is this particular issue being debated/considered (in other words, what motivations are operative)? What means are being examined to achieve what ends?

2. Seeking all the wisdom that is available is the mark of good

ethics and involves giving attention to a variety of sources. It takes seriously the processes of rational analysis that uncover and compare the empirical facts; it means listening to principles that have come to us in the course of history; it involves attending to the affective side of our lives, to feelings and emotions, to the sentiments of moral outrage and repulsion, and of moral beauty and attraction. (Of these three sources—reasoning processes, principles from history, and feelings—the role of feeling is the one most often regarded with suspicion and distrust and consequently is frequently disregarded. Without doubt, there is often a conflict between reason and feeling, between one's head and one's heart, that makes listening to both problematic. Yet there is no doubt that both affect our moral perceptions and both influence our moral behavior, for good and for ill. For these two very important reasons, both need to be confronted, explored, directed. I will say more about this issue at a later point in the essay.)

3. Ethical reflection includes the activity of anticipating the future implications of considered courses of action and of imagining, comparing, and evaluating a variety of alternative possibilities. In this way, one extends and expands one's view through the powers of creative imagination before coming to a judgment.

4. In light of these previous processes of getting clear about the dilemma and sources of insight, one is able to come to a decision whereby a particular course of action is chosen, approved, or perhaps recommended as ethically acceptable/advisable. At this point in the process, one needs to keep in mind, of course, the distinction between the moral norm according to which one wishes to operate (such as justice) and the social strategy employed to meet that end (revolution, busing, boycott).

In this process, reflection lifts one out of the mire of confusion that is generated by experience onto step one of the ladder. The problem is identified and the conflict analyzed, values are called upon to give direction to thought, and an attempt is made to translate those values into recommended actions or action patterns. At this level, ethical thinkers and ethically reflective doers engage in processes of addressing, assessing, analyzing, and recommending the concrete questions that invite, or, more often, beg for resolution. It is possible to limit the ethical task to level one. But the art and the science of religious ethics is refined and made more rigorous and more honest when the ethicist makes use of steps to levels two and three.

The *second level* offers the opportunity to see more broadly by giving extended consideration to one's interpretive framework, one's worldview, metaphysic, or vision of life. The first level of doing ethics presupposes and makes use of this second level. Here one's fundamental outlook regarding the nature of reality, of the good, human rights to self-determination, relationships to other humans and to nature, honesty, justice, and care of the sick and the vulnerable depends upon one's view of what life is all about. To do ethics at this level is to deal with questions of whether and to what extent we are free agents or objects of determination from without; it is to examine whether and in what ways we are related to one another, to nonhuman realities, to transcendence, and what implications these statements of relatedness hold. It is to identify what loyalties are operative and to admit who or what we find worthy of our allegiance. Richard McCormick suggests that "our basic moral commitments are pre-thematic, pre-discursive in character"[4]; and I think he is right. Which is why we need, at level two, to examine those pre-thematic, pre-discursive commitments and bring them to consciousness yet one more time, reflect on them in order to recommit ourselves to them, modify them, or abandon them.

To do ethics at this level is to acknowledge the historical community that has shaped our vision about the importance of life and the limits of life and to acknowledge the current community that shapes our vision now. It is to surface the context of meaning from which we come and to admit what is that context of meaning with which we wish to be aligned.

This second level of doing ethics lifts up for self-critical reflection the convictions and presuppositions that comprise one's view of reality and the loyalties that affect one's approach to concrete problem-solving. It engages one in recognizing what principles inform one's imagination and guide one's decisions. And it engages one in pondering what principles one wants to inform the imagina-

---

4 Richard A. McCormick, "Response to Professor Curran," *Proceedings of the Catholic Theological Society of America* (New York: Manhattan College, 1974), 163.

tion and guide decision-making. Stanley Hauerwas' view of the ethical enterprise wisely and effectively captures the importance of giving attention to vision as well as to decision: "The moral life does not consist just in making one right decision after another," he writes; "it is the progressive attempt to widen and clarify our vision of reality."[5] John Cobb also has highlighted the importance vision has for the ethical task in a statement with which I identify fully: "I am persuaded that the basic vision of reality within which one thinks and experiences is more crucial for how ethical issues arise and are dealt with than is the formal analysis of moral experience."[6] A Chinese proverb tells us that "two-thirds of what we see is behind our eyes." Taking this to be the case, reflection at level two enables us to look behind our eyes and acknowledge what we find.

The *third level* that religious ethicists need to be concerned with discloses issues that are present in the first and second levels, yet often in hidden form. This is the epistemological level that addresses the question: how do I know what I know?—about reality, about the good, about human persons and their status in the universe, about the existence or nonexistence of a transcendent order. Where level two engages us in reflection on *what* our presuppositions and views of life are, level three ushers us into dealing with *how* we know them and *why* we hold them dear. At this point we have moved from the task of acknowledging the convictions and presuppositions that underlie our worldview to the twofold task of acknowledging their origin and of justifying their continuance. Level three allows for additional questions, metaethical in thrust, that deal with the meaning of moral concepts as well as the justification of ultimate moral and metaphysical principles. Since it focuses attention on epistemological presuppositions, level three deals with a realm that is "above" or "behind" practical ethics proper.

Individual ethicists attending to specific problems may enter this process at any level and need not proceed in the order I describe.

---

5 Stanley Hauerwas, "The Significance of Vision: Toward an Aesthetic Ethic," *Vision and Virtue: Essays in Christian Ethical Reflection* (Notre Dame, IN: Fides/Claretian, 1974), 44.

6 John Cobb, "Response to Reynolds," in *John Cobb's Theology in Process*, ed. David Ray Griffin and Thomas J. J. Altizer (Philadelphia: Westminster, 1977), 182.

One can skip over the first rung of a ladder and begin at level two, moving up or down, as one chooses. Or one might make a grand leap to level three if one is convinced, for example, that the epistemological questions should be settled before those of worldview and decision procedures. But if the process proceeds in the order I describe, the ethicist in one sense relives history. For from the historical point of view, epistemology developed relatively late, as a critical reflection on metaphysics, which was prior. (Only after people identified the nature of reality were they inclined to ponder the more radical question of how they came to their conclusions, how they knew anything at all.) Similarly, metaphysical thought developed as a critical reflection on the knowledge of physical realities. (When some sense of clarity was gained with respect to the concrete, tangible components of our lives, people became curious about what universals could be discovered that pertained to this variety and multiplicity.)

In summary form, the three levels of ethical inquiry and reflection can be visualized in vertical form in the chart at the end of this article.

In my view, to do religious ethics is to move up and down this three-leveled ladder, stepping out of the dilemma at hand (ground level) in order to gain perspective that will enhance the possibility of a judgment born of wisdom. Wisdom is more likely to occur where thoughtful examination of the issues together with reflection self-critically directed combine with a presumed desire to do the right, the good, the fitting. Inquiry often begins at the practical level where a question or crisis precipitates the need and desire for reflection; such reflection, however, leads one beyond the realm of crisis to step two of the ladder, enabling one to reach out for direct contact with one's philosophical and theological presuppositions as one seeks value referents in order to give direction to thought. As one identifies these values and the vision of life out of which they come, seeking to appropriate and apply them to the problem at hand, still another step beckons the professional ethicist. This third step, designated the epistemological level, enables one to reach more radical levels of self-reflection by taking notice of the sources of one's knowledge about the now-identified values and by seeking to justify them. How one knows what is valuable needs to be reviewed continuously because of our capacity for self-deception and because of the overwhelmingly influential role that our values play in the decisions and determinations that are ultimately made at level one. One needs to bring one's values and their sources to the fore, acknowledging them explicitly and deliberately. The alternative is to deceive oneself and to mislead others by keeping them unexplicit and unarticulated, though they are present and pervasive nonetheless.

One of the strengths of so defining the religio-ethical task and of engaging in it is the mobility it affords for achieving a variety of standpoints in the way that a wooden ladder enables a variety of standpoints for its climber. Each ascent offers a new level of abstraction in perception, and provides a new possibility for seeing more broadly and more comprehensively, and thereby for understanding more fully the context in which the problem at hand is being met, addressed, and resolved. This variety of standpoints also carries with it the possibility of discerning areas of illusion and deception and can thereby function as a corrective force. Such movement enables one to touch both the concrete (level one) and the theoretical (levels two and three) and the concrete (level one) once again, as one examines difficult decisions that invade our lives and demand thoughtful resolution. In this view, the discipline of religious ethics is intimately involved with and singularly expressive of the rhythm of life itself as this characterizes those who live reflectively. For ethical inquiry and reflection are rooted in the natural rhythms of doing and thinking and doing with new insight, of acting and analyzing and acting once again with added perspective and deliberation.

Insofar as the image of the ladder suggests movement and variety of standpoints, it is an appropriate analogy for the task I describe. Yet every analogy contains dissimilarities as well as similarities and insofar as the ladder suggests a thing, a static structure, its appropriateness is lessened. Nor is it intended to imply a hierarchy of value (where higher is better, as in climbing the ladder of success). The primary analogue, rather, is that of movement, process, the climbing activity of ascending and descending from the concrete to the abstract to the concrete once again. The image is employed because of the functional value of a ladder: each step is important in terms of what it lets me do, that is, what it enables me to bring within view, and to reach for.

This three-tiered view of the nature and scope of the ethical task seems to me to have a decided edge over a more restrictive view which narrows the focus of ethics to metaethics or to analysis and the logic of moral argument. I am not alone in this dissatisfaction and find that Arthur Dyck, for one, registers his own discontent in the form of a recommendation: "philosophical ethics must once more attend to metaphysics."[7] The difference alluded to between religious ethics and philosophical ethics is not an intrinsic difference, however, and need not be present in practice. The distinctive difference between religious ethics and philosophical ethics is not method but content. Both forms of ethical inquiry can benefit from reflection on the three levels enumerated in this paper. What differentiates them from one another (and what differentiates one religion from another and one philosophy from another) are the presuppositions they bring to their work, that is, the *content of their visions of life, what they see* (regarding the presence or absence of an ultimate Reality, regarding the nature of human persons, and of freedom and determinism and the like). George Thomas makes this point about presuppositions clearly: "In brief, there is no such thing as an ethic which has been developed by pure reason without the aid of presuppositions. The difference between Christian ethics and secular moral philosophy is not that the former has presuppositions while the latter is free from them; it is that they derive their presuppositions from different sources."[8]

For example, although the Christian ethicist may give privileged status to the experience of the Hebrew prophets and the Christian disciples, and although the Hindu ethicist very likely grants special status to the Vedas or the Bhagavad Gita, the philosophical ethicist (moral philosopher) also has his heroes. He grants privileged status to Socrates, perhaps, or to Kant or to G. E. Moore—or to whomever else is seen to be the wisest and best. When pressed to articulate why he views them as models, it becomes clear that this affirmation/

---

7 Dyck, "Questions of Ethics," 481. See also Stanley Hauerwas, "Obligation and Virtue Once More," *Journal of Religious Ethics* 3 (Spring 1975), 34–35.

8 George Thomas, *Christian Ethics and Moral Philosophy* (New York: Charles Scribner's Sons, 1955), 377. See also Gustafson, "Theology and Ethics," 90.

June O'Connor

admiration rests *ultimately* upon metaphysical and ethical assumptions that are not demonstrable but are accepted in a kind of faith.[9]

In saying this, I do not thereby suggest that the use of reason and the rational processes of justification are dispensable. On the contrary, their presence is indispensable if we are to seek clarity and even, at times, conversion (both cognitive and moral), not by coercion but by persuasion. Because everyone who thinks, thinks out of passions and commitments, loves and hates, critical reason is essential as a freeing force and as a common ground enabling communication among those with conflicting commitments and diverse loves. What I do wish to suggest, however, is that energy spent directing attention to the rational justification of certain actions and the logic of moral argument, though appropriate, is insufficient. In addition to analyzing the meanings of "moral" and the reasons for recommending specific moral behaviors, ethicists should be doing something else besides, namely, acknowledging those visions of reality that have become part of them through their communities of shared faith (whether religious or a-religious, whether theistic or atheistic), making explicit the values that these visions of life offer, and reexamining the sources from which they come. Doing ethics within a cross-cultural consciousness enables one to recognize these assumptions and presuppositions more easily, more sharply, and more quickly than when one remains within the boundaries of one's own culture.

The role of reason in ethical relection is a particularly important concern in western ethics. Often reason has been assigned a position of such great importance that other forms of knowledge, such as the knowledge that comes through feeling, have been devalued. This is unfortunate.[10] Insistence on the centrality of reason in ethics is

9 Thomas, *Christian Ethics,* 377. See also Stephen C. Toulmin, *An Examination of the Place of Reason in Ethics* (Cambridge: Cambridge University Press, 1950), 154–60.

10 When the place of feeling is not disvalued altogether, it is likely to be acknowledged but then dropped from discussion, as in William K. Frankena's *Ethics* (Englewood Cliffs, NJ: Prentice-Hall, 1963 [Second edition, 1973]). In Chapter One he identifies the six factors in morality as: 1) forms of judgment, 2) reasons to justify judgments, 3) rules, principles and ideals and virtues that form the background for particular judgments, 4) ways of feeling that accompany judgment, 5) sanctions such as holding responsible, praising, blaming, 6) a point

understandable as a corrective to and a defense against occasionally exaggerated exaltations of feeling as source of ethical insight, yet we need to remember from time to time that an uncritical esteem for reason is also unwise and can be dangerous.

Two chief ways in which reason in ethics has functioned in the West are relevant to this discussion. One view sees rationality as content; it seeks to identify what the rational is in a particular case and to label that discovery as normative. If feeling does not conform

of view which is taken in the various activities of judging, reasoning and feeling. Having identified these six factors in morality, Frankena acknowledges his intent to center most of his discussion on items one, two, three, and five—thereby removing from view factors four and six (first edition p. 8, second edition p. 9). As I hope to make clear in the course of this essay, I wish to lift up these latter items—feelings and point of view—and urge that they also be given equal time, due consideration, for I find them crucial factors in morality that cannot be dismissed if we are to analyze and engage in ethical reflection adequately and realistically.

Daniel Maguire's comprehensive appreciation of the diverse factors in morality leads him to acknowledge in more detail than most the place of feeling or affective knowledge in doing ethics. See "Ethics: How To Do It," Chapter 4 of his excellent book, *Death By Choice* (Garden City, NY: Doubleday, 1974), 77–114, for an abbreviated statement of his method; for an extended treatment, consult his *The Moral Choice*, a remarkable and rewarding study that details his theory of moral knowledge.

Bernard Lonergan's brief but penetrating discussion on feelings in *Method in Theology* (London: Darton, Longman and Todd, 1971), 30–34, also merits serious reading as does Alfred North Whitehead's philosophy in *Process and Reality* (New York: The Free Press, 1969), 205, in which he grants feelings a metaphysical status: "the philosophy of organism attributes 'feeling' throughout the actual world." Also: "Each actual entity is conceived as an act of experience arising out of data. It is a process of 'feeling' the many data, so as to absorb them into the unity of one individual 'satisfaction.' Here 'feeling' is the term used for the basic generic operation of passing from the objectivity of the data to the subjectivity of the actual entity in question" (*Process and Reality*, 54). Feelings are thus intrinsic to that process whereby the ultimate metaphysical reality, the actual occasion, is what it is. Although Whitehead's view of feelings is more nuanced and more technical than I wish to pursue here, it provides a fresh view that leads us to reconsider the place and power of feelings in a new way. One final passage from Whitehead is relevant to the content of this paper: "In our own relatively high grade of human existence, this doctrine of feelings and their subject is best illustrated by our notion of moral responsibility. The subject is responsible for being what it is in virtue of its feelings. It is also derivatively responsible for the consequences of its existence because they flow from its feelings" (*Process and Reality*, 259). This is a highly suggestive sentence for rethinking the relationship between moral responsibility and feeling.

to what is understood to be rational in a given system or setting, feeling is dismissed as undeserving of serious attention. The reason-as-content view identifies reason and the rational with particular assertions and proceeds to subordinate feeling as source of knowledge to reason as source of knowledge.

A second view, one that I wish to lift up for consideration in this paper, sees rationality as process rather than as content. This means that reason is employed to reflect upon knowledge discovered by reason but also to reflect upon the knowledge that comes through feeling. Both reason and feeling are to be recognized as legitimate sources of truth and are therefore to be given an equal hearing. To say that they are given an equal hearing, however, is not to say that they are granted an equal following. Our capacity to rationalize—to abuse the language of reason in an effort to satisfy self-interest—is a well-developed capacity that needs constant vigilance. And our proclivity for aborting the reasoning process by indulging in raw feeling can ambush the total enterprise of serious ethical reflection. In this view, then, rationality maintains a position of priority but it is a priority of reason-as-process (reflection) not as content.

Reason and feeling can be vehicles to the insight and wisdom that are prerequisites for moral judgment, but they can also function as barriers to insight and wisdom. There is little in life that is unambiguous. On the one hand, the feelings of empathy and compassion, for example, can aid one in discerning one's proper ethical response by orienting one to recognize the virtue and value of justice. Such feelings might even prompt one to channel one's energies to see that justice is brought about. On the other hand, these same feelings of empathy and compassion, normally thought of as noble and admirable qualities, might function to restrict discernment and foster selfishness, for such feelings can be narrowly directed to one's own social class or business associations, thereby preventing one from recognizing the needs of people outside one's familiar circles.

In either case, for good or for evil, the feelings need to be attended to. Bernard Lonergan rightly states,

> it is much better to take full cognizance of one's feelings, however deplorable they may be, than to brush them aside, overrule them, ignore them. To take cognizance of them makes it possible for one to know oneself, to uncover the inattention, obtuseness, silliness, irresponsibility that

gave rise to the feeling one does not want, and to correct the aberrant attitude.[11]

And, conversely (to paraphrase and complete Lonergan's thought), to take cognizance of one's feelings also makes it possible for one to recognize one's strengths: to uncover the attentiveness, sensitivity, seriousness, responsibility that gave rise to the feelings one *does* want, and to nourish and foster them as worthy and noble components of one's moral self.

Just as feeling can function as both vehicle and barrier, so, too, can reason. As a positive force, reason can provide psychic distance from a given dilemma and enable one to see more clearly, that is, to assess the benefits and dangers of a potential response by giving attention to communal concerns as well as personal preferences. In this way, reason frees one from following the raw, instinctive movement of immediate self-interest and enables one to think in universals. But reason is not without its dangers. Its negative potential is twofold. First, reason's capacity for dispassion and disinterest can render ethics impotent: in the name of dispassionate reflection and breadth of view, reason can lure one into a heady delight, prompting one to forget that in ethics, reflection is means and decision is end. If reason is exalted to the point where it becomes an end in itself, reason usurps the place of decision and thwarts the purpose for which the reflection was intended. A second abuse to which reason is vulnerable occurs when the phrase "the rational" is used as a synonym for "the acceptable" or "the convincing." Since reason in ethics often takes the form of a person giving *reasons* to justify certain actions, the reasons articulated become subject to scrutiny by others. Reasons found to be unacceptable are often labeled "unreasonable" or "irrational" when what is really meant (and therefore should be stated) is that the reasons cited are unacceptable because unconvincing. An example: in speaking about reasons for loving one's neighbor, for practicing genuine other-concern as a life style over against self-concern as a life style, the British philosopher John Hick has made the claim that such a choice is "rational" only if it is ultimately rooted in a belief in God and an afterlife.[12] For a nontheistic

11 Lonergan, *Method in Theology*, 33.
12 From a lecture entitled "The Eschatological Meaning of Life," delivered at

humanist to choose a life of altruism, believing that this life is all that there is, is, for Hick, "irrational." But the humanist counters, "nontheistic altruism is not irrational, but is an utterly rational choice, available to all reasonable people. One need not believe in God and life hereafter to be genuinely concerned about other people." In fact, the secular humanist might continue, "altruism is possible only for the unbeliever. To love and serve one's fellow human beings because God wills it and because there is a life beyond suggest motivations of self-interest that make no claim on the secular humanist." (There are undoubtedly other forms of self-interest present to both secular humanist and religious believer, but that point need not be developed here.) And the dialogue goes on.

The point I wish to make is that although Hick finds nontheistic altruism an unacceptable reason and calls it irrational, what he really means is that he judges such a reason to be insufficient or unacceptable. Rational persons—reasoning and reasonable persons —often root their choices in very different, sometimes opposing, grounds. To label the other as irrational or not rational, does not, I think, further the ethical dialogue. On the contrary it aborts such dialogue, often alienates its participants, and most important, misnames what is happening. To love other people in a sustained, deep, and generous way because one believes that God is real and has called all persons to a destiny of communion with him and with one another is a rational choice based on a particular view of the world. To love other people in a sustained, deep, and generous way simply because that in itself is better than living a life which gives primacy to self-concern is also a rational choice rooted in a different worldview. Both choices are rational but what is sufficient or satisfying to the one is insufficient or incredible for the other because of differing worldviews, because they are operating out of totally different presuppositions. To label the other's reason as irrational is specious. When "the rational" is identified with *particular reasons*, grounded in a particular interpretive framework, the language of reason becomes abused and misused and functions as a cover for something else entirely that is really going on. One need not be irrational to be wrong. It can be argued, for example, that Hitler's policy of geno-

the University of California, Riverside, 30 November 1977.

cide was rational and consistent with his hopes for a pure Aryan race. But this is also to say that "the rational" can be outrageously immoral. To be rational is not necessarily to be morally right.

In sum, the rationality-as-process view recognizes that "the rational" is as ambiguous as feeling. It can ennoble; it can also destroy. And so rationality-as-process examines the contents of both reason and feeling before it decides which to nurture in a given case. Precisely which one is to be nourished and encouraged will be determined by the norms valued; justice, love, liberty, and truthfulness are those most frequently repeated in western ethics, although others could be added to the list as well.

Ideally, the visions of reality examined at level two are not accepted blindly but are, as level three is lived, continually examined in order that uncritical acceptance be prevented. Thus, reason in the form of self-critical reflection is thereby nourished at every stage in the process, for reason-as-process is viewed as a necessary foundation and integral component of the ethical task, both religious and philosophical.

Good ethics as I envision it and work at it, looks to multiple voices for wisdom and insight in decision-making. It looks to the experience described as revelation as well as to the experience of reason; it taps the wisdom that comes from intuition, from history, from both group experience and personal experience; it listens to creative imagination and to feeling, for it recognizes that truth and goodness can be perceived affectively as well as intellectually; it welcomes myths, rituals, proverbs, experiences, beliefs, and traditions as sources pertinent to furthering the religio-ethical task. No one of these sources alone is, or can be, sufficient. But each can offer its voice, shedding light on the question at hand. Religious ethics and philosophical ethics, benefitting from the breadth of view offered by specific historical traditions, should place all of these sources on their agenda for inquiry and assess their contribution in relation to one another. Besides being climbers of ladders, ethicists function as jugglers as well, for they seek to maintain contact with a variety of sources, giving serious attention to each; they do not allow themselves to simplify (and distort) their task by holding tightly onto just one.

If this view makes the ethical task seem unwieldy because of the broad range of questions with which it deals and the broad base of wisdom it seeks to tap, it is to be remembered that the moral life (that with which ethics is concerned) is no less complex. Ethical reflection is prompted by confusion that invades the attempt to live a moral life. One's response to this confusion involves reason and reflection but it demands a good deal more from us as well, for although the moral life is rational, it is also nonrational. At times it is clearly ordered and at other times terribly messy; it is often marked by incoherence and ambiguity. I agree with Richard Hoehn who recently said that while he believes that consciousness is the prime mover in the moral life he also believes that consciousness is like a lake into which streams flow from all other dimensions of the self: imagination, memory, feeling, reasoning, volition, emotion.[13] Each needs to be attended to.

The attentive reader has by now discerned several presuppositions that inform this view of ethics: that it is catholic in orientation, that is to say, comprehensive in outlook and interested in tapping wisdom from a multiplicity of forms; that it affirms an intimate relationship among epistemology, metaphysics, and problem-solving procedures; that it takes for its starting point the concreteness of human existence, fully acknowledging its dilemmas and its possibilities; that ethics refers primarily not to a code of conduct or system of moral thought but to a many-sided and many-leveled process of reflection prompted by the need for decision.

The three-tiered process here outlined can function for one who is attuned to doing normative religious ethics as well as the person more interested in studying (describing) the religious ethics lived or articulated by a given person or community. To do religious ethics engages one in a process of thought that demand a clear method, a sensitive heart, and an honest, critical, and discerning mind. It is to be concerned with duties and with values, with *oughts* (how ought I respond?), but also with *mights* (how might I respond?), with rules and laws but also with creative and imaginative possibilities. It is, more often than not, to address a specific question and move to

13 From a paper entitled "The Self as Center: Phenomenological Analysis and Implications for the Teaching of Ethics," with a citation to Larry Castillo-Wilson, presented before the Ethics Section of the American Academy of Religion at the 1977 annual meeting.

insight, judgment, and resolution through disciplined and systematic entry into each of the three levels described in this essay: concern with problem-solving, concern with point of view, concern with the roots of knowing.

SUMMARY OF THE THREE LEVELS
OF ETHICAL REFLECTION

Ground level refers to experience and the confusion and uncertainty that are generated by experience. This is the basis out of which ethics emerges. One faces induction into war, commitment in friendship, a ballot calling for approval or disapproval of a bill to legalize capital punishment. One wonders how to respond, what to do . . . and ethical reflection is begun.

Level one expresses a person's concern with decision and action (right action, good action, moral behavior). Here one reflects upon the practical questions that arise from experience and that call for resolution. This first step enables one to engage in procedures for identifying and analyzing the given problem through a variety of activities (collecting the facts, seeking wisdom from diverse sources, anticipating future implications, imagining alternatives, judging and deciding).

Level two enables one to give attention to one's standpoint, interpretive framework, or worldview, that is, to the philosophical and theological presuppositions that comprise one's view of reality. At this level, one confronts one's basic understanding regarding such issues as the nature of the good, the meaning of human agency, the relationship of the human to the nonhuman world, people's power (capacity) or lack of it to act with some significant measure of freedom and responsibility, the presence or absence of an ultimate in human life and its role in human affairs. This level directs attention to those convictions and loyalties that inform one's imagination and guide one's decisions.

Level three makes it possible for one to examine the epistemological presuppositions that affect one's view of those elements considered at step two; this third level affords a broader view than the lower levels allowed. Here one is called to recognize one's sources of knowledge for the presuppositions, convictions, and loyalties examined at level two and to engage in the process of justifying them. Most simply put, the question is, how do you know what you know? (What are your sources of knowledge and why do you trust them?) Or: it's not enough for you to tell me what you see. I want to know where you are standing as you see and speak, and also why you stand there.

19

Feminist Theology and Bioethics

Margaret A. Farley

The aim of this essay is to explore the connections between feminist theology and issues in the field of bioethics. I shall try to indicate basic contours of feminist theology and some ways its values bear on the vast network of ethical issues related to the biological sciences, technology, and medicine. In order to press the question of possible contributions by feminist theology to bioethics, I shall focus on the implications of feminist theology for reproductive technology.

To some extent, the connection between the concerns of feminist theology and bioethics is obvious. Feminist theology proceeds from a methodological focus on the experience of women, and feminist ethics begins with a central concern for the well-being of women. Medical ethics (as a part of bioethics) can be expected to share this focus and this concern, if for no other reason than that women constitute the majority of those who receive and provide health care.[1] Beyond this, however, traditional religious views of women associate them symbolically and literally with nature, with the body, with human relationships, with reproduction—all themes for feminist theological critique, all foci for major concerns of bioethics. Three caveats are in order. It is helpful to identify some forms of relation which we should *not* expect to find.

First, we should not expect to find feminist theology articulating

1 Caroline Whitbeck, "Women and Medicine: An Introduction," *The Journal of Medicine and Philosophy* 7 (1983), 119, 125, and B. K. Rothman, "Women, Health and Medicine," in *Women: A Feminist Perspective*, ed. Jo Freeman (Palo Alto: Mayfield, 1979), 27–40.

for bioethics fundamental values or moral principles which are in every way unique. Few contemporary theological ethicists claim for their theologies exclusive access to moral insight in the formulation of commonly held norms.[2] It is not only religious belief, or theology, or a particular theology that can ground, for example, a requirement to respect persons, or a principle of equality, or a rational system of distributive justice. Likewise, it is not only feminist theology that can ground a view of human persons as fundamentally interpersonal and social, or that can formulate a view of nature that requires human stewardship rather than exploitation. Still, the critical function of feminist theology may provide a new perspective on some issues in bioethics.

Second, there is no one definitive form of feminist theology. Theology in general is pluralistic on many levels. Feminist theology is one among many options in theology, but it is itself as pluralistic as is theology generally. Thus, there are feminist theologies centered in Goddess worship, and others that locate themselves in the Jewish and Christian biblical traditions, and still others that move beyond any historical traditions at all. So clear have the differences in feminist theologies become that typologies abound in a growing effort to compare and contrast them.[3] This divergence must be kept in mind while we explore the convergence of basic ethical concerns, values, and norms for action.

Third, feminist theology is at beginning points in its systematic formulation. While monumental strides have been taken by feminist biblical scholars, theologians, and historians,[4] sustained theological

2 Richard A. McCormick, *How Brave a New World? Dilemmas in Bioethics* (Garden City, NY: Doubleday, 1981), 9, and "Bioethics in the Public Forum," *Milbank Memorial Fund Quarterly* 61 (1983), 119; Beverly Wildung Harrison, *Our Right to Choose: Toward a New Ethic of Abortion* (Boston: Beacon Press, 1983), 84–90; James M. Gustafson, *The Contributions of Theology to Medical Ethics* (Milwaukee: Marquette University Press, 1975), 26. For a contrary emphasis, see Stanley Hauerwas, "Can Ethics Be Theological?" *Hastings Center Report* 8 (1978), 48.

3 Rosemary Radford Ruether, *Sexism and God-Talk: Toward A Feminist Theology* (Boston: Beacon Press, 1983), 214–34; Elisabeth Schüssler Fiorenza, *In Memory of Her: A Feminist Reconstruction of Christian Origins* (New York: Crossroad, 1983), 7–36; and Carol S. Robb, "A Framework for Feminist Ethics," supra.

4 Mary Daly, *Beyond God the Father* (Boston: Beacon, 1973); Ruether, *Sexism*

synthesis is new on the horizon, at least for the Christian tradition.[5] Even newer is a systematic comprehensiveness and depth on the ethical side of feminist theology.[6] There is no easy route from the sources of religious faith to the specific insights needed for the radically new questions generated by scientific and medical capabilities. This conviction is mirrored in the reservations which many feminist theologians and ethicists express regarding some technologies of reproduction.[7] It is also mirrored in the recognition of the necessity of collaboration with disciplines other than theology and ethics for the gradual forging of moral perspectives on the multitude of issues which a comprehensive bioethics may address.

There are limits, then, to the connections presently discernible between feminist theology and bioethics. Within those limits, however, lie meeting points, challenges, resources, of potential critical importance to both disciplines. We turn first to the methods, sources, and relevant themes of feminist theology.

FEMINIST THEOLOGY

Three themes in feminist theology can be raised up for central consideration: 1) relational patterns among human persons, 2) human embodiment, and 3) human assessment of the meaning and value of the world of "nature." Feminist theology's development of these themes includes an articulation of basic ethical perceptions and leads to the formulation of some ethical action-guides. Moreover, these themes illuminate important methodological decisions which constitute not only central commitments for feminist theology but possible warrants for ethical arguments in bioethics.

Patterns of Relation   Feminism, in its most fundamental sense, is opposed to discrimination on the basis of sex. This opposition has the ultimate aim of equality among persons regardless of gender. To

and God-Talk; Letty Russell, *The Future of Partnership* (Philadelphia: Westminster, 1979); Schüssler Fiorenza, *In Memory of Her;* and Phyllis Trible, *God and the Rhetoric of Sexuality* (Philadelphia: Fortress Press, 1978).

5 See Ruether's *Sexism and God-Talk.*
6 Harrison, *Our Right to Choose.*
7 Harrison, *Our Right to Choose,* 37, and Ruether, *Sexism and God-Talk,* 226.

achieve this aim, feminism is necessarily pro-woman. Since discrimination on the basis of sex remains pervasively discrimination against women, feminism aims to correct this bias by a bias for women, however temporary or prolonged that bias must be. A bias for women includes a focal concern for the well-being of women and a taking of account of women's experience in coming to understand what well-being demands for women and men.

Feminist theology perceives profound discrimination against women in traditions of religious patriarchy. There are massive tendencies in religious traditions to justify patterns of relationship in which men dominate women. Within the history of Christianity, for example, the major pattern of relationship between women and men has been one of dominance and subjugation, sustained through beliefs about the essential inferiority of women to men and the need for a hierarchical order in social arrangements. Theological assessments of woman's nature were based on a fundamental dualism within humanity. Women and men are distinguished as polar opposites, representing body or mind, emotion or reason, passivity or activity, dependence or autonomy. The female-identified pole is always inferior to the male. More than this, women are often symbolically associated with evil, perceived as temptresses, feared as the threat of chaos to order, carnality to spirituality, weakness to strength. Even when women are exalted as symbols of virtue rather than vice, they bear the liabilities of imposed expectations and the burden of mediating "femininity" to men.[8]

Feminist theology's critique of religious tradition extends to the central symbols of faith. Christianity's traditional formulations of a doctrine of God have often served as sexist warrants for discrimination against women. Personal metaphors for God are strongly masculine in the biblical tradition as well as in theological formulations of the Trinity. Moreover, Christian faith is centered in a savior who is male. Hence, there is a strong tendency in this tradition to consider men more appropriate as representatives of God in the human family, society, and the church. Indeed, traditional Christian theology has often granted the fullness of the *imago Dei* to men,

---

8 Rosemary Radford Ruether, ed., *Religion and Sexism: Images of Women in the Jewish and Christian Traditions* (New York: Simon and Schuster, 1974).

yielding it only derivatively and partially to women. But more than this, characterizations of the Christian God as sovereign, transcendent, requiring submission from human persons,[9] have offered a model of relationship (dominance and submission) on which human relationships are then patterned. Along with this goes a view of the human self in which the height of Christian virtue is patient suffering and self-sacrificial love, and the only mode of Christian action is humble servanthood. Women are socialized into these ideals in a way that men are not, for men can imitate the autonomy and agency of God in their role as God's representatives. Doctrines of sin which stress the evil of prideful self-assertion only reinforce the submissiveness which already characterizes women.[10]

What emerges in feminist theology is an analysis of oppressive patterns of relationship and ideologies which foster them. These patterns of oppression are identified in every human relation where the pattern is one of domination and subjugation on the basis of sex or race or class. Given the radical nature of a critique which reaches every major doctrine, feminist theologians either move away from Christianity altogether, or take up the task of critical reconstruction of Christian theology. In either case, they have by and large moved to develop a view of human relations characterized by equality and mutuality, in which both autonomy and relationality are respected.

Feminist theologians who seek to reconstruct Christian theology "beyond the feminist critique" argue that there are fundamental resources within the tradition which are not ultimately sexist and which can be brought to bear precisely as a challenge to sexism. With feminist hermeneutical methods, biblical resources reveal a God who does not need to compete with human beings for sovereignty, who comes forth with freedom in order to call forth freedom from human persons; a God who is able to be imagined in feminine as well as masculine terms,[11] for whom "friend" or "partner" are more apt metaphors than "king" or "logos."[12] Historical and theolog-

9 Carol P. Christ, "The New Feminist Literature: A Review of Literature," *Religious Studies Review* 3 (1977), 203–12, and Daly, *Beyond God the Father.*

10 Judith Plaskow, *Sex, Sin and Grace* (Washington, DC: University Press of America, 1980).

11 Trible, *God and the Rhetoric of Sexuality.*

12 Sallie McFague, *Metaphorical Theology* (Philadelphia: Fortress, 1982) and

ical resources yield a view of human community that challenges the domination of one group over another, one class of persons over another.[13]

It has not been open to feminist theology simply to appropriate a view of the human person which makes autonomy paramount as the ground of respect or the primary principle to be protected in social relations. Relationality has pressed itself on feminist theologians from the experience of women. It is this that has demanded continued analysis of the nature of human relations and has led to historical and biblical studies of, for example, Christian communities, and to theological studies of the very nature of God (as relational). But if feminist theology cannot ignore relationality, neither has it been able to let go of autonomy as an essential feature of personhood.[14] Romantic returns to organic notions of society where relation is all, each in her place, without regard for free agency or for personal identity and worth which transcends roles—these are options that feminists judge can only repeat forms of oppression for women.

Pluralism in feminist theology, of course, leads to some profoundly different choices regarding historical forms of human relationships. Disagreements are on the level of strategy (is there any possibility of radically transforming existing religious traditions?); or on the analysis of the cause of oppression (whether it is most fundamentally religion, or culture in a more general sense, or the conspiracy of men, or economics, etc.); or on the model of relation (do exclusivity and separatism contradict the values of equality and mutuality?). Such disagreements are extremely serious, and it would be a mistake to underestimate them. Still, there is basic unanimity among feminist theologians on the values that are essential for nonoppressive human relationships—the values of equality, mutuality, and freedom.[15]

Russell, *The Future of Partnership.*

13 Ruether, *Sexism and God-Talk*, 23; Schüssler Fiorenza, *In Memory of Her.*

14 Valerie Saiving, "Androgynous Life: A Feminist Appropriation of Process Thought," *Feminism and Process Thought*, ed. Sheila G. Davaney (New York: Edwin Mellon Press, 1981).

15 To the argument that separatist feminist movements do indeed contradict these values (by affirming a new form of elitism, by simply "reversing" the order

Embodiment   The second theme in feminist theology which has particular bearing on issues of bioethics is human embodiment. There is a clear history of association of ideas that we must trace if we are to see the import of this theme both for feminist theology and bioethics.

Body/spirit is in many ways the basic dualism with which historical religions have struggled since late antiquity. Women, as we have already noted, have been associated with body, men with mind. Women's physiology has been interpreted as "closer to nature" than men's in that many areas and functions of a women's body seem to serve the human species as much or more than they serve the individual woman.[16] Women's bodies, in this interpretation, are subject to a kind of fate—more so than men's. Women are immersed in "matter," in an inertness which has not its own agency. This is manifest not only in the determined rhythms of their bodily functions, but in a tendency to act from emotion rather than from reason, and in women's "natural" work which is the caring for the bodies of children and men.

Women have also been associated with the ongoing evaluations of human bodiliness˙ and matter in general. Despite resistance from basically world-affirming attitudes in Judaism, and despite an ongoing conflict with positive Christian doctrines of creation and incarnation, both of these traditions incorporated negative views of the human body (and especially women's bodies). In late antiquity, Judaism was influenced by world-denying attitudes of Near Eastern gnosticism and mysticism. Christianity absorbed these same influences in its very foundations, along with Greek philosophical distrust of the transitoriness of bodily being.

Integral to views of the human body have been views of human sexuality. Despite traditional influences toward positive valuation (of

---

in the hierarchy of men and women, etc.), the response is sometimes given that separation does not entail domination, and that elitism is no more a necessarily substantial charge against separatist feminism than it is against any religious sectarianism. It is more difficult for some separatists to answer the criticism that they are duplicating oppressive patterns of "identifying an enemy."

16 Sherry B. Ortner, "Is Female to Male as Nature Is to Culture?" in *Woman, Culture and Society,* ed. Michelle Zimbalist Rosaldo and Louise Lamphere (Stanford: Stanford University Press, 1974).

sexuality as a part of creation, as implicated in the very covenant with God, etc.), strongly negative judgments have been brought in. From ancient blood taboos, to stoic prescriptions for the control of sexual desire by reason, to Christian doctrines of the consequences of original sin, fear and suspicion regarding the evil potentialities of sex have reigned strong in the western conscience. So great, in fact, has been the symbolic power of sex in relation to evil that there seems to have been "from time immemorial," as Paul Ricoeur puts it, "an indissoluble complicity between sexuality and defilement."[17]

Women's sexuality has been seen as more "carnal" than men's, "closer to nature," more animal-like, less subject to rational control. Disclosure of this historical view of women's sexuality came as a surprise to many feminists whose direct learning from religious traditions had tended to be the opposite—that is, that women are less passionate than men, and hence more responsible for setting limits to sexual activity. The reversal in this regard has its roots, too, in religious traditions and reflects the tendency we have seen before to identify women with evil, on one hand, and place them on a pedestal, on the other.[18] In either case, women's identity remains closely tied to the way they relate to their bodies, and in either case, women have learned to devalue their bodies. For women themselves, Freud's comment on beliefs about menstruation, pregnancy, and childbirth held true: " ... it might almost be said that women are altogether taboo."[19]

The rise of feminist consciousness called into question all past interpretations of the meaning of women's bodies. Women's turn to their own experience for new interpretations of embodiment was not a simple process. A beginning feminist response was a rejection of this association. Anatomy was *not* destiny; women were not to be identified with their bodies any more than were men; women could transcend their bodies through rational choices. Such a response paradoxically freed women, however, to take their bodies more seriously. Women soon moved to "reclaim" their bodies—to claim them as their own, as integral to their selfhood and their woman-

---

17 Paul Ricoeur, *The Symbolism of Evil* (New York: Harper and Row, 1967), 28.

18 Nancy F. Cott, "Passionlessness," *Signs* 4 (1978), 227–28.

19 Sigmund Freud, "The Taboo of Virginity," *Collected Papers*, 8:75.

hood. This entailed new practical and theoretical approaches. Reflecting on their experiences, women shared insights and interpretation, formulated new symbols, expanded and revised understandings of human embodiment as such.[20]

Feminist philosophers and theologians used a phenomenological method to describe what it means to *be* a body as well as *have* a body, to understand their own bodies as ways of being inserted into the world, as structured centers of personal activity, as body-subjects not just body-objects.[21] From an understanding of themselves as embodied subjects, women "reclaim" their bodies not just by taking them seriously and "living" them integrally, but by refusing to yield control of them to men. New intimate self-understandings and new philosophical and theological anthropologies yield new personal and political decisions.

The World of Nature The third theme in feminist theology relevant to bioethics is the meaning and value of the world of nature. Feminist theologians' concern for this theme is directly influenced by their concern for patterns of human relations and for the world as the place of human embodiment.

Just as women have been thought of in religious and cultural traditions as "close to nature," so the world of nature has been symbolized as female. This is a clue to the difficulties which feminist theologians have with past beliefs and attitudes regarding nature. They find, in fact, a correlation between patterns of domination over women and efforts at domination over nature.[22]

Perceptions of nature change through history, of course. Nature has been exalted beyond the being and culture of humans, or reduced to a tool for humans; it has been viewed as the cosmic source of life and goodness, or a mysterious force to be feared and fled or controlled. All of these interpretations of nature mirror similar identifications of the essence of woman.

20 Penelope Washbourn, *Becoming Woman: The Quest for Spiritual Wholeness in Female Experience* (New York: Harper and Row, 1979).

21 Mary Crenshaw Rawlinson, "Psychiatric Discourse and the Feminine Voice," *Journal of Medicine and Philosophy* 7 (1982), 153–77.

22 Ruether in *Sexism and God-Talk*, 72–85 and in *To Change the World* (New York: Crossroad, 1981), 57–70, Griscom, supra.

Despite the fact that a Christian worldview and specific Christian teachings have supported "sacramental" views of the whole of creation, Christianity has also tended to trivialize nature. Ascetic theologies sometimes reduced nature to a transitory illusion, a distraction from "higher things." Christian leaders sometimes forbade the study of nature as dangerous or a waste of time. When nature and culture were paired among traditional dualisms, nature was assigned the value of the negative pole. Similarly, while there is a strong tradition in Christian thought requiring reverence for and stewardship of nature, there is also strong support for a way of relating to nature which sees it only as something to be used, dominated, controlled by human persons.[23]

Rosemary Ruether traces a history of western attitudes toward nature from an early ascetical "flight" from nature to a modern "return" to nature.[24] The rise of scientific research in the seventeenth century helped secularize nature, fostered a perception of it as intrinsically rational, penetrable, manageable. Unintended negative consequences of scientific and technological development produced romantic reactions calling for a different return to nature—a restoration of "pure" nature, uncontaminated and unalienated by human intervention. All of these attitudes toward nature represented the pattern of hierarchical domination and subjugation—domination through possession and control, whether through denigration, or exploitation, or the expectation of mediated happiness and identity through "keeping" nature as a haven for some (despite the suffering this in turn might cause for others).[25]

Feminist theology argues, alternatively, for a view of nature consonant with a view of a God who takes the whole of creation seriously, and a view of creation which does not see predatory hierarchy as the basis of order. Nature, in this view, is valuable according to its concrete reality, which includes an interdependence with embodied humanity. It is limited in its possibilities, which precludes its moral use as the battleground for the ultimate chal-

---

23 McCormick, *How Brave a World?*, 7.
24 Ruether, *Sexism and God-Talk*, 82.
25 Ruether, *Sexism and God-Talk*, 85 and in *To Change the World*.

lenge to human freedom. Human intelligence and freedom are not barred from addressing nature, but measures for understanding and just use are lodged both in nature itself and in ethical requirements for relations among persons.

We have seen enough of feminist theology to draw some conclusions regarding the *methods* likely to characterize any ethics that derives from it. First in this regard, there is a sense in which feminist theology and ethics can be said to be concerned with objective reality, and hence to presuppose methodologically some access to an intelligible reality. Like feminism in general, feminist theology had its origins in women's growing awareness of the disparity between received traditional interpretations of their identity and function within the human community and their own experience of themselves and their lives. The corresponding claim that gender role-differentiation and gender-specific limitations on opportunities for education, political participation, economic parity, etc., are discriminatory was based on the argument that past interpretations of women's reality were simply wrong. That is, past theories failed to discover the concrete reality of women and represented, in fact, distorted perceptions of that reality.

It would be a mistake, however, to label feminist theology and ethics in any simple sense "naturalistic." Feminist theology does not, obviously, reduce to a natural or behavioral science. Nor does it rely for its access to reality on human reason alone. And while feminist theological ethics searches for and proposes universally valid norms, it does so in a way that acknowledges the historical nature of human knowledge and the social nature of the interpretation of human experience. The fact that present insights may be superseded by future ones, and that present formulations of specific principles may change, does not contradict either the methodological requirement of attending to concrete reality or the methodological presupposition that the accuracy and adequacy of theories can be tested against that reality.

Closely aligned with all of this is the methodological commitment to begin with and continue a primary focus on the experience of

295

women.[26] This is often coupled with the qualification that no claims are made for the universality of women's experience in relation to human experience. There is a claim made, however, that until a theology based on women's experience is developed, traditionally assumed universal claims for a theology based on men's experience will continue to render inadequate if not inaccurate the major formulations of religious belief.

A methodological commitment to the primacy of women's experience as a source for theology and ethics yields, in addition, a feminist hermeneutical principle which functions in the selection and interpretation of all other sources. While not every feminist theologian articulates this principle in exactly the same way, it can be expressed as strongly as, "Whatever diminishes or denies the full humanity of women must be presumed not to reflect the divine or an authentic relation to the divine, or to reflect the authentic nature of things, or to be the message or work of an authentic redeemer or a community of redemption."[27] This principle functions in different ways in different feminist theologies. In some, it leads to the rejection of the authority of the Bible altogether;[28] in others it allows the relativization of the authority of some texts;[29] in still others, it leaves all texts standing as a part of an authoritative revelation, but renders their meaning transformed under a new feminist paradigm.[30] The same is true for theological doctrines, historical events, and for other sources of theology and ethics.

A focus on women's experience, the use of a feminist hermeneutical principle, and a concern for the lived experience of women precisely as disadvantaged, constitute for feminist theological ethics the bias for women which is the earmark of feminism in general. If this is chosen as a strategic priority, feminist theological ethics can be methodologically oriented ultimately as an ethic whose concerns include the well-being of both women and men, both humanity and the world of nature. Its theological center will depend on its ultimate warrants for these concerns.

26 Plaskow, *Sex, Sin and Grace* and Ruether, *Sexism and God-Talk*, 12–13.
27 Ruether, *Sexism and God-Talk*, 19.
28 Elizabeth Cady Stanton, ed., *The Original Feminist Attack on the Bible: The Woman's Bible* (New York: Arno Press, 1974).
29 Schüssler Fiorenza, *In Memory of Her.*
30 Trible, *The Rhetoric of Sexuality.*

Finally, feminist theological ethics has been open to both deonto-logical and teleological patterns of reasoning.[31] On one hand, the very notion of "strategic-priority," as well as a strongly "ecological" view of reality, imply a concern for consequences, an ethical evalution of means in relation to ends and parts in relation to wholes, a relativization of values in situations of conflict. On the other hand, demands of the concrete reality of persons are such that some attitudes and actions can be judged unethical precisely because they contradict values intrinsic to that reality. Neither of these modes of reasoning is ruled out for feminist theological ethics.

When we turn from method to *substance* in feminist theological ethics, we need only summarize the ethical import of feminist theological themes. Thus, an ethic derived from feminist theology understands the well-being of persons in a way that takes account of their reality as *embodied* subjects, in relation to an historical world. This ethic also gives important status to equality and mutuality. It holds together autonomy and relationality. It gives ethical priority to models of relationship characterized by collaboration rather than competition or hierarchical gradation. Finally, it does not isolate an ethic of human relations from ethical obligations to the whole of nature.

Some test of this ethic can be made by turning now to issues in bioethics.

FEMINIST THEOLOGY AND BIOETHICS

Feminist theology offers a distinctive perspective on many issues under bioethics, because women's lives are deeply implicated in personal medical care, public health, and the development and use of biomedical technologies. Here the lived experience of women reveals some of the central opportunities and limitations of the human condition. Here it is that "reflection upon the goals, prac-tices, and theories of medicine validates philosophical reflection upon many issues that have traditionally been of concern to women," but ignored by the traditional disciplines of philosophy and theology.[32]

31 Harrison, *Our Right to Choose*, 12–13.
32 Whitbeck, "Women and Medicine," 120.

Margaret A. Farley

We can explore the interrelation between feminist theology and bioethics in a number of ways. From a feminist perspective, we can examine general principles of bioethics, such as autonomy, beneficence, and justice; and specific issues such as abortion, medical care of the elderly, psychiatric biases in the treatment of women, hierarchical ordering of medical professions. Let me focus upon the issue of the development and use of reproductive technologies.[33] A feminist theological approach to this issue may show some of the implications of feminist theology for understanding both context and principles in the area of bioethics.

The potentialities of reproductive technology have for some time caught the attention of feminists, though without unanimity of analysis. Some feminists have argued that the ultimate source of women's oppression is their physiological capability of bearing children. While physical motherhood can constitute individual and social power, it also renders women powerless—before nature, before men, before their children, before society (which judges and determines the conditions under which their children must grow). In the face of this powerlessness, and the suffering it entails, technology offers a solution. Indeed, in an extreme view, women's liberation can only be achieved with a revolution not only against forms of society, but against nature itself. Thus, Shulamith Firestone argued for the "freeing of women from the tyranny of their reproductive biology by every means available," including technology which could separate women once and for all from a gender-identified responsibility for reproduction.[34]

This was a relatively early position, however, and strong disagreement came from other feminists on a variety of grounds. Many consider the analysis of the causes of oppression to be wrong.[35] Others see in the development of reproductive technologies a new

33 Reproductive technologies include all those technologies which relate to human reproduction. They are sometimes differentiated from technologies of genetic engineering, though I do not in this essay maintain a sharp separation. For some helpful distinctions, see President's Commmission for the Study of Ethical Problems in Medicine and Biomedical and Behavioral Research, *Splicing Life* (Washington, DC: U.S. Government Printing Office, 1982), 8–10.

34 Shulamith Firestone, *The Dialectic of Sex: The Case for Feminist Revolution* (New York: Bantam Books, 1971), 238.

35 Juliet Mitchell, *Woman's Estate* (New York: Vintage Books, 1971), 87–91.

means of devaluing women, rendering them "expendable in the procreative process."[36] Still others argue that some uses of technology, such as amniocentesis for the purpose of gender selection, will pit women against themselves.[37]

Feminists agree, however, on at least two things in regard to these questions. First, the history of women's experience in relation to the power and process of reproduction is a history of great pain. While fertility, pregnancy, and childbirth have been a source of women's happiness and fulfillment, and occasions for powerful expressions of great human love and enduring fidelity to duty, they have also been the locus of a cumulative burden of immense oppression and suffering. The twentieth century incursion of technology into reproduction (the "medicalization" of pregnancy and childbirth) has often added to this suffering, extended this oppression.

Secondly, feminists agree that the development and use of reproductive technology cannot be evaluated apart from its concrete, socio-cultural context. This context remains an "historically specific social order in which positions of power and privilege are disproportionately occupied by men."[38] As long as sexism continues to characterize the lived world which women know, technology will have different consequences for women and for men. Far from freeing women from unnecessary burdens in reproduction, further technological development may result in greater bondage.

Neither feminism in general nor feminist theology render wholly negative judgments on reproductive technology. One obvious reason is that such technology can take many forms. Evaluations of developments of contraceptives, childbirth procedures, methods of abortion, artificial insemination, *in vitro* fertilization, fetal diagnosis, cloning, and many other technologies can hardly be lumped together in a single comprehensive judgment. Generally, despite deep ambivalence toward reproductive technologies, feminists can affirm that "natural-scientific breakthroughs represent genuine gains

36 Harrison, *Our Right to Choose*, 37.

37 Tabitha M. Powledge, "Unnatural Selection: On Choosing Children's Sex," in *The Custom-Made Child: Women Centered Perspectives,* ed. Holmes, Hoskins, and Gross (Clifton, NJ: Humana Press, 1981), 193–99.

38 Jean Bethke Elshtain, "A Feminist Agenda on Reproductive Technology," *Hastings Center Report* 12 (1982), 41.

in human self-understanding. The widespread social irresponsibility of medical practice, exacerbated by male monopoly of the medical profession that is only now changing, must not be confused with the value of scientific discoveries."[39] Science and technology have been instruments of reform at times, even in regard to sexism.[40]

It will be helpful to narrow our focus still more to one form of reproductive technology. The form that I will consider is *in vitro* fertilization for the purpose of producing a child. As a technology, it raises the issue of profound change in human modes of reproduction.

One place to begin a feminist analysis of *in vitro* fertilization (with embryo transfer or some other form of providing for gestation) is with women's experience to date of technology in the area of pregnancy and birth. As we have already noted, in many respects this is not a happy experience. Recent studies have helped to make visible the difficulties women have had.[41] Recalling these difficulties can help us to formulate the questions that need to be asked of *in vitro* fertilization. The use of medical technology in relation to childbirth has contributed to the alienation of women from their bodies, their partners, and their children (by, for example, moving childbirth into settings appropriate primarily for the treatment of disease, isolating mothers both from "women's culture" and their spouses, regimenting the presence of mothers with their babies, etc.);[42] and it has placed women in a network of professional

---

39 Harrison, *Our Right to Choose*, 169–70.

40 Rosalind Rosenberg, *Beyond Separate Spheres: Intellectual Roots of Modern Feminism* (New Haven: Yale University Press, 1982), 22, 83, 136.

41 Richard W. Wertz and Dorothy C. Wertz, *Lying-In: A History of Childbirth in America* (New York: Free Press, 1977); Ann Oakley, "A Case of Maternity," *Signs* 4 (1979), 606–31; Adrienne Rich, *Of Woman Born: Motherhood as Experience and Institution* (Buffalo: Prometheus, 1976); Karen Lebacqz, "Reproductive Research and the Image of Woman," *Women in a Strange Land*, ed. Clare B. Fisher (Philadelphia: Fortress, 1975); and Mary Daly, *Gyn/Ecology: The Metaethics of Radical Feminism* (Boston: Beacon Press, 1978).

42 "Tales of horror" are told more and more in recent sociological studies in this regard. However, it should be noted that very recently there have come significant changes—changes, for example, such as an increase in home birthing, the provision of birthing rooms in hospitals, the rise once again of the profession of midwifery, etc. Some feminists express concern that some new movements, such as natural childbirth, incorporate an alienating technology just as previous

relations which unjustifiably limit their autonomy (as "patient"). Does the development and use of *in vitro* fertilization hold this same potential for alienation, albeit in different ways? Does *in vitro* fertilization violate (or is it in accord with) feminist understandings of embodiment, norms for relationships, and concerns for the common good?

For many feminists the sundering of the power and process of reproduction from the bodies of women constitutes a loss of major proportions. Hence, the notion of moving the whole process to the laboratory (using not only *in vitro* fertilization but artificial placentas, et al.) is not one that receives much enthusiasm. On the other hand, *in vitro* fertilization does not necessarily violate the essential embodying of reproduction. If its purpose is to enable women who would otherwise be infertile to conceive a child, it becomes a means precisely to mediate embodiment. Feminists generally oppose the sacralization of women's reproductive organs and functions that would prohibit all technological intervention. In fact, desacralization in this regard is a necessary step in the breaking of feminine stereotypes and the falsification of anatomy as destiny. Moreover, feminist interpretations are very clear on the validity of separating sexuality from reproduction. Without contradiction, however, they also affirm reproduction as a significant potential dimension of sexuality. Yet feminists do not give an absolute value to a series of "natural" physical connections between sexual intercourse and the fertilization of an ovum by male sperm. It is a failure of imagination which sees this as the only way in which integrated sexuality can be related to reproduction. All in all, then, while human embodiment remains a central concern in a feminist analysis of *in vitro* fertilization, it does not thereby rule out the ethical use of this technology.

Feminists are generally clear on the need to understand and experience childbearing in an active way. Pregnancy and childbirth are not events in relation to which women should be wholly passive.[43] Part of taking active control and responsibility regarding their reproductive power can include a willingness to use technology

methods did (Wertz and Wertz, *Lying-In*, 183–98 and Oakley, "A Case of Maternity," 628–30).

43 Harrison, *Our Right to Choose*, 169, 246–47.

in so far as it makes childbearing more responsible, less painful, and more safe. Sometimes discernment of just these consequences for technology is difficult, but the fact that it is called for indicates, again, that *in vitro* fertilization is not ruled out in principle.

Perhaps the most troubling aspect of *in vitro* fertilization, and other technologies which actually empower reproduction, is the question of primary agency and responsibility. Women's previous experience with reproductive technology suggests that women's own agency is likely to be submerged in the network of multiple experts needed to achieve *in vitro* fertilization. Far from this accomplishing a liberation of women from childbearing responsibilities, it can entail "further alienation of our life processes."[44] Moreover, efforts to restrict and share the agency of professionals often move only in the direction of what some feminists fear as collectivism or state control, the "total alienation of one's life to institutions external to one's own control and governed by a managerial elite."[45] Without a drastic change in the composition of society and the professions, widespread use of *in vitro* fertilization could make it difficult for women to achieve or sustain control of human reproduction.

Does it matter whether women or men, parents or scientists, control reproduction? Feminists argue that those who will bear the responsibility for childrearing should have primary agency in decisions about childbearing—not just because it is their right if they are to bear the burden of such responsibility, but because this is required for the well-being of offspring. "Only those who are deeply realistic about what it takes to nourish human life *from birth onward* have the wisdom to evaluate procreative choice."[46] Reproductive technologies that divorce decisions for childbearing from childrearing fail to take seriously the basic needs of children for not only material resources but personal relation and support, in contexts which allow the awakening of basic trust and the development of fundamental

44 Ruether, *Sexism and God-Talk*, 227.
45 Ruether, *Sexism and God-Talk*, 226.
46 Harrison, *Our Right to Choose*, 173. I am not, here, focusing on the grounds for women's right to procreative choice which are often central to feminist arguments—that is, a right to bodily integrity or a right to privacy. One reason I am not focusing on those grounds is that *in vitro* fertilization *can* be understood to prescind from women's bodies in a way that, for example, abortion cannot.

autonomy.[47] It is not only women who, in principle, can make these choices,[48] but it is "parents," not just "scientific facilitators" or society at large or any persons unprepared to take responsibility at an intimate and comprehensive level for our children. Such problems of agency are complex and sobering in the face of technological capabilities such as *in vitro* fertilization. They are not, in principle, intractable, perhaps not even in practice. They need not rule out the ethical use of *in vitro* fertilization. But they occasion grave moral caution.

Yet another consideration regards the developing capability for "selection" of offspring from among many candidates (differentiated by gender, bodily health, intellectual capacity, etc.). The problem of "discards" in *in vitro* fertilization is larger than the discernment of grave embryonic anomalies. For some feminists this capability can erode moral and religious obligation to accept all sorts of persons into the human community. In so doing, it undermines basic feminist principles of equality, inclusiveness, mutuality, and toleration of difference and of "imperfection."[49] *In vitro* fertilization need not, of course, be used in this way. But once again, a voice of caution is raised.

Underlying all of these considerations is the need to measure *in vitro* fertilization according to norms of justice. If justice in its deepest sense can be understood as treating persons in truthful accordance with their concrete reality, then all the issues of embodiment, nondiscrimination, agency, responsibility, inclusive care, are issues of justice. They are not focused only on individuals, but on the human community. They converge in the fundamental question, "How are we to reproduce ourselves as human persons?" They press us to new theories of justice which extend a requirement for "just parenting" in relation to all human children. They include, too, questions of the meaning and value of *in vitro* fertilization in a

47 Sara Ruddick, "Maternal Thinking," *Signs* 6 (1980), 358 and President's Commission, *Splicing Life,* 65. This can be maintained without conflicting with contemporary concerns for "too much mothering," etc.
48 Ruddick, "Maternal Thinking," 262. Nor should it be the exclusive prerogative of women. When it is this, it justifies a male dismissal of obligation regarding childrearing—something feminists have long been concerned to oppose.
49 Elshtain, "A Feminist Agenda," 42.

world threatened by overpopulation, in countries where not every existing child is yet cared for, in communities where grave needs of children require the resources of science and technology. Questions of macroallocation of scarce goods and services may finally be unresolvable, but they cannot be ignored. At the very least, in this instance, they preclude justifications of *in vitro* fertilization on the basis of any absolute right to procreate.

A feminist analysis of *in vitro* fertilization remains, then, provisional. It yields, however, the following position. Negatively, there are not grounds for an absolute prohibition of the development and use of technology such as *in vitro* fertilization. Positively, such technology may aid just and responsible human reproduction. The presence of certain circumstances, or certain conditions, sets limits to its ethical development and use—circumstances such as 1) high risk of injury to the well-being of either parent or child; 2) a context unconducive to the growth and development of any child produced (unconducive because, for example, no one is prepared to offer the child a basic human personal relationship); 3) an intention to produce a child to be used as a means only, in relation to the producers' ends (as, for example, if the child is produced merely for the sake of the advance of scientific research, or for the duplication of one's own self without regard for the child's development into an autonomous self); 4) failure to meet criteria of distributive justice (when it is determined that other basic human needs place legitimate prior claims on the resources involved). Such conditions rule out spectres of human laboratory "farms." They also tell us something about the conditions for any ethical decisions regarding human reproduction, not just decisions made in the context of reproductive technology.

With this, then, we have one example of the relation between feminist theology and an issue of bioethics. My development of the issue is more suggestive than exhaustive of the particular ethical values and ultimate theological warrants that feminist theologians may offer. Future work in bioethics will bring careful reflection on questions that I have not addressed at all—questions, for example, of women's interpretation not only of birth but of death, and women's evaluation of the strength of "quality of life" claims in relation to sanctity of life principles. Whatever lines along which a feminist bioethics may develop, however, it will never be far from central concerns for human embodiment, for the well-being of women-persons on a par with the well-being of men-persons, for newly just patterns of relationship among all persons, and for the balanced care of the whole world of both nonpersonal and personal beings.

Contributors

Barbara Hilkert Andolsen earned her Ph.D. in religion at Vanderbilt University. She has written essays for *Commonweal, Concilium,* and the *Journal of Religious Ethics.* She teaches ethics and women's studies in the Religion Department at Rutgers University. As a Ford Research Associate at Harvard Divinity School, she is investigating the impact of office automation on women's work.

Nancy Bancroft is Assistant Professor in the Lincoln University Masters Program. She has published articles in *Horizons, Cross Currents, Radical Religion, Religious Studies Review* and the *Journal of Ecumenical Studies* among others, and frequently delivers papers at meetings of professional societies in the areas of religion and social theory. For twenty years she has been active in movements against racism and classism.

Toinette Eugene serves as Assistant Professor of Education, Society, and Black Church Studies at Colgate Rochester Divinity School–Bexley Hall–Crozer Theological Seminary in Rochester, New York, where she teaches pastoral theology. Dr. Eugene has published a variety of articles in professional journals and is often engaged as a consultant for pastoral and educational conferences where she demonstrates her concern for integrating issues of spirituality and sociology within the context of church and society.

Margaret A. Farley is currently Professor of Christian Ethics at Yale Divinity School. She holds a Ph.D. in religious studies from Yale University. She has published articles on feminist ethics, medical ethics, sexual ethics, and social ethics in journals such as *The Journal of Religious Ethics, The Journal of Religion,* and *Theological Studies.* She is coauthor of *A Metaphysics of Being and God.* Her next book will be on conflict and commitment.

Elisabeth Schüssler Fiorenza has taught at Notre Dame University and is presently Talbot Professor of New Testament at Episcopal Divinity School. She is the author of several books including *In Memory of Her: A Feminist Theological Reconstruction of Christian Origins; Bread not Stone: The Challenge of Feminist Biblical Interpretation;* and *Claiming the Center: A Feminist Critical Theology of Liberation* (forthcoming).

307

Contributors

Joan L. Griscom lives in the woods of northern New Jersey. She is completing a Ph.D. in Counseling Psychology at New York University and also holds degrees from Vassar College and Union Theological Seminary (New York). She is currently working with battered women. Her perspective has been shaped by her participation in the communal research of the Northeast Consultation on Social Ethics in Feminist Perspective.

Christine E. Gudorf is Associate Professor of Theology at Xavier University, Cincinnati. She has written *Catholic Social Teaching on Liberation Themes* and articles in *Horizons, National Catholic Reporter, Commonweal,* and other journals.

Beverly Wildung Harrison holds a Ph.D. from Union Theological Seminary (New York) where she is Professor of Christian Social Ethics. In addition to *Our Right to Choose* from which her essay in this volume is taken, she has written essays collected as *Making the Connections: Essays in Feminist Christian Social Ethics* (forthcoming) and is a collaborator in *God's Fierce Whimsy: The Implications of Feminism for Theological Education.*

Ada Maria Isasi-Diaz was born in Havana, Cuba, the third child in a close family of eight children. She has done graduate work in history, theology, and education in various places in the United States, Spain, and Peru, and is now completing theological studies at Union Theological Seminary. Since 1975 she has been actively involved in the United States women's movement, particularly on the issue of women's rights in the Roman Catholic church, and in the Hispanic movement at both local and national levels. As a Christian Hispanic feminist, Isasi-Diaz has published many articles in newspapers, journals, and books.

June Jordan is a poet, journalist, and activist. She is the author of numerous books, several of them award winners. Her articles, essays and poems have appeared in the *New York Times, The Village Voice, New Republic, Ms., Essence, New Black Poetry, Partisan Review, American Poetry Review,* and others. She is Professor of English at the State University of New York at Stony Brook.

Catherine Keller teaches and writes in religious studies, connecting psychological, philosophical, and mythological interests within the matrix of feminist theory, and is currently completing *From a Broken Web: Separation, Sexism and Self.* After studies at the University of Heidelberg, she earned the M.Div at Eden Theological Seminary in conjunction with pastoral work, and then her Ph.D. at Claremont Graduate School in 1983. She is now Assistant Professor of Theology at Xavier University.

308

Contributors

June O'Connor is Associate Professor of Religious Studies at the University of California, Riverside. She has authored articles in *Horizons: Journal of the College Theology Society, Listening: Journal of Religion and Culture, The Christian Century, Journal of Religious Ethics*, and a book on Aurobindo Ghose entitled *The Quest for Political and Spiritual Liberation: A Study in the Thought of Sri Aurobindo Ghose.*

Mary D. Pellauer met the women's movement at the University of Chicago while studying social ethics in the Divinity School. She has taught women's studies courses in several seminaries, including Union Theological Seminary (New York), 1977–83. She is presently thinking about what to do in her second career, weaving, and baking in St. Paul, Minnesota.

Judith Plaskow is Associate Professor of Religious Studies at Manhattan College. She writes and lectures on feminist theology in general and Jewish feminism in particular. Author of *Sex, Sin and Grace* and co-editor of *Womanspirit Rising*, she is currently working on a book entitled *Turning, a Jewish Feminist Theology.*

Janice Raymond is Associate Professor of Women's Studies and Medical Ethics at the University of Massachusetts, Amherst. She is the author of *The Transsexual Empire* and a forthcoming book, *On Female Friendship.*

Carol S. Robb is Assistant Professor of Religious Studies at the University of Massachusetts, Boston Harbor campus. The article by her included in this collection was written for the Consultation on Social Ethics in Feminist Perspective, and completed while she was a Research Associate in Women's Studies in Ethics at Harvard Divinity School.

Rosemary Radford Ruether holds a Ph.D. in Classics and Patristics from Claremont Graduate School. She is Georgia Harkness Professor of Theology at Garrett-Evangelical Theological Seminary. She is the author of many books including: *Faith and Fratricide: The Theological Roots of Anti-Semitism; Religion and Sexism; New Woman, New Earth; Women and Religion in America: the Nineteenth Century;* and *Sexism and God-Talk.*

Ruth L. Smith teaches religion and philosophy in the Humanities Department at Worcester Polytechnic Institute in Worcester, Massachusetts. She has also taught in the English Department at Berea College and at Andover Newton Theological School and Ohio Wesleyan University. Her Ph.D. in Social Ethics is from Boston University. Currently her research is focused on the meaning of sociality for ethics and she is writing a book on Reinhold Niebuhr.

Contributors

Starhawk is the author of *The Spiral Dance: The Rebirth of the Ancient Religion of the Great Goddess* and *Dreaming the Dark: Magic, Sex and Politics.* A feminist and peace activist, she teaches the European Goddess tradition often called witchcraft at several Bay Area colleges. She is co-founder of the Reclaiming Collective in San Francisco which offers classes, workshops, and public rituals in Goddess worship.